Acknowledgements

"I have learned from my teachers;
from my colleagues more;
and from my students more than all."
—Talmud Ta'anit 7b

Special thanks to the Rabbis of the Pacific Northwest, especially Rabbi Joshua Stampfer, Rabbi Dov Gartenberg, Rabbi Jack Izakson, as well as all of the other Rabbis that have and continue to inspire us.

Sources

Hebrew text and translations adapted from:
Isaacs, Rabbi Ronald and Rabbi Daniel Pressman. *Siddur Shir Chadash for Youth and Family*. Hoboken, NJ: Ktav, 1994.

The Rabbinical Assembly of the United Synagogue of Conservative Judaism. *Siddur Sim Shalom*. Ed. and Trans. Rabbi Jules Harlow. New York: The Rabbinical Assembly, 1985.

The Rabbinical Assembly of the United Synagogue of Conservative Judaism. *Siddur Sim Shalom for Shabbat and Festivals*. New York: The Rabbinical Assembly, 1998.

The Sabbath Prayer (p. 66) adapted from:
Stein, Joseph. *Fiddler on the Roof*. Lyrics by Sheldon Harnick. Music by Jerry Bock. New York: Crown, 1965.

Quotations throughout the text from:
Congregation Beth El. *V'taheir Libeinu*. Sudbury, MA: Congregation Beth El, 1980.

Levy, Rabbi Naomi. *To Begin Again*. New York: Baal Antine Books, 1998.

Rav Nachman of Breslov. *Likutey Moharan*. Vol. I & 2. N.p.: Chasidei Breslov, n.d.

Rav Nachman of Breslov. *The Alef-Bet Book*. Jerusalem: Breslov Research Institute, 1986.

Birkat Ha-Yeladim: Blessing of the Children

*Commissioned in honor of Leslie Wexner and his family
by the Portland Wexner Fellows of 1995-97*

    May God bless you and keep you.
    May God's face shine upon you and be gracious to you.
    May God's face be lifted up to you and grant you peace.

You were born to a legacy of Torah, brighter than gold.
Let it illuminate your heart and your mind and nourish your soul.
    Torah's wisdom waits for you;
    Dig for meaning, seek the truth.
    Learn to question, learn to teach,
    Learn to expand your reach.
Learn our history, handed down, that you may pass it along.

May you be blessed in your coming, and your going, daytime and night.
Seek to know the ways of God by doing what's right:
    Welcome guests with open door,
    Comfort sorrow, feed the poor.
    Keep your tongue from hurtful speech,
    Stand for justice, work for peace.
May your deeds, both great and small, help to heal us all.

You're a link in the chain of generations, gift from above,
Seed of our future, fruit of our past, surrounded by love.
    May you someday make a home
    Joined with one you love alone,
    Sharing struggle, laughing, tears,
    Strengthening through the years.
And if children come to you, bless them as we bless you:

(for girls)	*(for boys)*
Y'simeich Elohim k'Sarah, Rivkah, Rachel v'Leah.	*Y'simcha Elohim k'Ephraim v'chi-Menasheh.*
Like our mothers, strong and courageous, bring forth your vision.	Lead a fruitful life of peace and honor our tradition.

based on the liturgy for Brit Milah and the blessing of children on Shabbat
Copyright 1997, Barbara Slader, Portland, OR (503)281-0403

Prayers For Other Occasions

Everyday Blessings

Upon smelling fragrant spices:

Praised are You, Adonai our God, Ruler of the universe, Creator of different kinds of spices.

Baruch atah Adonai, Eloheinu melech ha-olam, borei meenei v'sameem.

Upon smelling fragrant trees or shrubs:

Praised are You, Adonai our God, Ruler of the universe, Creator of fragrant trees.

Baruch atah Adonai, Eloheinu melech ha-olam, borei atzei v'sameem.

Upon seeing wonders of nature, including lightning, shooting stars, high mountains, and a sunrise:

Praised are You, Adonai our God, Ruler of the universe, Source of Creation.

Baruch atah Adonai, Eloheinu melech ha-olam, oseh ma-aseh v'reshit.

Upon hearing thunder:

Praised are You, Adonai our God, Ruler of the universe, whose power and might fill the world.

Baruch atah Adonai, Eloheinu melech ha-olam, shekocho ug'vurato maleh olam.

Upon seeing a rainbow:

Praised are You, Adonai our God, Ruler of the universe, Who remembers the covenant, is faithful to it, and keeps a promise.

Baruch atah Adonai, Eloheinu melech ha-olam, zocher hab'reet v'ne-eman biv'reeto v'kayam b'ma-amaro.

Upon seeing trees or creatures of striking beauty:

Praised are You, Adonai our God, Ruler of the universe, Who has such beauty in the world.

Baruch atah Adonai, Eloheinu melech ha-olam, shekacha lo b'olamo.

Upon using something new for the first time:

Praised are You, Adonai our God, Ruler of the universe, for granting us life, for sustaining us, and for helping us to reach this time.

Baruch atah Adonai, Eloheinu melech ha-olam, shehecheiyanu v'kee'manu v'higee-anu laz'man hazeh.

בִּרְכוֹת הוֹדָאָה

Upon smelling fragrant spices:

בָּרוּךְ אַתָּה יְיָ, אֱלֹהֵינוּ מֶלֶךְ הָעוֹלָם, בּוֹרֵא מִינֵי בְשָׂמִים:

Upon smelling fragrant trees or shrubs:

בָּרוּךְ אַתָּה יְיָ, אֱלֹהֵינוּ מֶלֶךְ הָעוֹלָם, בּוֹרֵא עֲצֵי בְשָׂמִים:

Upon seeing wonders of nature, including lightning, shooting stars, high mountains, and a sunrise:

בָּרוּךְ אַתָּה יְיָ, אֱלֹהֵינוּ מֶלֶךְ הָעוֹלָם, עֹשֶׂה מַעֲשֵׂה בְרֵאשִׁית:

Upon hearing thunder:

בָּרוּךְ אַתָּה יְיָ, אֱלֹהֵינוּ מֶלֶךְ הָעוֹלָם, שֶׁכֹּחוֹ וּגְבוּרָתוֹ מָלֵא עוֹלָם:

Upon seeing a rainbow:

בָּרוּךְ אַתָּה יְיָ, אֱלֹהֵינוּ מֶלֶךְ הָעוֹלָם, זוֹכֵר הַבְּרִית וְנֶאֱמָן בִּבְרִיתוֹ וְקַיָּם בְּמַאֲמָרוֹ:

Upon seeing trees or creatures of striking beauty:

בָּרוּךְ אַתָּה יְיָ, אֱלֹהֵינוּ מֶלֶךְ הָעוֹלָם, שֶׁכָּכָה לוֹ בְּעוֹלָמוֹ:

Upon using something new for the first time:

בָּרוּךְ אַתָּה יְיָ, אֱלֹהֵינוּ מֶלֶךְ הָעוֹלָם, שֶׁהֶחֱיָנוּ וְקִיְּמָנוּ וְהִגִּיעָנוּ לַזְּמַן הַזֶּה:

Prayers For Other Occasions

Havdallah

While holding the candle, spices, and wine, we sing:

Look! God is my Redeemer, I will trust and not be afraid. For God is my strength and my song, and has been my Redeemer. You will draw water with joy from the wellsprings of redemption. Deliverance is Adonai's. You will bless Your people. *Adonai Tz'vaot* is with us, the God of Jacob protects us. *Adonai Tz'vaot*, blessed is the person who trusts in You. Save us, Adonai, Ruler who will answer us when we call.

Hineh El y'shu-atee, ev'tach v'lo ef'chad, kee ozee v'zim'rat Yah Adonai, vay'hee lee leeshu-ah. ush'av'tem mayim b'sason mima-ay'nei hay'shu-ah. LAdonai hay'shu-ah al am'cha vir'chatecha selah. Adonai tz'va-ot imanu mis'gav lanu Elohei Ya-akov selah. Adonai tz'va-ot ash'rei adam bote-ach bach. Adonai hoshee-ah hamelech ya-anenu v'yom kor'enu.

To our ancestors there was light, gladness, joy, and honor. So may we be blessed. I lift the cup of deliverance and call upon Adonai.

Lay'hudeem hay'tah orah v'simchah v'sason vee-kar.
Ken ti'yeh lanu, kos y'shu-ot esa. Uv'shem Adonai ek'ra.

We say the blessing over the wine (but don't drink it yet):

Praised are You, Adonai our God, Ruler of the universe, Creator of the fruit of the vine.

Baruch atah Adonai, Eloheinu melech ha-olam, borei p'ri hagafen.

We say the blessing over the spices, then smell them:

Praised are You, Adonai our God, Ruler of the universe, Creator of different kinds of spices.

Baruch atah Adonai, Eloheinu melech ha-olam, borei meenei v'sameem.

We say the blessing over the light. As we say this blessing, hold your hands up to the light then look at the reflection in your fingernails:

Praised are You, Adonai our God, Ruler of the universe, Creator of the lights of the fire.

Baruch atah Adonai, Eloheinu melech ha-olam, borei m'orei ha-esh.

Praised are You, Adonai our God, Ruler of the universe, Who separates between the holy and the ordinary, between light and darkness, between Israel and the other peoples, between the seventh day and the six work days. Praised are You, Adonai, Who separates the holy and the ordinary.

Baruch atah Adonai, Eloheinu melech ha-olam, hamav'dil bein kodesh l'chol, bein or l'choshech, bein Yisra-el la-ameem, bein yom hash'vee-ee, l'sheshet y'mei hama-aseh. Baruch atah Adonai, hamav'deel bein kodesh l'chol.

Drink some of the wine and then put the candle out in it.

הַבְדָּלָה

DID YOU KNOW THAT... *Havdallah* is the very last moment of Shabbat. We want to enjoy Shabbat to this very last moment, so we make a point of experiencing it through all five of our senses: we *see* the light of the candle, we *feel* its warmth on our hands, we *smell* the spices, we *taste* the wine, and we *hear* the candle sizzle as it is put out in the wine.

While holding the candle, spices, and wine, we sing:

הִנֵּה אֵל יְשׁוּעָתִי, אֶבְטַח וְלֹא אֶפְחָד, כִּי עָזִּי וְזִמְרָת יָהּ יְיָ, וַיְהִי לִי לִישׁוּעָה: וּשְׁאַבְתֶּם מַיִם בְּשָׂשׂוֹן מִמַּעַיְנֵי הַיְשׁוּעָה: לַיְיָ הַיְשׁוּעָה עַל עַמְּךָ בִרְכָתֶךָ סֶּלָה: יְיָ צְבָאוֹת עִמָּנוּ מִשְׂגָּב לָנוּ אֱלֹהֵי יַעֲקֹב סֶלָה: יְיָ צְבָאוֹת אַשְׁרֵי אָדָם בֹּטֵחַ בָּךְ: יְיָ הוֹשִׁיעָה הַמֶּלֶךְ יַעֲנֵנוּ בְיוֹם קָרְאֵנוּ:

לַיְּהוּדִים הָיְתָה אוֹרָה וְשִׂמְחָה וְשָׂשׂוֹן וִיקָר:
כֵּן תִּהְיֶה לָּנוּ, כּוֹס יְשׁוּעוֹת אֶשָּׂא וּבְשֵׁם יְיָ אֶקְרָא:

We say the blessing over the wine (but don't drink it yet):

בָּרוּךְ אַתָּה יְיָ, אֱלֹהֵינוּ מֶלֶךְ הָעוֹלָם, בּוֹרֵא פְּרִי הַגָּפֶן.

We say the blessing over the spices, then smell them:

בָּרוּךְ אַתָּה יְיָ, אֱלֹהֵינוּ מֶלֶךְ הָעוֹלָם, בּוֹרֵא מִינֵי בְשָׂמִים:

We say the blessing over the light. As we say this blessing, hold your hands up to the light then look at the reflection in your fingernails:

בָּרוּךְ אַתָּה יְיָ, אֱלֹהֵינוּ מֶלֶךְ הָעוֹלָם, בּוֹרֵא מְאוֹרֵי הָאֵשׁ:

בָּרוּךְ אַתָּה יְיָ, אֱלֹהֵינוּ מֶלֶךְ הָעוֹלָם, הַמַּבְדִּיל בֵּין קֹדֶשׁ לְחוֹל, בֵּין אוֹר לְחֹשֶׁךְ, בֵּין יִשְׂרָאֵל לָעַמִּים, בֵּין יוֹם הַשְּׁבִיעִי, לְשֵׁשֶׁת יְמֵי הַמַּעֲשֶׂה: בָּרוּךְ אַתָּה יְיָ, הַמַּבְדִּיל בֵּין קֹדֶשׁ לְחוֹל:

Drink some of the wine and then put the candle out in it.

Prayers For Other Occasions

Avinu Malkenu

On sad days such as Fast Days, we add Avinu Malkenu after our prayers.

Our Parent, our Ruler answer us though we have no deeds to plead our cause; save us with mercy and lovingkindness.	Aveenu mal'kenu, chanenu va-anenu, Kee ein banu ma-aseem, Aseh imanu tz'dakah vachesed V'hoshee-enu.

Blessing of a New Month

On the Shabbat before Rosh Chodesh, we add this blessing to the Torah Service before returning the Torah to the Ark.

May it be your will, Adonai our God and God of our ancestors, To renew our lives in the coming month. Grant us long life, A peaceful life with goodness and blessing, Sustenance and physical vitality, A life of reverence and piety, A life free from shame and reproach, A life of abundance and honor, A reverent life guided by the love of Torah, A life in which our worthy aspirations will be fulfilled. Amen.

Y'hee ratzon mil'faneicha Adonai Eloheinu vElohei avoteinu, Shet'chadesh aleinu et hachodesh habah l'tovah v'liv'racha, V'titen lanu chayeem arukeem, Chayeem shel shalom, Chayeem she tovah, Chayeem shel b'racha, Chayeem shel par'nasah, Chayeem shel chilutz atzamot, Chayeem she'yesh bahem yir'at shamayim v'yir'at chet. Chayeem she-ein bahem bushah uch'limah, Chayeem shel oser v'chavod, Chayeem shet'heh vanu ahavat torah v'yir'at shamayim, Chayeem she-y'mal'u mish'alot libenu l'tovah, amen selah.

The leader holds the Torah and continues:

May God who made miracles for our ancestors, redeeming them from slavery to freedom, redeem us soon and gather our dispersed from the four corners of the earth in the fellowship of the entire people Israel. And let us say, amen.

Mee she-asah niseem la-avoteinu, v'ga-al otam me-av'dut l'cherut, hu yig'al otanu b'karov, veekabetz nidacheinu me-ar'ba kan'fot ha-aretz. Chavereem kol Yisrael, v'nomar amen.

The new month of _____ will begin on _____. May it hold blessing for us and for all the people Israel.

Rosh Chodesh _____ yih'yeh b'yom _____ haba aleinu v'al kol Yisrael l'tovah.

May the Holy One bless this new month for us and for all God's people, the House of Israel, with life and peace, joy and gladness, deliverance and consolation. And let us say, amen.

Y'chad'shehu hakadosh baruch hu, aleinu v'al kol amo beit Yisrael, l'chayeem ul'shalom. L'sason ul'sim'cha. Leeshu-ah ul'nechamah. V'nomar amen.

אָבִינוּ מַלְכֵּנוּ

On sad days such as Fast Days, we add Avinu Malkenu after our prayers.

אָבִינוּ מַלְכֵּנוּ, חָנֵּנוּ וַעֲנֵנוּ, כִּי אֵין בָּנוּ מַעֲשִׂים,
עֲשֵׂה עִמָּנוּ צְדָקָה וָחֶסֶד וְהוֹשִׁיעֵנוּ.

בִּרְכַּת הַחֹדֶשׁ

On the שבת *before* ראש חדש,
we add this blessing to the Torah Service before returning the Torah to the Ark.

יְהִי רָצוֹן מִלְּפָנֶיךָ יְיָ אֱלֹהֵינוּ וֵאלֹהֵי אֲבוֹתֵינוּ,
שֶׁתְּחַדֵּשׁ עָלֵינוּ אֶת הַחֹדֶשׁ הַבָּא לְטוֹבָה וְלִבְרָכָה,
וְתִתֶּן לָנוּ חַיִּים אֲרוּכִּים, חַיִּים שֶׁל שָׁלוֹם,
חַיִּים שֶׁל טוֹבָה, חַיִּים שֶׁל בְּרָכָה,
חַיִּים שֶׁל פַּרְנָסָה, חַיִּים שֶׁל חִלּוּץ עֲצָמוֹת,
חַיִּים שֶׁיֵּשׁ בָּהֶם יִרְאַת שָׁמַיִם וְיִרְאַת חֵטְא:
חַיִּים שֶׁאֵין בָּהֶם בּוּשָׁה וּכְלִמָּה,
חַיִּים שֶׁל עֹשֶׁר וְכָבוֹד,
חַיִּים שֶׁתְּהֵא בָּנוּ אַהֲבַת תּוֹרָה וְיִרְאַת שָׁמַיִם,
חַיִּים שֶׁיִּמָּלְאוּ מִשְׁאֲלוֹת לִבֵּנוּ לְטוֹבָה, אָמֵן סֶלָה:

The leader holds the Torah and continues:

מִי שֶׁעָשָׂה נִסִּים לַאֲבוֹתֵינוּ, וְגָאַל אוֹתָם מֵעַבְדוּת לְחֵרוּת, הוּא
יִגְאַל אוֹתָנוּ בְּקָרוֹב, וִיקַבֵּץ נִדָּחֵינוּ מֵאַרְבַּע כַּנְפוֹת הָאָרֶץ. חֲבֵרִים
כָּל יִשְׂרָאֵל, וְנֹאמַר אָמֵן:

רֹאשׁ חֹדֶשׁ _____ יִהְיֶה בְּיוֹם _____ הַבָּא עָלֵינוּ וְעַל כָּל
יִשְׂרָאֵל לְטוֹבָה:

יְחַדְּשֵׁהוּ הַקָּדוֹשׁ בָּרוּךְ הוּא, עָלֵינוּ וְעַל כָּל עַמּוֹ בֵּית יִשְׂרָאֵל,
לְחַיִּים וּלְשָׁלוֹם. (אָמֵן)
לְשָׂשׂוֹן וּלְשִׂמְחָה. (אָמֵן)
לִישׁוּעָה וּלְנֶחָמָה. וְנֹאמַר אָמֵן:

Prayers For Other Occasions

Prayers For Other Occasions

Prayer for Peace in Israel

Our Parent in heaven, Rock and Redeemer of the people Israel: Bless the state of Israel, with its promise of redemption. Shield it with your love; spread over it the shelter of your peace. Guide its leaders and advisors with Your light and Your truth. Help them with Your good counsel. Strengthen the hands of those who defend our Holy Land. Deliver them; crown their efforts with triumph. Bless the land with peace, and its inhabitants with lasting joy. And let us say: Amen.

Aveenu shebashamayim, tzur Yisra-el v'go-alo, barech et m'deenat yis'ra-el, resheet tz'meechat g'ulatenu. Hagen aleiha b'ev'rat chas'decha uf'ros aleiha sukat sh'lomecha ush'lach or'cha va-amit'cha l'rasheiha, sareiha v'yo-atzeiha, v'tak'nem b'etzah tovah mil'faneicha. Chazek et y'dei m'ginei eretz kod'sheinu, v'han'cheelem Eloheinu y'shu-ah, va-ateret nitzachon t'at'rem, v'natata shalom ba-arezt v'simchat olam l'yosh'veiha. V'nomar amen.

Traveller's Prayer

May it be Your will, Adonai our God and God of our ancestors, to guide us in peace, to sustain us in peace, to lead us to our desired destination in health and joy and peace, and to bring us home in peace. Save us from every enemy and disaster on the way, and from all calamities that threaten the world. Bless the work of our hands. May we find grace, love and compassion in Your sight and in the sight of all who see us. Hear our supplication, for You listen to prayer and supplication. Praised are You, Adonai, who hears prayer.

Y'hi ratzon mil'faneicha Adonai Eloheinu velohei avoteinu, shetoleechenu l'shalom v'tatz'eedenu l'shalom v'tis'm'chenu l'shalom, v'tagee-enu lim'choz chef'tzenu l'chayim ul'sim'cha ul'shalom, v'tachazeerenu l'veitenu l'shalom. V'tatzeelenu mikaf kol oyev v'orev baderech umikol meenei pur'anee-ot hamit'rag'shot lavo la-olam v'tish'lach b'racha b'ma-aseh yadeinu, v'tit'nenu l'chen ul'chesed ul'rachameem b'eineicha uv'einei chol ro-einu, v'tish'ma kol tachanuneinu, kee el shome-a t'filah v'tachanun atah. Baruch atah Adonai, shome-a t'filah.

בְּרָכוֹת

> There are many special things that we do at Camp Solomon Schechter that have special prayers. These prayers are not found anywhere else in our Siddur. This section has some blessings for special things and some for special times like *Havdallah*.

תְּפִלָּה לִשְׁלוֹם הַמְּדִינָה

אָבִינוּ שֶׁבַּשָּׁמַיִם, צוּר יִשְׂרָאֵל וְגוֹאֲלוֹ, בָּרֵךְ אֶת מְדִינַת יִשְׂרָאֵל, רֵאשִׁית צְמִיחַת גְּאֻלָּתֵנוּ. הָגֵן עָלֶיהָ בְּאֶבְרַת חַסְדֶּךָ וּפְרוֹשׂ עָלֶיהָ סֻכַּת שְׁלוֹמֶךָ וּשְׁלַח אוֹרְךָ וַאֲמִתְּךָ לְרָאשֶׁיהָ, שָׂרֶיהָ וְיוֹעֲצֶיהָ, וְתַקְּנֵם בְּעֵצָה טוֹבָה מִלְּפָנֶיךָ. חַזֵּק אֶת יְדֵי מְגִנֵּי אֶרֶץ קָדְשֵׁנוּ, וְהַנְחִילֵם אֱלֹהֵינוּ יְשׁוּעָה, וַעֲטֶרֶת נִצָּחוֹן תְּעַטְּרֵם, וְנָתַתָּ שָׁלוֹם בָּאָרֶץ וְשִׂמְחַת עוֹלָם לְיוֹשְׁבֶיהָ. וְנֹאמַר אָמֵן.

תְּפִלַּת הַדֶּרֶךְ

יְהִי רָצוֹן מִלְּפָנֶיךָ יְיָ אֱלֹהֵינוּ וֵאלֹהֵי אֲבוֹתֵינוּ, שֶׁתּוֹלִיכֵנוּ לְשָׁלוֹם וְתַצְעִידֵנוּ לְשָׁלוֹם וְתִסְמְכֵנוּ לְשָׁלוֹם, וְתַגִּיעֵנוּ לִמְחוֹז חֶפְצֵנוּ לְחַיִּים וּלְשִׂמְחָה וּלְשָׁלוֹם, וְתַחֲזִירֵנוּ לְבֵיתֵנוּ לְשָׁלוֹם. וְתַצִּילֵנוּ מִכַּף כָּל אוֹיֵב וְאוֹרֵב בַּדֶּרֶךְ וּמִכָּל מִינֵי פֻּרְעָנִיּוֹת הַמִּתְרַגְּשׁוֹת לָבוֹא לָעוֹלָם, וְתִשְׁלַח בְּרָכָה בְּמַעֲשֵׂה יָדֵינוּ, וְתִתְּנֵנוּ לְחֵן וּלְחֶסֶד וּלְרַחֲמִים בְּעֵינֶיךָ וּבְעֵינֵי כָל רוֹאֵינוּ, וְתִשְׁמַע קוֹל תַּחֲנוּנֵינוּ, כִּי אֵל שׁוֹמֵעַ תְּפִלָּה וְתַחֲנוּן אָתָּה. בָּרוּךְ אַתָּה יְיָ, שׁוֹמֵעַ תְּפִלָּה.

Prayers For Other Occasions

Halleluyah.	Hal'lu et Adonai kol goyim,
Praise Adonai, all nations,	Shab'chuhu kol ha'umeem.
Praise God, all peoples!	Kee gavar aleinu chas'do,
God's kindness overwhelmed us.	Ve-emet Adonai l'olam hal'luyah!
Adonai's truth is forever. Halleluyah!	

Thank Adonai for being good,	Hodu lAdonai kee tov,
God's kindness lasts forever.	Kee l'olam chas'do.
Let Israel say:	Yomar na Yisra-el,
God's kindness lasts forever.	Kee l'olam chas'do.
Let the House of Aaron say:	Yom'ru na veit Aharon,
God's kindness lasts forever.	Kee l'olam chas'do.
Let those who respect Adonai say:	Yom'ru na yir'ei Adonai,
God's kindness lasts forever.	Kee l'olam chas'do.

Each of the following lines is recited twice:

I thank You for answering me	Od'cha kee aneetanee
And rescuing me.	Vat'hee lee leeshu-ah.
The stone which the builders rejected	Even ma'asu haboneem
Is now the cornerstone.	Hai'ta l'rosh pinah.
This is Adonai's doing.	Me-et Adonai hai'ta zot,
It is wonderful in our eyes.	Hee nif'lat b'eineinu.
This is the day that Adonai has made;	Zeh hayom asah Adonai,
Let us rejoice and be glad on it.	Nageelah v'nism'cha vo.

Each of the following lines is repeated after the leader:

Please Adonai, save us!	Ana Adonai hoshee-ah na.
Please Adonai, save us!	Ana Adonai hoshee-ah na.
Please Adonai, cause us to succeed!	Ana Adonai hatz'leecha na.
Please Adonai, cause us to succeed!	Ana Adonai hatz'leecha na.

We are seated.

Praised are you, Adonai, who is a Ruler	Baruch atah Adonai, Melech m'hulal
praised with songs or praise.	batish'bahchot.

הַלְלוּ אֶת יְיָ, כָּל גּוֹיִם, שַׁבְּחוּהוּ כָּל הָאֻמִּים.
כִּי גָבַר עָלֵינוּ חַסְדּוֹ, וֶאֱמֶת יְיָ לְעוֹלָם הַלְלוּיָהּ:

PSALM 117

הוֹדוּ לַיְיָ כִּי טוֹב, כִּי לְעוֹלָם חַסְדּוֹ:
יֹאמַר נָא יִשְׂרָאֵל, כִּי לְעוֹלָם חַסְדּוֹ:
יֹאמְרוּ נָא בֵית אַהֲרֹן, כִּי לְעוֹלָם חַסְדּוֹ:
יֹאמְרוּ נָא יִרְאֵי יְיָ, כִּי לְעוֹלָם חַסְדּוֹ:

PSALM 118:1–4

Each of the following lines is recited twice:

אוֹדְךָ כִּי עֲנִיתָנִי וַתְּהִי לִי לִישׁוּעָה.
אֶבֶן מָאֲסוּ הַבּוֹנִים, הָיְתָה לְרֹאשׁ פִּנָּה.
מֵאֵת יְיָ הָיְתָה זֹּאת, הִיא נִפְלָאת בְּעֵינֵינוּ.
זֶה הַיּוֹם עָשָׂה יְיָ, נָגִילָה וְנִשְׂמְחָה בוֹ.

PSALM 118:21–24

Each of the following lines is repeated after the leader:

אָנָּא יְיָ הוֹשִׁיעָה נָּא:
אָנָּא יְיָ הוֹשִׁיעָה נָּא:
אָנָּא יְיָ הַצְלִיחָה נָא:
אָנָּא יְיָ הַצְלִיחָה נָא:

בָּרוּךְ אַתָּה יְיָ, מֶלֶךְ מְהֻלָּל בַּתִּשְׁבָּחוֹת.

We are seated.

Hallel

Psalms of Praise

We rise.

Praised are You, Adonai our God, Ruler of the universe, who made us holy through mitzvot and commanded us to read the Hallel.

Baruch atah Adonai Eloheinu melech haolam, asher kid'shanu b'mitz'votav v'tzivanu lik'ro et hahalel.

When Israel went of out Egypt,
The House of Jacob from a foreign people,
Judah became God's holy people,
Isreal, God's nation.
The sea saw and turned back,
the Jordan fled.
The mountains jumped like rams,
the hills, like lambs.
What is with you, sea, that you flee;
Jordan, that you turn back?
Mountains, that you jump like rams;
hills, like lambs?
Quake, earth, before the Ruler,
before the God of Jacob,
Who turns the rock into a pool of water;
Who turns flint into fountains.

B'tzet Yisra-el miMitz'rayim
Beit Ya'akov mei-am lo-ez.
Hai'tah Yehudah l'kod'sho,
Yisra-el mam'sh'lotav.
Hayam ra-ah vayanos,
HaYar'den yisov l'achor.
Hehareem rak'du ch'eileem,
G'va-ot kiv'nei tzon.
Ma l'cha hayam kee tanus,
HaYar'den tisov l'achor.
Hehareem tir'k'du ch'eileem,
G'va'ot kiv'nei tzon.
Milif'nei adon chuli aretz,
Milif'nei Eloha Ya-akov.
Hahof'chi hatzur agam mayim,
Chalameesh l'mai'no mayim.

God will remember us and bless us,
God will bless the House of Israel.
God will bless the House of Aaron.
God will bless those who respect Adonai,
everyone alike.
May Adonai increase you and your children.
You are blessed by Adonai,
Who made heaven and earth.
The heavens belong to Adonai,
But the earth was given to human beings.
The dead do not praise God,
Nor do those that death silences.
But we will praise God now and forever.
Halleluyah!

Adonai z'charanu y'varech,
Y'varech et beit Yisra-el,
Y'varech et beit Aharon.
Y'varech yir'ei Adonai,
Hak'taneem im hag'doleem.
Yosef Adonai aleichem,
Aleichem v'al b'neichem.
B'rucheem atem lAdonai,
Oseh shamayim va-aretz.
Hashamayim shamayim lAdonai,
V'ha-aretz natan liv'nei adam.
Lo hameteem y'hal'lu Yah,
V'lo kol yor'dei dumah.
Va-anach'nu n'varech Yah,
May-atah v'ad olam. Hal'luyah.

> On special days such as Holidays and Rosh Chodesh, we add this special group of *t'hilim* (psalms) to the *Shacharit* service, all of which praise God.

We rise.

בָּרוּךְ אַתָּה יְיָ אֱלֹהֵינוּ מֶלֶךְ הָעוֹלָם, אֲשֶׁר קִדְּשָׁנוּ בְּמִצְוֹתָיו וְצִוָּנוּ לִקְרֹא אֶת הַהַלֵּל.

בְּצֵאת יִשְׂרָאֵל מִמִּצְרָיִם, בֵּית יַעֲקֹב מֵעַם לֹעֵז.
הָיְתָה יְהוּדָה לְקָדְשׁוֹ, יִשְׂרָאֵל מַמְשְׁלוֹתָיו.
הַיָּם רָאָה וַיָּנֹס, הַיַּרְדֵּן יִסֹּב לְאָחוֹר:
הֶהָרִים רָקְדוּ כְאֵילִים, גְּבָעוֹת כִּבְנֵי צֹאן.
מַה לְּךָ הַיָּם כִּי תָנוּס הַיַּרְדֵּן תִּסֹּב לְאָחוֹר.
הֶהָרִים תִּרְקְדוּ כְאֵילִים, גְּבָעוֹת כִּבְנֵי צֹאן.
מִלִּפְנֵי אָדוֹן חוּלִי אָרֶץ, מִלִּפְנֵי אֱלוֹהַּ יַעֲקֹב.
הַהֹפְכִי הַצּוּר אֲגַם מָיִם, חַלָּמִישׁ לְמַעְיְנוֹ מָיִם:

PSALM 114

יְיָ זְכָרָנוּ יְבָרֵךְ,
יְבָרֵךְ אֶת בֵּית יִשְׂרָאֵל, יְבָרֵךְ אֶת בֵּית אַהֲרֹן.
יְבָרֵךְ יִרְאֵי יְיָ, הַקְּטַנִּים עִם הַגְּדֹלִים.
יֹסֵף יְיָ עֲלֵיכֶם, עֲלֵיכֶם וְעַל בְּנֵיכֶם.
בְּרוּכִים אַתֶּם לַיְיָ, עֹשֵׂה שָׁמַיִם וָאָרֶץ.
הַשָּׁמַיִם שָׁמַיִם לַיְיָ, וְהָאָרֶץ נָתַן לִבְנֵי אָדָם.
לֹא הַמֵּתִים יְהַלְלוּ יָהּ, וְלֹא כָּל יֹרְדֵי דוּמָה.
וַאֲנַחְנוּ נְבָרֵךְ יָהּ, מֵעַתָּה וְעַד עוֹלָם,
הַלְלוּיָהּ:

PSALM 115:12–18

Hallel

Mourner's Kaddish

Mourners:

May God's great name be made great and holy in the world which God created according to God's will. May God establish Divine rule soon, in our days, quickly and in the near future, and let us say: Amen.

Yit'gadal v'yit'kadash sh'meh rabah. B'al'mah dee v'rah chir'utei, v'yam'leech mal'chutei b'chayeichon uv'yomeichon uv'chayei d'chol beit Yisra-el. Ba-agalah uviz'man kareev v'im'ru amen.

Everyone:

May God's great name be praised for ever and ever.

Y'heh sh'meh rabah m'varach l'alam ul'al'mei al'mayah.

Mourners:

Blessed, praised, glorified and raised high, honored and elevated be the name of the Holy Blessed One, far beyond all blessings and songs, praises and words of comfort which people can say, and let us say: Amen.

Yit'barach v'yishtabach v'yitpa-ar v'yit'romam v'yit'naseh v'yit'hadar v'yit'aleh v'yit'halal sh'meh d'kud'shah b'reech hu l'elah min kol bir'chatah v'sheeratah tush'b'chatah v'nechematah, da-ameeran b'al'mah, v'im'ru amen.

May there be abundant peace from heaven and life for us and for all Israel, and let us say: Amen.

Y'hei sh'lamah rabah min sh'mayah v'chayeem aleinu v'al kol Yisra-el, v'im'ru amen.

May the One who makes peace in the high heavens make peace for us and for all Israel, and let us say: Amen.

Oseh shalom bim'romav, hu ya-aseh shalom aleinu, v'al kol Yisra-el v'im'ru amen.

קדִּישׁ יָתוֹם

Mourners:

יִתְגַּדַּל וְיִתְקַדַּשׁ שְׁמֵהּ רַבָּא. בְּעָלְמָא דִּי בְרָא כִרְעוּתֵיהּ, וְיַמְלִיךְ מַלְכוּתֵהּ בְּחַיֵּיכוֹן וּבְיוֹמֵיכוֹן וּבְחַיֵּי דְכָל בֵּית יִשְׂרָאֵל. בַּעֲגָלָא וּבִזְמַן קָרִיב וְאִמְרוּ אָמֵן:

Everyone:

יְהֵא שְׁמֵהּ רַבָּא מְבָרַךְ לְעָלַם וּלְעָלְמֵי עָלְמַיָּא:

Mourners:

יִתְבָּרַךְ וְיִשְׁתַּבַּח וְיִתְפָּאַר וְיִתְרוֹמַם וְיִתְנַשֵּׂא וְיִתְהַדָּר וְיִתְעַלֶּה וְיִתְהַלָּל שְׁמֵהּ דְּקֻדְשָׁא בְּרִיךְ הוּא לְעֵלָּא מִן כָּל בִּרְכָתָא וְשִׁירָתָא תֻּשְׁבְּחָתָא וְנֶחֱמָתָא, דַּאֲמִירָן בְּעָלְמָא, וְאִמְרוּ אָמֵן:

יְהֵא שְׁלָמָא רַבָּא מִן שְׁמַיָּא וְחַיִּים עָלֵינוּ וְעַל כָּל יִשְׂרָאֵל, וְאִמְרוּ אָמֵן:

עֹשֶׂה שָׁלוֹם בִּמְרוֹמָיו הוּא יַעֲשֶׂה שָׁלוֹם עָלֵינוּ וְעַל כָּל יִשְׂרָאֵל, וְאִמְרוּ אָמֵן:

Aleinu

We rise.

We should praise God for not making us like the other peoples and families of the earth. We bend the knee and bow and give thanks to the Ruler of all earthly rulers, the Blessed Holy One. God spread out the heavens and built the earth's foundations. God's mighty presence is in the highest heights. God is our God—no one else. Our Ruler is true. There is nothing besides God, as it is written in God's Torah: "You shall know therefore this day and keep in mind that Adonai alone is God in heaven above and on earth below; there is no other."

And so we hope in You, Adonai our God, soon to see Your power used in a wonderful way: removing false gods from the earth, fixing the brokenness of the world so that it will be a world truly ruled by God. All humanity will call Your name, and all the wicked of the earth will turn toward You. All who live in the world will know and understand that everyone should accept You as their God. They will bow to You, Adonai our God, honoring the glory of Your name. For You will rule the world, and You will always rule over it in glory, as it is written in the Torah: "Adonai will rule for ever and ever." And as the prophet Zechariah said: "Then God will be Ruler over all the earth. On that day Adonai will be One and God's name will be One."

Aleinu l'shabe-ach la-adon hakol, latet g'dulah l'yotzer b'resheet, shelo asanu k'goyei ha-aratzot, v'lo samanu k'mish'p'chot ha-adamah, shelo sam chel'kenu kahem, v'goralenu k'chol hamonam. Va-anachnu kor'eem umish'tachaveem umodeem, lifnei melech, malchei ham'lacheem, hakadosh baruch hu. Shehu noteh shamayeem v'yosed aretz, umoshav y'karo bashamayim mima-al, ush'cheenat uzo b'gav'hei m'romeem, hu Eloheinu ein od. Emet malkenu efes zulato, kakatuv b'Torato: V'yada'ta hayom vahashevota El l'vavecha, kee Adonai hu haEloheem bashamayim mima-al, v'al ha-aretz mitachat, ein od.

Al ken n'kaveh l'cha Adonai Eloheinu, lir'ot m'hera b'tif'eret uzecha, l'ha-aveer giluleem min ha-aretz v'ha-eleeleem karot yikaretun. L'taken olam b'mal'chut shadai, v'chol b'nei vasar yik'r'u vish'mecha. L'haf'not eleicha kol rish'ei aretz. Yakeeru v'yed'u kol yosh'vei tevel, kee l'cha tich'ra kol berech, tishava kol lashon. L'faneicha Adonai Eloheinu yich'r'u v'yipolu. V'lich'vod shim'cha y'kar yitenu. Veekab'lu chulam et ol mal'chutecha. V'tim'loch aleihem m'herah l'olam va-ed.
❖ Kakatuv b'toratecha, Adonai yim'loch l'olam va-ed. V'ne-emar, v'haya Adonai l'melech al kol ha-aretz, bayom hahu yih'yeh Adonai echad, ush'mo echad.

We are seated.

מנחה לשבת

עָלֵינוּ
We rise.

עָלֵינוּ לְשַׁבֵּחַ לַאֲדוֹן הַכֹּל, לָתֵת גְּדֻלָּה לְיוֹצֵר בְּרֵאשִׁית, שֶׁלֹּא עָשָׂנוּ כְּגוֹיֵי הָאֲרָצוֹת, וְלֹא שָׂמָנוּ כְּמִשְׁפְּחוֹת הָאֲדָמָה, שֶׁלֹּא שָׂם חֶלְקֵנוּ כָּהֶם, וְגֹרָלֵנוּ כְּכָל הֲמוֹנָם:
וַאֲנַחְנוּ כּוֹרְעִים וּמִשְׁתַּחֲוִים וּמוֹדִים,
לִפְנֵי מֶלֶךְ, מַלְכֵי הַמְּלָכִים, הַקָּדוֹשׁ בָּרוּךְ הוּא.
שֶׁהוּא נוֹטֶה שָׁמַיִם וְיֹסֵד אָרֶץ, וּמוֹשַׁב יְקָרוֹ בַּשָּׁמַיִם מִמַּעַל, וּשְׁכִינַת עֻזּוֹ בְּגָבְהֵי מְרוֹמִים, הוּא אֱלֹהֵינוּ אֵין עוֹד. אֱמֶת מַלְכֵּנוּ אֶפֶס זוּלָתוֹ, כַּכָּתוּב בְּתוֹרָתוֹ: וְיָדַעְתָּ הַיּוֹם וַהֲשֵׁבֹתָ אֶל לְבָבֶךָ, כִּי יְיָ הוּא הָאֱלֹהִים בַּשָּׁמַיִם מִמַּעַל, וְעַל הָאָרֶץ מִתָּחַת, אֵין עוֹד:

עַל כֵּן נְקַוֶּה לְּךָ יְיָ אֱלֹהֵינוּ, לִרְאוֹת מְהֵרָה בְּתִפְאֶרֶת עֻזֶּךָ, לְהַעֲבִיר גִּלּוּלִים מִן הָאָרֶץ, וְהָאֱלִילִים כָּרוֹת יִכָּרֵתוּן. לְתַקֵּן עוֹלָם בְּמַלְכוּת שַׁדַּי, וְכָל בְּנֵי בָשָׂר יִקְרְאוּ בִשְׁמֶךָ. לְהַפְנוֹת אֵלֶיךָ כָּל רִשְׁעֵי אָרֶץ. יַכִּירוּ וְיֵדְעוּ כָּל יוֹשְׁבֵי תֵבֵל, כִּי לְךָ תִּכְרַע כָּל בֶּרֶךְ, תִּשָּׁבַע כָּל לָשׁוֹן: לְפָנֶיךָ יְיָ אֱלֹהֵינוּ יִכְרְעוּ וְיִפֹּלוּ. וְלִכְבוֹד שִׁמְךָ יְקָר יִתֵּנוּ. וִיקַבְּלוּ כֻלָּם אֶת עוֹל מַלְכוּתֶךָ. וְתִמְלֹךְ עֲלֵיהֶם מְהֵרָה לְעוֹלָם וָעֶד. כִּי הַמַּלְכוּת שֶׁלְּךָ הִיא, וּלְעוֹלְמֵי עַד תִּמְלוֹךְ בְּכָבוֹד:
❖ כַּכָּתוּב בְּתוֹרָתֶךָ, יְיָ יִמְלֹךְ לְעוֹלָם וָעֶד: וְנֶאֱמַר: וְהָיָה יְיָ לְמֶלֶךְ עַל כָּל הָאָרֶץ, בַּיּוֹם הַהוּא יִהְיֶה יְיָ אֶחָד, וּשְׁמוֹ אֶחָד:

We are seated.

Shabbat Afternoon Prayers

Kaddish Shalem

Leader:

May God's great name be made great and holy in the world which God created according to God's will. May God establish Divine rule soon, in our days, quickly and in the near future, and let us say: Amen.

Yit'gadal v'yit'kadash sh'meh rabah. B'al'mah dee v'rah chir'utei, v'yam'leech mal'chutei b'chayeichon uv'yomeichon uv'chayei d'chol beit Yisra-el. Ba-agalah uviz'man kareev v'im'ru amen.

Everyone:

May God's great name be praised for ever and ever.

Y'heh sh'meh rabah m'varach l'alam ul'al'mei al'mayah.

Leader:

Blessed, praised, glorified and raised high, honored and elevated be the name of the Holy Blessed One, far beyond all blessings and songs, praises and words of comfort which people can say, and let us say: Amen.

Yit'barach v'yishtabach v'yitpa-ar v'yit'romam v'yit'naseh v'yit'hadar v'yit'aleh v'yit'halal sh'meh d'kud'shah b'reech hu l'elah min kol bir'chatah v'sheeratah tush'b'chatah v'nechematah, da-ameeran b'al'mah, v'im'ru amen.

May the prayers and pleas of the entire House of Israel be accepted before their Parent in heaven. And let us say: Amen.

Tit'kabal tz'lot'hon uva-ut'hon d'chol Yisra-el kadam avuhon dee vish'mayah v'im'ru amen.

May there be abundant peace from heaven and life for us and for all Israel, and let us say: Amen.

Y'hei sh'lamah rabah min sh'mayah v'chayeem aleinu v'al kol Yisra-el, v'im'ru amen.

May the One who makes peace in the high heavens make peace for us and for all Israel, and let us say: Amen.

Oseh shalom bim'romav, hu ya-aseh shalom aleinu, v'al kol Yisra-el v'im'ru amen.

מנחה לשבת

קַדִישׁ שָׁלֵם

Leader:

יִתְגַּדַּל וְיִתְקַדַּשׁ שְׁמֵהּ רַבָּא. בְּעָלְמָא דִּי בְרָא כִרְעוּתֵיהּ, וְיַמְלִיךְ מַלְכוּתֵהּ בְּחַיֵּיכוֹן וּבְיוֹמֵיכוֹן וּבְחַיֵּי דְכָל בֵּית יִשְׂרָאֵל. בַּעֲגָלָא וּבִזְמַן קָרִיב וְאִמְרוּ אָמֵן:

Everyone:

יְהֵא שְׁמֵהּ רַבָּא מְבָרַךְ לְעָלַם וּלְעָלְמֵי עָלְמַיָּא:

Leader:

יִתְבָּרַךְ וְיִשְׁתַּבַּח וְיִתְפָּאַר וְיִתְרוֹמַם וְיִתְנַשֵּׂא וְיִתְהַדָּר וְיִתְעַלֶּה וְיִתְהַלָּל שְׁמֵהּ דְּקֻדְשָׁא בְּרִיךְ הוּא לְעֵלָּא מִן כָּל בִּרְכָתָא וְשִׁירָתָא תֻּשְׁבְּחָתָא וְנֶחֱמָתָא, דַּאֲמִירָן בְּעָלְמָא, וְאִמְרוּ אָמֵן:

תִּתְקַבֵּל צְלוֹתְהוֹן וּבָעוּתְהוֹן דְּכָל יִשְׂרָאֵל קֳדָם אֲבוּהוֹן דִּי בִשְׁמַיָּא וְאִמְרוּ אָמֵן:

יְהֵא שְׁלָמָא רַבָּא מִן שְׁמַיָּא וְחַיִּים עָלֵינוּ וְעַל כָּל יִשְׂרָאֵל, וְאִמְרוּ אָמֵן:

עֹשֶׂה שָׁלוֹם בִּמְרוֹמָיו הוּא יַעֲשֶׂה שָׁלוֹם עָלֵינוּ וְעַל כָּל יִשְׂרָאֵל, וְאִמְרוּ אָמֵן:

May we see Your merciful return to Zion. Praised are You, Adonai, who restores Your presence to Zion.

We thank You for being our God and God of our ancestors for ever and ever. You are the Rock of our lives and our saving Shield. In every generation we will thank and praise You for our lives which are in Your power, for our souls which are in Your keeping, for Your miracles which are with us every day, and for Your wonders and good deeds that are with us at all times, evening, morning, and noon. O Good One, Your mercies have never stopped. O Merciful One, Your kindness has never stopped. We have always placed our hope in You.

For all these things, our Ruler, may Your name be blessed and honored forever.

May every living thing thank You and praise You sincerely, O God, our rescue and help. Praised are You, Your name is the Good One, and it is good to thank You.

Give peace to Your people Israel and to the whole world forever, for You are the Ruler of peace. May it please You always to bless Your people Israel with Your peace.

Praised are You, Adonai, who blesses Your people Israel with peace.

My God, help me not to say bad things or to tell lies. Help me to ignore people who say bad things about me. Open my heart to Your Torah, so that I can do Your mitzvot. Quickly stop the ideas and spoil the plans of anyone who wants to hurt me. Do this because of Your love, Your holiness, and Your Torah: so that those You love will be free. May the words of my mouth and the thoughts of my heart find favor with You, my Rock and my Protector. May the One who makes peace up above give peace to us and to all the people of Israel. Amen.

V'techezeinah eineinu b'shuv'cha l'tzee-on b'rachameem. Baruch atah Adonai, hamachazeer sh'cheenato l'tzee-on.

Modeem anach'nu lach, sha-atah hu, Adonai Eloheinu vElohei avoteinu, l'olam va-ed, tzur chayeinu, magen yish'enu, atah hu l'dor vador nodeh l'cha un'saper t'hilatecha. Al chayeinu ham'sureem b'yadecha, v'al nish'moteinu hap'kudot lach, v'al niseicha sheb'chol yom imanu, v'al nif'l'oteicha v'tovoteicha sheb'chol et, erev vavoker v'tzohorayim, hatov kee lo chalu rachameicha, v'ham'rachem kee lo tamu chasadeicha me-olam kiveenu lach.

V'al kulam yitbarach v'yit'romam shim'cha, mal'kenu, tameed l'olam va-ed.

V'chol hachayeem yoducha selah, veehal'lu et shim'cha be-emet, ha-El y'shu-atenu v'ez'ratenu selah. Baruch atah Adonai, hatov shim'cha ul'cha na-eh l'hodot.

Shalom rav al Yisra-el am'cha taseem l'olam, kee atah hu melech adon l'chol hashalom. V'tov b'eineicha l'varech et am'cha Yisra-el b'chol et uv'chol sha-ah bish'lomecha.

Baruch atah Adonai, ham'varech et amo Yisra-el bashalom.

Elohai, n'tzor l'shonee mera. Us'fatai midaber mir'mah. V'lim'kal'lai naf'shee tidom, v'naf'shee ke-afar lakol tih'yeh. P'tach libee b'Torahtecha, uv'mitzvoteicha tir'dof naf'shee. V'chol hachosh'veem alai ra-ah, m'herah hafer atzatam v'kal'kel macahshav'tam. Aseh l'ma-an Toratecha. Lama-an yechal'tzun y'deedeicha, hoshee-ah y'meen'cha va-anenee. Yih'yu l'ratzon im'rei fee v'heg'yon libee l'faneicha, Adonai tzuree v'go-alee. Oseh shalom bim'romav, hu ya-aseh shalom aleinu, v'al kol Yisra-el v'im'ru amen.

מנחה לשבת

וְתֶחֱזֶינָה עֵינֵינוּ בְּשׁוּבְךָ לְצִיּוֹן בְּרַחֲמִים. בָּרוּךְ אַתָּה יְיָ, הַמַּחֲזִיר שְׁכִינָתוֹ לְצִיּוֹן.

מוֹדִים אֲנַחְנוּ לָךְ, שָׁאַתָּה הוּא, יְיָ אֱלֹהֵינוּ וֵאלֹהֵי אֲבוֹתֵינוּ, לְעוֹלָם וָעֶד, צוּר חַיֵּינוּ, מָגֵן יִשְׁעֵנוּ, אַתָּה הוּא לְדוֹר וָדוֹר נוֹדֶה לְךָ וּנְסַפֵּר תְּהִלָּתֶךָ. עַל חַיֵּינוּ הַמְּסוּרִים בְּיָדֶךָ, וְעַל נִשְׁמוֹתֵינוּ הַפְּקוּדוֹת לָךְ, וְעַל נִסֶּיךָ שֶׁבְּכָל יוֹם עִמָּנוּ, וְעַל נִפְלְאוֹתֶיךָ וְטוֹבוֹתֶיךָ שֶׁבְּכָל עֵת, עֶרֶב וָבֹקֶר וְצָהֳרָיִם, הַטּוֹב כִּי לֹא כָלוּ רַחֲמֶיךָ, וְהַמְרַחֵם כִּי לֹא תַמּוּ חֲסָדֶיךָ מֵעוֹלָם קִוִּינוּ לָךְ.

וְעַל כֻּלָּם יִתְבָּרַךְ וְיִתְרוֹמַם שִׁמְךָ, מַלְכֵּנוּ, תָּמִיד לְעוֹלָם וָעֶד.

וְכֹל הַחַיִּים יוֹדוּךָ סֶּלָה, וִיהַלְלוּ אֶת שִׁמְךָ בֶּאֱמֶת, הָאֵל יְשׁוּעָתֵנוּ וְעֶזְרָתֵנוּ סֶלָה. בָּרוּךְ אַתָּה יְיָ, הַטּוֹב שִׁמְךָ וּלְךָ נָאֶה לְהוֹדוֹת.

שָׁלוֹם רָב עַל יִשְׂרָאֵל עַמְּךָ תָּשִׂים לְעוֹלָם, כִּי אַתָּה הוּא מֶלֶךְ אָדוֹן לְכָל הַשָּׁלוֹם. וְטוֹב בְּעֵינֶיךָ לְבָרֵךְ אֶת עַמְּךָ יִשְׂרָאֵל בְּכָל עֵת וּבְכָל שָׁעָה בִּשְׁלוֹמֶךָ.

בָּרוּךְ אַתָּה יְיָ, הַמְבָרֵךְ אֶת עַמּוֹ יִשְׂרָאֵל בַּשָּׁלוֹם.

אֱלֹהַי, נְצוֹר לְשׁוֹנִי מֵרָע. וּשְׂפָתַי מִדַּבֵּר מִרְמָה: וְלִמְקַלְלַי נַפְשִׁי תִדֹּם, וְנַפְשִׁי כֶּעָפָר לַכֹּל תִּהְיֶה. פְּתַח לִבִּי בְּתוֹרָתֶךָ, וּבְמִצְוֹתֶיךָ תִּרְדּוֹף נַפְשִׁי. וְכָל הַחוֹשְׁבִים עָלַי רָעָה, מְהֵרָה הָפֵר עֲצָתָם וְקַלְקֵל מַחֲשַׁבְתָּם. עֲשֵׂה לְמַעַן שְׁמֶךָ, עֲשֵׂה לְמַעַן יְמִינֶךָ, עֲשֵׂה לְמַעַן קְדֻשָּׁתֶךָ. עֲשֵׂה לְמַעַן תּוֹרָתֶךָ. לְמַעַן יֵחָלְצוּן יְדִידֶיךָ, הוֹשִׁיעָה יְמִינְךָ וַעֲנֵנִי. יִהְיוּ לְרָצוֹן אִמְרֵי פִי וְהֶגְיוֹן לִבִּי לְפָנֶיךָ, יְיָ צוּרִי וְגוֹאֲלִי. עֹשֶׂה שָׁלוֹם בִּמְרוֹמָיו, הוּא יַעֲשֶׂה שָׁלוֹם עָלֵינוּ, וְעַל כָּל יִשְׂרָאֵל וְאִמְרוּ: אָמֵן.

We are seated.

You are one, Your name is One, and who is like Your people Israel, unique throughout the world? Singular splendor, crown of salvation, a day of rest and sanctity You have given to Your people. Abraham was glad, Isaac rejoiced, Jacob and his children found rest on this day—a rest reflecting Your lavish love and true faithfulnes in peace and tranquility, contentment and quietude a perfect rest in which You delight. May Your children acknowledge You as their source of rest. And through their rest may they sanctify Your name.

Atah echad v'shim'cha echad, umee k'am'cha Yisra-el goi echad ba-aretz, tif'eret g'dulah, va-ateret y'shu-ah, yom m'nuchah uk'dushah l'am'cha natata, Avraham yagel, Yitzchak y'ranen, Ya-akov uvanav yanuchu vo, m'nuchat ahavah un'davah, m'nuchat emet ve-emunah, m'nuchat shalom v'shal'vah v'hash'ket vavetach, m'nuchah sh'lemah sha-atah rotzeh bah, yakeeru vaneicha v'yed'u kee me-it'cha hee m'nuchatam, v'al m'nuchatam yak'deeshu et sh'mecha.

Our God and God of our ancestors, be pleased with our Shabbat rest, make us holy with Your mitzvot and let us share in Your Torah. Satisfy us with Your goodness and make us happy with Your help. Purify our hearts so that we can serve You truly. Adonai our God, let us receive Your holy Shabbat with love and favor, so that Your people Israel who make Your name holy will rest on it. Praised are You Adonai, who makes the Shabbat holy.

Eloheinu vElohei avoteinu, r'tzeh vim'nuchatenu, kad'shenu b'mitz'voteicha v'ten chel'kenu b'toratecha, sab'enu mituvecha v'sam'chenu beeshu-atecha, v'taher libenu l'ov'd'cha be-emet, v'han'cheelenu Adonai Eloheinu b'ahavah uv'ratzon Shabbat kod'shecha, v'yanuchu vah Yisra-el m'kad'shei sh'mecha. Baruch atah Adonai, m'kadesh haShabbat.

Adonai, be pleased with Your people Israel and with their prayer. Restore worship to Your Temple. May the prayer of Your people Israel always be accepted with love and favor.

R'tzeh, Adonai Eloheinu, b'am'cha Yisra-el uvit'filatam, v'hashev et ha-avodah lid'veer beitecha, ut'filatam b'ahavah t'kabel b'ratzon, ut'hee l'ratzon tameed avodat Yisra-el amecha.

On Rosh Chodesh, add the following:

Our God and God of our ancestors, please remember us, our ancestors, the Messiah, Your holy city Jerusalem, and Your people Israel. Remember them for good, with mercy and lovingkindness, for life and peace on this day of the New Moon.
Remember us, Adonai our God; keep us in mind for blessing, and give us life. You promised to protect and save us, have mercy on us and save us, for our eyes turn to You, for You are a kind and merciful Ruler.

Eloheinu vElohei avoteinu, ya-aleh v'yavo, v'yagee-a, v'yera-eh, v'yeratzeh, v'yishama, v'yipaked, v'yizacher zich'ronenu ufikdonenu, v'zich'ron avoteinu mashiach ben David av'decha, v'zich'ron Y'rushalayim eer kod'shecha, v'zich'ron kol am'cha beit Yisra-el l'faneicha, lif'leitah, l'tovah, l'chen ul'chesed ul'rachameem, l'chayim ul'shalom, b'yom Rosh Hachodesh hazeh.
Zochrenu, Adonai, Eloheinu, bo l'tovah, ufok'denu vo liv'rachah, v'hoshee-enu vo l'chayim, uvid'var y'shu-ah v'rachameem, chus v'chonenu, v'rachem aleinu v'hoshee-enu, kee eleicha eineinu, kee El melech chanun v'rachum atah.

אַתָּה אֶחָד וְשִׁמְךָ אֶחָד, וּמִי כְּעַמְּךָ יִשְׂרָאֵל גּוֹי אֶחָד בָּאָרֶץ, תִּפְאֶרֶת גְּדֻלָּה, וַעֲטֶרֶת יְשׁוּעָה, יוֹם מְנוּחָה וּקְדֻשָּׁה לְעַמְּךָ נָתָתָּ, אַבְרָהָם יָגֵל, יִצְחָק יְרַנֵּן, יַעֲקֹב וּבָנָיו יָנוּחוּ בוֹ, מְנוּחַת אַהֲבָה וּנְדָבָה, מְנוּחַת אֱמֶת וֶאֱמוּנָה, מְנוּחַת שָׁלוֹם וְשַׁלְוָה וְהַשְׁקֵט וָבֶטַח, מְנוּחָה שְׁלֵמָה שָׁאַתָּה רוֹצֶה בָּהּ, יַכִּירוּ בָנֶיךָ וְיֵדְעוּ כִּי מֵאִתְּךָ הִיא מְנוּחָתָם, וְעַל מְנוּחָתָם יַקְדִּישׁוּ אֶת שְׁמֶךָ.

אֱלֹהֵינוּ וֵאלֹהֵי אֲבוֹתֵינוּ, רְצֵה בִמְנוּחָתֵנוּ, קַדְּשֵׁנוּ בְּמִצְוֹתֶיךָ וְתֵן חֶלְקֵנוּ בְּתוֹרָתֶךָ, שַׂבְּעֵנוּ מִטּוּבֶךָ וְשַׂמְּחֵנוּ בִּישׁוּעָתֶךָ, וְטַהֵר לִבֵּנוּ לְעָבְדְּךָ בֶּאֱמֶת, וְהַנְחִילֵנוּ יְיָ אֱלֹהֵינוּ בְּאַהֲבָה וּבְרָצוֹן שַׁבַּת קָדְשֶׁךָ, וְיָנוּחוּ בָהּ יִשְׂרָאֵל מְקַדְּשֵׁי שְׁמֶךָ. בָּרוּךְ אַתָּה יְיָ, מְקַדֵּשׁ הַשַּׁבָּת:

רְצֵה, יְיָ אֱלֹהֵינוּ, בְּעַמְּךָ יִשְׂרָאֵל וּבִתְפִלָּתָם, וְהָשֵׁב אֶת הָעֲבוֹדָה לִדְבִיר בֵּיתֶךָ, וּתְפִלָּתָם בְּאַהֲבָה תְקַבֵּל בְּרָצוֹן, וּתְהִי לְרָצוֹן תָּמִיד עֲבוֹדַת יִשְׂרָאֵל עַמֶּךָ.

On ראש חדש, *add the following:*

אֱלֹהֵינוּ וֵאלֹהֵי אֲבוֹתֵינוּ, יַעֲלֶה וְיָבֹא, וְיַגִּיעַ וְיֵרָאֶה, וְיֵרָצֶה וְיִשָּׁמַע, וְיִפָּקֵד וְיִזָּכֵר זִכְרוֹנֵנוּ וּפִקְדוֹנֵנוּ, וְזִכְרוֹן אֲבוֹתֵינוּ, וְזִכְרוֹן מָשִׁיחַ בֶּן דָּוִד עַבְדֶּךָ, וְזִכְרוֹן יְרוּשָׁלַיִם עִיר קָדְשֶׁךָ, וְזִכְרוֹן כָּל עַמְּךָ בֵּית יִשְׂרָאֵל לְפָנֶיךָ, לִפְלֵיטָה, לְטוֹבָה, לְחֵן וּלְחֶסֶד וּלְרַחֲמִים, לְחַיִּים וּלְשָׁלוֹם, בְּיוֹם רֹאשׁ הַחֹדֶשׁ הַזֶּה.

זָכְרֵנוּ, יְיָ אֱלֹהֵינוּ, בּוֹ לְטוֹבָה, וּפָקְדֵנוּ בוֹ לִבְרָכָה, וְהוֹשִׁיעֵנוּ בוֹ לְחַיִּים, וּבִדְבַר יְשׁוּעָה וְרַחֲמִים, חוּס וְחָנֵּנוּ, וְרַחֵם עָלֵינוּ וְהוֹשִׁיעֵנוּ, כִּי אֵלֶיךָ עֵינֵינוּ, כִּי אֵל מֶלֶךְ חַנּוּן וְרַחוּם אָתָּה.

Shabbat Afternoon Prayers

K'dushah

When the Amidah is chanted out loud, the K'dushah is substituted for "You are holy..." at the bottom of the page.

We shall tell of Your holiness on earth just as it is told in the heavens above. As Your prophet wrote, the angels called to one another, saying:

> Holy, holy, holy is *Adonai Tzeva'ot*, the whole world is filled with God's glory.

Then the Serafim responded in a mighty chorus:

> Praised is God's glory from God's place.

With Your holy words it is written:

> Adonai will rule forever, your God, O Zion, for all generations. Halleluyah.

For all generations we will tell Your greatness, and forever and ever we will add our holiness to Yours. We will never stop praising You, for You are a great and holy God. Praised are You Adonai, the holy God.

N'kadesh et shim'cha ba-olam, k'shem shemakdisheem oto bish'mei marom, kakatuv al yad n'vee-echa, v'kara zeh el zeh v'amar:

> Kadosh, kadosh, kadosh Adonai Tzeva-ot, m'lo chol ha-aretz k'vodo.

L'umatam baruch yomeru:

> Baruch k'vod Adonai mim'komo.

Uv'div'rei kod'sh'cha katuv lemor:

> Yimloch Adonai l'olam, Elohayich Tzion l'dor vador, hal'luyah.

L'dor vador nageed god'lecha, ul'netzach n'tzacheem k'dushat'cha nakdeesh, v'shiv'chacha, Eloheinu, mipeenu lo yamush l'olam va-ed, kee El melech gadol v'kadosh atah. Baruch atah Adonai, ha-El hakadosh.

When the Amidah is recited silently:

You are holy and Your name is holy and holy beings praise You every day. Praised are You Adonai, the holy God.

Atah kadosh v'shim'cha kadosh uk'dosheem b'chol yom y'hal'lucha, selah. Baruch atah Adonai, ha-El hakadosh.

מנחה לשבת

קְדוּשָׁה

When the עמידה *is chanted out loud,*
the קדושה *is substituted for* קדוש אתה *at the bottom of the page.*

נְקַדֵּשׁ אֶת שִׁמְךָ בָּעוֹלָם, כְּשֵׁם שֶׁמַּקְדִּישִׁים אוֹתוֹ בִּשְׁמֵי מָרוֹם, כַּכָּתוּב עַל יַד נְבִיאֶךָ: וְקָרָא זֶה אֶל זֶה וְאָמַר:

קָדוֹשׁ, קָדוֹשׁ, קָדוֹשׁ יְיָ צְבָאוֹת, מְלֹא כָל הָאָרֶץ כְּבוֹדוֹ.

לְעֻמָּתָם בָּרוּךְ יֹאמֵרוּ:

בָּרוּךְ כְּבוֹד יְיָ מִמְּקוֹמוֹ.

וּבְדִבְרֵי קָדְשְׁךָ כָּתוּב לֵאמֹר:

יִמְלֹךְ יְיָ לְעוֹלָם, אֱלֹהַיִךְ צִיּוֹן לְדֹר וָדֹר, הַלְלוּיָהּ.

לְדוֹר וָדוֹר נַגִּיד גָּדְלֶךָ, וּלְנֵצַח נְצָחִים קְדֻשָּׁתְךָ נַקְדִּישׁ, וְשִׁבְחֲךָ, אֱלֹהֵינוּ, מִפִּינוּ לֹא יָמוּשׁ לְעוֹלָם וָעֶד, כִּי אֵל מֶלֶךְ גָּדוֹל וְקָדוֹשׁ אָתָּה. בָּרוּךְ אַתָּה יְיָ, הָאֵל הַקָּדוֹשׁ.

When the עמידה *is recited silently:*

אַתָּה קָדוֹשׁ וְשִׁמְךָ קָדוֹשׁ וּקְדוֹשִׁים בְּכָל יוֹם יְהַלְלוּךָ, סֶּלָה. בָּרוּךְ אַתָּה יְיָ, הָאֵל הַקָּדוֹשׁ.

Shabbat Afternoon Prayers

Shabbat Afternoon Amidah

We rise and take three steps back and three steps forward as we say:

Adonai, open my lips so I may speak Your praise.

Adonai s'fatai tif'tach ufi yagid t'hilatecha.

Praised are You, Adonai our God and God of our ancestors, God of Abraham, God of Isaac, and God of Jacob, God of Sarah, God of Rebecca, God of Rachel, and God of Leah, the great, strong and awe-inspiring God, God on high. You act with lovingkindness and create everything. God remembers the loving deeds of our ancestors, and will bring a redeemer to their children's children because that is God's loving nature.

Baruch atah Adonai Eloheinu vElohei avoteinu, Elohei Av'raham, Elohei Yitz'chak, vElohei Ya-akov, Elohei Sarah, Elohei Riv'ka, Elohei Rachel, vElohei Le-ah. Ha-El hagadol hagibur v'hanora, El el'yon, gomel chasideem toveem, v'koneh hakol, v'zocher chasdei avot, umevee go-el liv'nei v'neihem l'ma-an sh'mo b'ahavah.

You are a helping, guarding, saving and shielding Ruler. Praised are You, Adonai, Shield of Abraham and Guardian of Sarah.

Melech ozer ufoked umoshee-a umagen. Baruch atah Adonai, magen Av'raham ufoked Sarah.

You are mighty forever, Adonai. You give life to the dead with Your great saving power.

Atah gibor l'olam Adonai, m'chayeh meteem atah rav l'hoshee-a.

From Shemini Atzeret until Pesach:

You cause the wind to blow and the rain to fall.

Masheev haru-ach umoreed hagashem.

You support the living with kindness. You give life to the dead with great mercy. You support the fallen, heal the sick and set free those in prison. You keep faith with those who sleep in the dust. Who is like You, mighty Ruler, and who can compare to You, Ruler of life and death who causes salvation to bloom.

M'chal'kel chayim b'chesed, m'chayeh meteem b'rachameem rabeem, somech nofleem, v'rofeh choleem, umateer asureem, um'kayem emunato leeshenei afar, mee chamocha ba-al g'vurot umee domeh lach, melech memeet um'chayeh umatz'mee-ach y'shu-ah.

You are trustworthy in giving life to the dead. Praised are You Adonai, who gives life to the dead.

V'ne-eman atah l'hachayot meteem. Baruch atah Adonai, m'chayeh hameteem.

עֲמִידָה שֶׁל מִנְחָה לְשַׁבָּת

We rise and take three steps back and three steps forward as we say:

אֲדֹנָי שְׂפָתַי תִּפְתָּח וּפִי יַגִּיד תְּהִלָּתֶךָ:

בָּרוּךְ אַתָּה יְיָ אֱלֹהֵינוּ וֵאלֹהֵי אֲבוֹתֵינוּ, אֱלֹהֵי אַבְרָהָם, אֱלֹהֵי יִצְחָק, וֵאלֹהֵי יַעֲקֹב, אֱלֹהֵי שָׂרָה, אֱלֹהֵי רִבְקָה, אֱלֹהֵי רָחֵל וֵאלֹהֵי לֵאָה. הָאֵל הַגָּדוֹל הַגִּבּוֹר וְהַנּוֹרָא, אֵל עֶלְיוֹן, גּוֹמֵל חֲסָדִים טוֹבִים, וְקוֹנֵה הַכֹּל, וְזוֹכֵר חַסְדֵי אָבוֹת, וּמֵבִיא גוֹאֵל לִבְנֵי בְנֵיהֶם לְמַעַן שְׁמוֹ בְּאַהֲבָה.

מֶלֶךְ עוֹזֵר וּפוֹקֵד וּמוֹשִׁיעַ וּמָגֵן: בָּרוּךְ אַתָּה יְיָ, מָגֵן אַבְרָהָם וּפוֹקֵד שָׂרָה:

אַתָּה גִבּוֹר לְעוֹלָם אֲדֹנָי, מְחַיֵּה מֵתִים אַתָּה, רַב לְהוֹשִׁיעַ:

From Shemini Atzeret until Pesach:
מַשִּׁיב הָרוּחַ וּמוֹרִיד הַגֶּשֶׁם:

מְכַלְכֵּל חַיִּים בְּחֶסֶד, מְחַיֵּה מֵתִים בְּרַחֲמִים רַבִּים, סוֹמֵךְ נוֹפְלִים, וְרוֹפֵא חוֹלִים, וּמַתִּיר אֲסוּרִים, וּמְקַיֵּם אֱמוּנָתוֹ לִישֵׁנֵי עָפָר, מִי כָמוֹךָ בַּעַל גְּבוּרוֹת וּמִי דּוֹמֶה לָךְ, מֶלֶךְ מֵמִית וּמְחַיֶּה וּמַצְמִיחַ יְשׁוּעָה: וְנֶאֱמָן אַתָּה לְהַחֲיוֹת מֵתִים. בָּרוּךְ אַתָּה יְיָ, מְחַיֵּה הַמֵּתִים:

Shabbat Afternoon Prayers

We rise to return the Torah to the Ark. The leader chants:

Praise Adonai whose name alone is highly praised.	Y'hal'lu et shem Adonai, kee nis'gav sh'mo l'vado.

Everyone responds:

God's majesty is over the earth and the heavens. God will increase the pride and the praise of the people of Israel, the people close to God. Halleluyah.	Hodo al eretz v'shamayim. Vayarem keren l'amo, T'hilah l'chol chaseedav, liv'nei Yisra-el am k'rovo, hal'luyah.

The Torah is returned to the Ark, and we sing:

It is a tree of life for those who hold fast to it, And all its supporters are happy. Its paths are pleasant and all its ways are peaceful. Return us to You, Adonai, and we shall return.	Etz chayeem hee lamachazeekeem bah, v'tomcheiha m'ushar. D'racheiha dar'chei no-am, v'chol n'titvoteiha shalom. Hasheevenu Adonai, eleicha v'nashuvah, chadesh yameinu k'kedem.

Chatzi Kaddish

Leader:

May God's great name be made great and holy in the world which God created according to God's will. May God establish Divine rule soon, in our days, quickly and in the near future, and let us say, Amen.	Yit'gadal v'yit'kadash sh'meh rabah. B'al'mah dee v'rah chir'utei, v'yam'leech mal'chutei b'chayeichon uv'yomeichon uv'chayei d'chol beit Yisra-el. Ba-agalah uviz'man kareev v'im'ru amen.

Everyone:

May God's great name be praised for ever and ever.	Y'heh sh'meh rabah m'varach l'alam ul'al'mei al'mayah.

Leader:

Blessed, praised, glorified and raised high, honored and elevated be the name of the Blessed Holy One, far beyond all blessings and songs, praises and words of comfort which people can say, and let us say: Amen.	Yit'barach v'yishtabach v'yitpa-ar v'yit'romam v'yit'naseh v'yit'hadar v'yit'aleh v'yit'halal sh'meh d'kud'shah b'reech hu l'elah min kol bir'chatah v'sheeratah tush'b'chatah v'nechematah, da-ameeran b'al'mah, v'im'ru amen.

We rise to return the Torah to the Ark. The leader chants:

יְהַלְלוּ אֶת שֵׁם יְיָ, כִּי נִשְׂגָּב שְׁמוֹ לְבַדּוֹ.

Everyone responds:

הוֹדוֹ עַל אֶרֶץ וְשָׁמָיִם. וַיָּרֶם קֶרֶן לְעַמּוֹ,
תְּהִלָּה לְכָל חֲסִידָיו, לִבְנֵי יִשְׂרָאֵל עַם קְרוֹבוֹ, הַלְלוּיָהּ.

The Torah is returned to the Ark, and we sing:

עֵץ חַיִּים הִיא לַמַּחֲזִיקִים בָּהּ, וְתֹמְכֶיהָ מְאֻשָּׁר.
דְּרָכֶיהָ דַרְכֵי נֹעַם, וְכָל נְתִיבוֹתֶיהָ שָׁלוֹם.
הֲשִׁיבֵנוּ יְיָ, אֵלֶיךָ וְנָשׁוּבָה, חַדֵּשׁ יָמֵינוּ כְּקֶדֶם.

חֲצִי קַדִּישׁ

Leader:

יִתְגַּדַּל וְיִתְקַדַּשׁ שְׁמֵהּ רַבָּא. בְּעָלְמָא דִּי בְרָא כִרְעוּתֵיהּ, וְיַמְלִיךְ מַלְכוּתֵהּ בְּחַיֵּיכוֹן וּבְיוֹמֵיכוֹן וּבְחַיֵּי דְכָל בֵּית יִשְׂרָאֵל. בַּעֲגָלָא וּבִזְמַן קָרִיב וְאִמְרוּ אָמֵן:

Everyone:

יְהֵא שְׁמֵהּ רַבָּא מְבָרַךְ לְעָלַם וּלְעָלְמֵי עָלְמַיָּא:

Leader:

יִתְבָּרַךְ וְיִשְׁתַּבַּח וְיִתְפָּאַר וְיִתְרוֹמַם וְיִתְנַשֵּׂא וְיִתְהַדָּר וְיִתְעַלֶּה וְיִתְהַלָּל שְׁמֵהּ דְּקֻדְשָׁא בְּרִיךְ הוּא לְעֵלָּא מִן כָּל בִּרְכָתָא וְשִׁירָתָא תֻּשְׁבְּחָתָא וְנֶחֱמָתָא, דַּאֲמִירָן בְּעָלְמָא, וְאִמְרוּ אָמֵן:

Shabbat Afternoon Prayers

Torah Blessings

The leader sings:

Praise Adonai, who is to be praised.　　Bar'chu et Adonai ham'vorach.

Everyone replies, then the leader repeats:

Praised be Adonai who is to be praised for ever and ever.　　Baruch Adonai ham'vorach l'olam va-ed.

Praised are You, Adonai our God, Ruler of the universe, who chose us from among all peoples by giving us God's Torah. Praised are You, Adonai, who gives the Torah.　　Baruch atah Adonai, Eloheinu melech ha-olam, asher bachar banu mikol ha-ameem v'natan lanu et Torato. Baruch atah Adonai, noten haTorah.

After the Torah is read:

Praised are You, Adonai our God, Ruler of the universe, who gave us a Torah of truth and planted within us lasting life. Praised are You, Adonai, who gives the Torah.　　Baruch atah Adonai, Eloheinu melech ha-olam, asher natan lanu Torat emet, v'chayei olam nata b'tocheinu. Baruch atah Adonai, noten haTorah.

We rise as the Hagbah lifts up the Torah and shows its written side to us and chant:

This is the Torah that Moses placed before the Israelites, by God's authority, through Moses.　　V'zot haTorah asher sam Moshe lif'nei b'nei Yisra-el al pee Adonai b'yad Moshe.

The Torah which Moses handed down to us is the heritage of the community of Jacob.　　Torah tzivah lanu Moshe, Morasha k'hilat Ya-akov.

מנחה לשבת

בִּרְכוֹת הַתּוֹרָה

The leader sings:

בָּרְכוּ אֶת יְיָ הַמְבֹרָךְ:

Everyone replies, then the leader repeats:

בָּרוּךְ יְיָ הַמְבֹרָךְ לְעוֹלָם וָעֶד:

בָּרוּךְ אַתָּה יְיָ אֱלֹהֵינוּ מֶלֶךְ הָעוֹלָם, אֲשֶׁר בָּחַר בָּנוּ מִכָּל הָעַמִּים וְנָתַן לָנוּ אֶת תּוֹרָתוֹ: בָּרוּךְ אַתָּה יְיָ, נוֹתֵן הַתּוֹרָה:

After the Torah is read:

בָּרוּךְ אַתָּה יְיָ אֱלֹהֵינוּ מֶלֶךְ הָעוֹלָם, אֲשֶׁר נָתַן לָנוּ תּוֹרַת אֱמֶת, וְחַיֵּי עוֹלָם נָטַע בְּתוֹכֵנוּ: בָּרוּךְ אַתָּה יְיָ, נוֹתֵן הַתּוֹרָה:

We rise as the Hagbah lifts up the Torah and shows its written side to us and chant:

וְזֹאת הַתּוֹרָה אֲשֶׁר שָׂם מֹשֶׁה לִפְנֵי בְּנֵי יִשְׂרָאֵל, עַל פִּי יְיָ בְּיַד מֹשֶׁה:

תּוֹרָה צִוָּה לָנוּ מֹשֶׁה, מוֹרָשָׁה קְהִלַּת יַעֲקֹב:

Shabbat Afternoon Prayers

The Torah is carried around in procession as we sing:

Greatness, might, wonder, triumph, and majesty are Yours, Adonai-yes, all that is in heaven and on earth; to You, Adonai, belong kingship and rule over all. Praise Adonai and bow down to God's presence; God is holy! Praise Adonai, our God, bow to God's holy mountain. Adonai our God is holy.	L'cha Adonai hag'dulah v'hag'vurah v'hatif'eret v'hanetzach v'hahod, kee chol bashamayim uva-aretz. L'cha Adonai hamam'lacha v'hamit'naseh l'chol l'rosh: Rom'mu Adonai Eloheinu, v'hishtachavu lahadom rag'lav kadosh hu. Rom'mu Adonai Eloheinu, v'hishtachavu l'har kod'sho, kee kadosh Adonai Eloheinu.

Once the Torah is set down, we are seated.

The Gabbai calls up the first person to have an aliyah:

May God's sovereignty be revealed to us soon. May God favor the remnant of God's people Israel with grace and kindness, with compassion and love. And let us say: Amen. Let us all declare the greatness of God and give honor to the Torah.	V'tigaleh v'tera-eh mal'chuto aleinu biz'man karov, v'yachon p'letatenu uf'letat amo beit Yisra-el l'chein ul'chesed ul'rachameem ul'ratzon v'nomar amen. Hakol havu godel lEloheinu ut'nu chavod laTorah.
Let the first to be honored come forward.	Kohen, k'rav. Ya-amod _____ ben _____ hakohen. Bat kohen, kir'vee. Ta-amod _____ bat _____ hakohen. Ya-amod _____ ben _____ harishon. Ta-amod _____ bat _____ harishonah.
Praised is God who in holiness entrusted the Torah to God's people Israel.	Baruch shenatan Torah l'amo Yisra-el bik'dushto.

Everyone:

You who remain steadfast to Adonai your God have been sustained to this day.	V'atem had'vekeem bAdonai Eloheichem, chayeem kul'chem hayom.

מנחה לשבת

The Torah is carried around in procession as we sing:

לְךָ יְיָ הַגְּדֻלָּה וְהַגְּבוּרָה וְהַתִּפְאֶרֶת וְהַנֵּצַח וְהַהוֹד,
כִּי כֹל בַּשָּׁמַיִם וּבָאָרֶץ: לְךָ יְיָ הַמַּמְלָכָה וְהַמִּתְנַשֵּׂא לְכֹל לְרֹאשׁ:
רוֹמְמוּ יְיָ אֱלֹהֵינוּ, וְהִשְׁתַּחֲווּ לַהֲדֹם רַגְלָיו קָדוֹשׁ הוּא:
רוֹמְמוּ יְיָ אֱלֹהֵינוּ, וְהִשְׁתַּחֲווּ לְהַר קָדְשׁוֹ, כִּי קָדוֹשׁ יְיָ אֱלֹהֵינוּ:

Once the Torah is set down, we are seated.

The Gabbai calls up the first person to have an aliyah:

וְתִגָּלֶה וְתֵרָאֶה מַלְכוּתוֹ עָלֵינוּ בִּזְמַן קָרוֹב, וְיָחֹן פְּלֵטָתֵנוּ וּפְלֵטַת
עַמּוֹ בֵּית יִשְׂרָאֵל לְחֵן וּלְחֶסֶד וּלְרַחֲמִים וּלְרָצוֹן וְנֹאמַר אָמֵן.
הַכֹּל הָבוּ גֹדֶל לֵאלֹהֵינוּ וּתְנוּ כָבוֹד לַתּוֹרָה.

כֹּהֵן, קְרָב. יַעֲמֹד _____ בֶּן _____ הַכֹּהֵן.
בַּת כֹּהֵן, קִרְבִי. תַעֲמֹד _____ בַּת _____ הַכֹּהֵן.
יַעֲמֹד _____ בֶּן _____ הָרִאשׁוֹן.
תַעֲמֹד _____ בַּת _____ הָרִאשׁוֹנָה.
בָּרוּךְ שֶׁנָּתַן תּוֹרָה לְעַמּוֹ יִשְׂרָאֵל בִּקְדֻשָּׁתוֹ.

Everyone:

וְאַתֶּם הַדְּבֵקִים בַּיְיָ אֱלֹהֵיכֶם, חַיִּים כֻּלְּכֶם הַיּוֹם:

Shabbat Afternoon Prayers

Chatzi Kaddish

Leader:

May God's great name be made great and holy in the world which God created according to God's will. May God establish Divine rule soon, in our days, quickly and in the near future, and let us say, Amen.	Yit'gadal v'yit'kadash sh'meh rabah. B'al'mah dee v'rah chir'utei, v'yam'leech mal'chutei b'chayeichon uv'yomeichon uv'chayei d'chol beit Yisra-el. Ba-agalah uviz'man kareev v'im'ru amen.

Everyone:

May God's great name be praised for ever and ever.	Y'heh sh'meh rabah m'varach l'alam ul'al'mei al'mayah.

Leader:

Blessed, praised, glorified and raised high, honored and elevated be the name of the Blessed Holy One, far beyond all blessings and songs, praises and words of comfort which people can say, and let us say: Amen.	Yit'barach v'yishtabach v'yitpa-ar v'yit'romam v'yit'naseh v'yit'hadar v'yit'aleh v'yit'halal sh'meh d'kud'shah b'reech hu l'elah min kol bir'chatah v'sheeratah tush'b'chatah v'nechematah, da-ameeran b'al'mah, v'im'ru amen.

Torah Service

And as for me, may my prayer be offered to You, Adonai, at a favorable moment. God, in Your great kindness, answer me with Your true saving.	Va-anee t'filatee l'cha Adonai et ratzon, Eloheem b'rov chas'decha, anenee be-emet yish'echa.

We rise as the Ark is opened and sing:

Whenever the Ark would travel, Moses would say, Arise, Adonai, and scatter Your enemies; May those that hate You flee from You. For Torah shall come from Zion, The word of Adonai from Jerusalem. Blessed is the One who in holiness gave the Torah to Israel.	Vay'hee bin'so-a ha-aron vayomer Moshe, Kuma Adonai v'yafutzu oy'vecha, V'yanusu m'san'eicha mipaneicha. Kee mitzee-on tetzeh Torah, ud'var Adonai mirushalayim. Baruch shenatan Torah l'amo Yisra-el bik'dushato.

The leader faces the Ark, bows, and chants:

Declare Adonai's greatness with me; let us praise God together.	Gad'lu lAdonai itee, un'rom'mah sh'mo yach'dav.

חֲצִי קַדִישׁ

Leader:

יִתְגַּדַּל וְיִתְקַדַּשׁ שְׁמֵהּ רַבָּא. בְּעָלְמָא דִּי בְרָא כִרְעוּתֵיהּ, וְיַמְלִיךְ מַלְכוּתֵהּ בְּחַיֵּיכוֹן וּבְיוֹמֵיכוֹן וּבְחַיֵּי דְכָל בֵּית יִשְׂרָאֵל. בַּעֲגָלָא וּבִזְמַן קָרִיב וְאִמְרוּ אָמֵן:

Everyone:

יְהֵא שְׁמֵהּ רַבָּא מְבָרַךְ לְעָלַם וּלְעָלְמֵי עָלְמַיָּא:

Leader:

יִתְבָּרַךְ וְיִשְׁתַּבַּח וְיִתְפָּאַר וְיִתְרוֹמַם וְיִתְנַשֵּׂא וְיִתְהַדָּר וְיִתְעַלֶּה וְיִתְהַלָּל שְׁמֵהּ דְּקֻדְשָׁא בְּרִיךְ הוּא לְעֵלָּא מִן כָּל בִּרְכָתָא וְשִׁירָתָא תֻּשְׁבְּחָתָא וְנֶחֱמָתָא, דַּאֲמִירָן בְּעָלְמָא, וְאִמְרוּ אָמֵן:

סֵדֶר הוֹצָאַת הַתּוֹרָה

וַאֲנִי תְפִלָּתִי לְךָ יְיָ עֵת רָצוֹן,
אֱלֹהִים בְּרָב חַסְדֶּךָ, עֲנֵנִי בֶּאֱמֶת יִשְׁעֶךָ.

We rise as the Ark is opened and sing:

וַיְהִי בִּנְסֹעַ הָאָרֹן וַיֹּאמֶר מֹשֶׁה:
קוּמָה יְיָ, וְיָפֻצוּ אֹיְבֶיךָ, וְיָנֻסוּ מְשַׂנְאֶיךָ מִפָּנֶיךָ.
כִּי מִצִּיּוֹן תֵּצֵא תוֹרָה, וּדְבַר יְיָ מִירוּשָׁלָיִם.
בָּרוּךְ שֶׁנָּתַן תּוֹרָה לְעַמּוֹ יִשְׂרָאֵל בִּקְדֻשָּׁתוֹ.

The leader faces the Ark, bows, and chants:

גַּדְּלוּ לַיְיָ אִתִּי, וּנְרוֹמְמָה שְׁמוֹ יַחְדָּו:

ס God holds up all who fall, and helps all who are bent over to stand straight.

ע The eyes of all look to You with hope, and You give them their food at the right time.

פ You open Your hand, and feed everything alive to its heart's content.

צ Adonai is righteous in every way, and kind in every deed.

ק Adonai is near to all who call, to all who call to God's sincerity.

ר God does the wishes of those who respect God, God hears their cry and saves them.

ש Adonai protects all who love God, but God will destroy the wicked.

ת My mouth shall speak praises of God, and all beings shall bless God's holy name forever and ever.

We shall praise God, now and forever. Halleluyah.

Somech Adonai l'chol hanof'leem,
v'zokef l'chol hak'fufeem.

Einei chol eleicha y'saberu,
v'atah noten lahem et ach'lam b'ito.

Pote-ach et yadecha,
umas'bee-a l'chol chai ratzon.

Tzadeek Adonai b'chol d'rachav,
v'chaseed b'chol ma-asav.

Karov Adonai l'chol kor'av,
l'chol asher yik'ra-uhu ve-emet.

R'tzon y're-av ya-aseh,
v'et shav'atam yish'ma v'yoshee-em.

Shomer Adonai et kol ohavav,
v'et kol har'sha-im yash'meed.

❖ T'hilat Adonai y'daber pee,
Veevarech kol basar shem kod'sho, l'olam va-ed.

Va-anach'nu n'varech Yah, me-atah v'ad olam, hal'luyah.

Praised is our God who created us for God's glory,
setting us apart from those who go astray,
giving us The Torah which is truth,
and planting within us life eternal.

Baruch hu Eloheinu, sheb'ra-anu lich'vodo,
V'hiv'deelanu min hato-eem,
V'natan lanu Torat emet,
V'chayei olam nata b'tochenu.

Blessed are those who trusts in Adonai, for Adonai will be their protection.

Baruch hagever asher yiv'tach bAdonai,
v'hayah Adonai miv'tacho.

סוֹמֵךְ יְיָ לְכָל הַנֹּפְלִים, וְזוֹקֵף לְכָל הַכְּפוּפִים:

עֵינֵי כֹל אֵלֶיךָ יְשַׂבֵּרוּ, וְאַתָּה נוֹתֵן לָהֶם אֶת אָכְלָם בְּעִתּוֹ:
פּוֹתֵחַ אֶת יָדֶךָ, וּמַשְׂבִּיעַ לְכָל חַי רָצוֹן:

צַדִּיק יְיָ בְּכָל דְּרָכָיו, וְחָסִיד בְּכָל מַעֲשָׂיו:
קָרוֹב יְיָ לְכָל קֹרְאָיו, לְכֹל אֲשֶׁר יִקְרָאֻהוּ בֶאֱמֶת:

רְצוֹן יְרֵאָיו יַעֲשֶׂה, וְאֶת שַׁוְעָתָם יִשְׁמַע וְיוֹשִׁיעֵם:
שׁוֹמֵר יְיָ אֶת כָּל אֹהֲבָיו, וְאֵת כָּל הָרְשָׁעִים יַשְׁמִיד:

❖ תְּהִלַּת יְיָ יְדַבֶּר פִּי,
וִיבָרֵךְ כָּל בָּשָׂר שֵׁם קָדְשׁוֹ, לְעוֹלָם וָעֶד:
PSALM 145

וַאֲנַחְנוּ נְבָרֵךְ יָהּ, מֵעַתָּה וְעַד עוֹלָם, הַלְלוּיָהּ:
PSALM 115:18

בָּרוּךְ הוּא אֱלֹהֵינוּ, שֶׁבְּרָאָנוּ לִכְבוֹדוֹ,
וְהִבְדִּילָנוּ מִן הַתּוֹעִים,
וְנָתַן לָנוּ תּוֹרַת אֱמֶת,
וְחַיֵּי עוֹלָם נָטַע בְּתוֹכֵנוּ.

בָּרוּךְ הַגֶּבֶר אֲשֶׁר יִבְטַח בַּיְיָ, וְהָיָה יְיָ מִבְטַחוֹ:

Shabbat Afternoon Prayers

Shabbat Afternoon Prayers

Ashrei

Happy are they who live in Your house; They shall continue to praise You.

Ashrei yosh'vei veitecha, od y'hal'lucha selah.

Happy are the people for whom this is so; Happy are the people whose God is Adonai.

Ashrei ha-am shekacha lo, ashrei ha-am she-Adonai elohav.

A Psalm of David.

T'hilah l'David,

א I will honor You, my God and Ruler, I will praise Your name forever and ever.

Aromim'cha elohai hamelech, va-aver'chah shim'cha l'olam va-ed.

ב Every day I will praise You, and sing praises to Your name forever and ever.

B'chol yom avar'checha, va-ahal'lah shim'cha l'olam va-ed.

ג Great is Adonai and greatly praised; there is no limit to God's greatness.

Gadol Adonai um'hulal m'od, v'lig'dulato ein cheker.

ד One generation shall praise Your deeds to another, and tell about Your mighty deeds.

Dor l'dor y'shabach ma-aseicha, ug'vuroteicha yageedu.

ה I will speak about Your majesty, splendor and glory, and Your wonderful deeds.

Hadar k'vod hodecha, v'div'rei nif'l'oteicha aseechah.

ו They will talk about the power of Your mighty acts; and I will tell of Your greatness.

Ve-ezuz noroteicha yomeru, ug'dulat'cha asap'renah.

ז They recall Your great goodness, and sing of Your righteousness.

Zecher rav tuv'cha yabee-u, v'tzid'kat'cha y'ranenu.

ח Adonai is gracious and caring, patient and very kind.

Chanun v'rachum Adonai, erech apayim ug'dal chased.

ט Adonai is good to all, and merciful to everything God made.

Tov Adonai lakol, v'rachamav al kol ma-asav.

י All Your work shall praise You, Adonai, and Your faithful ones shall bless You.

Yoducha Adonai kol ma-aseicha, v'chaseedeicha y'varchucha.

כ They shall speak of the glory of Your rule, and talk of Your might.

K'vod mal'chut'cha yomeru, ug'vurat'cha y'daberu.

ל To announce to humanity God's greatness, the splendor and glory of God's rule.

L'hodee-ah liv'nei ha-adam g'vurotav, uch'vod hadar mal'chuto.

מ God, You rule eternally, Your kingdom is for all generations.

Mal'chut'cha mal'chut kol olameem, umem'shal't'cha b'chol dor vador.

מִנְחָה לְשַׁבָּת

> Shabbat Afternoon is kind of a melancholy time for us. On the one hand, we are happy because it is Shabbat, and on the other hand, we are sad because Shabbat is coming to an end. The special tunes that we sing for *Mincha* on Shabbat express these mixed feelings: some of the tunes are lively and upbeat, while some of them sound a little bit sad. At *Mincha*, we start to look to the coming week a little by reading the beginning of the next week's Torah portion.

אַשְׁרֵי

אַשְׁרֵי יוֹשְׁבֵי בֵיתֶךָ, עוֹד יְהַלְלוּךָ סֶּלָה:
PSALM 84:5

אַשְׁרֵי הָעָם שֶׁכָּכָה לּוֹ, אַשְׁרֵי הָעָם שֶׁיְיָ אֱלֹהָיו:
PSALM 144:15

תְּהִלָּה לְדָוִד,
אֲרוֹמִמְךָ אֱלוֹהַי הַמֶּלֶךְ, וַאֲבָרְכָה שִׁמְךָ לְעוֹלָם וָעֶד:
בְּכָל יוֹם אֲבָרְכֶךָ, וַאֲהַלְלָה שִׁמְךָ לְעוֹלָם וָעֶד:

גָּדוֹל יְיָ וּמְהֻלָּל מְאֹד, וְלִגְדֻלָּתוֹ אֵין חֵקֶר:
דּוֹר לְדוֹר יְשַׁבַּח מַעֲשֶׂיךָ, וּגְבוּרֹתֶיךָ יַגִּידוּ:

הֲדַר כְּבוֹד הוֹדֶךָ, וְדִבְרֵי נִפְלְאֹתֶיךָ אָשִׂיחָה:
וֶעֱזוּז נוֹרְאוֹתֶיךָ יֹאמֵרוּ, וּגְדֻלָּתְךָ אֲסַפְּרֶנָּה:

זֵכֶר רַב טוּבְךָ יַבִּיעוּ, וְצִדְקָתְךָ יְרַנֵּנוּ:
חַנּוּן וְרַחוּם יְיָ, אֶרֶךְ אַפַּיִם וּגְדָל חָסֶד:

טוֹב יְיָ לַכֹּל, וְרַחֲמָיו עַל כָּל מַעֲשָׂיו:
יוֹדוּךָ יְיָ כָּל מַעֲשֶׂיךָ, וַחֲסִידֶיךָ יְבָרְכוּכָה:

כְּבוֹד מַלְכוּתְךָ יֹאמֵרוּ, וּגְבוּרָתְךָ יְדַבֵּרוּ:
לְהוֹדִיעַ לִבְנֵי הָאָדָם גְּבוּרֹתָיו, וּכְבוֹד הֲדַר מַלְכוּתוֹ:

מַלְכוּתְךָ מַלְכוּת כָּל עוֹלָמִים, וּמֶמְשַׁלְתְּךָ בְּכָל דּוֹר וָדֹר:

Shabbat Afternoon Prayers

Adon Olam

Master of the universe
Who ruled before anything was created,
You are called Ruler
Because You created everything.

When everything ends at the end of time,
God will still rule alone.
God was, God is,
God always will be glorious.

God is one,
There is no other being that compares.
God is without beginning, without end,
Power and authority are God's.

My God and living Rescuer,
My sheltering Rock in times of trouble,
God is my banner and my shelter,
Filling my cup on the day I call.

Into God's hand I place my spirit,
When I sleep and when I awake,
And with my spirit, my body too.
Adonai is with me, I shall not fear.

Adon olam asher malach,
b'terem kol y'tzeer niv'ra.
L'et na-asah b'chef'tzo kol,
Azai melech sh'mo nik'ra.

V'acharei kich'lot hakol,
L'vado yim'loch nora.
V'hu hayah, v'hu hoveh,
V'hu yih'yeh, b'tif'arah.

V'hu echad v'ein shenee,
l'ham'sheel lo l'hach'beerah.
B'lee resheet b'lee tachleet,
V'lo ha-oz v'hamis'rah.

V'hu elee v'chai go-alee,
V'tzur chev'lee b'et tzarah.
V'hu nisee umanos lee
M'nat kosee b'yom ekra.

B'yado af'keed ruchee,
B'et eeshan v'a-eerah.
V'im ruchee g'vee-atee,
Adonai lee v'lo eera.

אֲדוֹן עוֹלָם

DID YOU KNOW THAT... The authors of our Jewish liturgy express their personal opinions of God and faith through their writings. What do you think the author of *Adon Olam* meant when he wrote "Adonai is with me, I shall not fear"?

אֲדוֹן עוֹלָם אֲשֶׁר מָלַךְ, בְּטֶרֶם כָּל יְצִיר נִבְרָא.
לְעֵת נַעֲשָׂה בְחֶפְצוֹ כֹּל, אֲזַי מֶלֶךְ שְׁמוֹ נִקְרָא.

וְאַחֲרֵי כִּכְלוֹת הַכֹּל, לְבַדּוֹ יִמְלוֹךְ נוֹרָא.
וְהוּא הָיָה, וְהוּא הֹוֶה, וְהוּא יִהְיֶה, בְּתִפְאָרָה.

וְהוּא אֶחָד וְאֵין שֵׁנִי, לְהַמְשִׁיל לוֹ לְהַחְבִּירָה.
בְּלִי רֵאשִׁית בְּלִי תַכְלִית, וְלוֹ הָעֹז וְהַמִּשְׂרָה.

וְהוּא אֵלִי וְחַי גֹּאֲלִי, וְצוּר חֶבְלִי בְּעֵת צָרָה.
וְהוּא נִסִּי וּמָנוֹס לִי, מְנָת כּוֹסִי בְּיוֹם אֶקְרָא.

בְּיָדוֹ אַפְקִיד רוּחִי, בְּעֵת אִישַׁן וְאָעִירָה.
וְעִם רוּחִי גְוִיָּתִי, יְיָ לִי וְלֹא אִירָא.

Shabbat Musaf Prayers

Mourner's Kaddish

Mourners:

May God's great name be made great and holy in the world which God created according to God's will. May God establish Divine rule soon, in our days, quickly and in the near future, and let us say: Amen.

Yit'gadal v'yit'kadash sh'meh rabah. B'al'mah dee v'rah chir'utei, v'yam'leech mal'chutei b'chayeichon uv'yomeichon uv'chayei d'chol beit Yisra-el. Ba-agalah uviz'man kareev v'im'ru amen.

Everyone:

May God's great name be praised for ever and ever.

Y'heh sh'meh rabah m'varach l'alam ul'al'mei al'mayah.

Mourners:

Blessed, praised, glorified and raised high, honored and elevated be the name of the Holy Blessed One, far beyond all blessings and songs, praises and words of comfort which people can say, and let us say: Amen.

Yit'barach v'yishtabach v'yitpa-ar v'yit'romam v'yit'naseh v'yit'hadar v'yit'aleh v'yit'halal sh'meh d'kud'shah b'reech hu l'elah min kol bir'chatah v'sheeratah tush'b'chatah v'nechematah, da-ameeran b'al'mah, v'im'ru amen.

May there be abundant peace from heaven and life for us and for all Israel, and let us say: Amen.

Y'hei sh'lamah rabah min sh'mayah v'chayeem aleinu v'al kol Yisra-el, v'im'ru amen.

May the One who makes peace in the high heavens make peace for us and for all Israel, and let us say: Amen.

Oseh shalom bim'romav, hu ya-aseh shalom aleinu, v'al kol Yisra-el v'im'ru amen.

קַדִּישׁ יָתוֹם

DID YOU KNOW THAT... The Mourner's Kaddish is a prayer for us to recite in honor of those loved ones who are no longer with us physically in this world. Out of respect for the memories of our loved ones and the millions of Jews that died in the Holocaust we say the Mourner's Kaddish.

Mourners:

יִתְגַּדַּל וְיִתְקַדַּשׁ שְׁמֵהּ רַבָּא. בְּעָלְמָא דִּי בְרָא כִרְעוּתֵיהּ, וְיַמְלִיךְ מַלְכוּתֵהּ בְּחַיֵּיכוֹן וּבְיוֹמֵיכוֹן וּבְחַיֵּי דְכָל בֵּית יִשְׂרָאֵל. בַּעֲגָלָא וּבִזְמַן קָרִיב וְאִמְרוּ אָמֵן:

Everyone:

יְהֵא שְׁמֵהּ רַבָּא מְבָרַךְ לְעָלַם וּלְעָלְמֵי עָלְמַיָּא:

Mourners:

יִתְבָּרַךְ וְיִשְׁתַּבַּח וְיִתְפָּאַר וְיִתְרוֹמַם וְיִתְנַשֵּׂא וְיִתְהַדָּר וְיִתְעַלֶּה וְיִתְהַלָּל שְׁמֵהּ דְּקֻדְשָׁא בְּרִיךְ הוּא לְעֵלָּא מִן כָּל בִּרְכָתָא וְשִׁירָתָא תֻּשְׁבְּחָתָא וְנֶחֱמָתָא, דַּאֲמִירָן בְּעָלְמָא, וְאִמְרוּ אָמֵן:

יְהֵא שְׁלָמָא רַבָּא מִן שְׁמַיָּא וְחַיִּים עָלֵינוּ וְעַל כָּל יִשְׂרָאֵל, וְאִמְרוּ אָמֵן:

עֹשֶׂה שָׁלוֹם בִּמְרוֹמָיו הוּא יַעֲשֶׂה שָׁלוֹם עָלֵינוּ וְעַל כָּל יִשְׂרָאֵל, וְאִמְרוּ אָמֵן:

Aleinu

We rise.

We should praise God for not making us like the other peoples and families of the earth. We bend the knee and bow and give thanks to the Ruler of all earthly rulers, the Blessed Holy One. God spread out the heavens and built the earth's foundations. God's mighty presence is in the highest heights. God is our God—no one else. Our Ruler is true. There is nothing besides God, as it is written in God's Torah: "You shall know therefore this day and keep in mind that Adonai alone is God in heaven above and on earth below; there is no other."

And so we hope in You, Adonai our God, soon to see Your power used in a wonderful way: removing false gods from the earth, fixing the brokenness of the world so that it will be a world truly ruled by God. All humanity will call Your name, and all the wicked of the earth will turn toward You. All who live in the world will know and understand that everyone should accept You as their God. They will bow to You, Adonai our God, honoring the glory of Your name. For You will rule the world, and You will always rule over it in glory, as it is written in the Torah: "Adonai will rule for ever and ever." And as the prophet Zechariah said: "Then God will be Ruler over all the earth. On that day Adonai will be One and God's name will be One."

Aleinu l'shabe-ach la-adon hakol, latet g'dulah l'yotzer b'resheet, shelo asanu k'goyei ha-aratzot, v'lo samanu k'mish'p'chot ha-adamah, shelo sam chel'kenu kahem, v'goralenu k'chol hamonam. Va-anachnu kor'eem umish'tachaveem umodeem, lifnei melech, malchei ham'lacheem, hakadosh baruch hu. Shehu noteh shamayeem v'yosed aretz, umoshav y'karo bashamayim mima-al, ush'cheenat uzo b'gav'hei m'romeem, hu Eloheinu ein od. Emet malkenu efes zulato, kakatuv b'Torato: V'yada'ta hayom vahashevota El l'vavecha, kee Adonai hu haEloheem bashamayim mima-al, v'al ha-aretz mitachat, ein od.

Al ken n'kaveh l'cha Adonai Eloheinu, lir'ot m'hera b'tif'eret uzecha, l'ha-aveer giluleem min ha-aretz v'ha-eleeleem karot yikaretun. L'taken olam b'mal'chut shadai, v'chol b'nei vasar yik'r'u vish'mecha. L'haf'not eleicha kol rish'ei aretz. Yakeeru v'yed'u kol yosh'vei tevel, kee l'cha tich'ra kol berech, tishava kol lashon. L'faneicha Adonai Eloheinu yich'r'u v'yipolu. V'lich'vod shim'cha y'kar yitenu. Veekab'lu chulam et ol mal'chutecha. V'tim'loch aleihem m'herah l'olam va-ed.

❖ Kakatuv b'toratecha, Adonai yim'loch l'olam va-ed. V'ne-emar, v'haya Adonai l'melech al kol ha-aretz, bayom hahu yih'yeh Adonai echad, ush'mo echad.

We are seated.

עָלֵינוּ

DID YOU KNOW THAT... The first paragraph of *Aleinu* praises God for our uniqueness as Jews, while the second looks to the future, hoping for the day when the world will belong to God and be a place of harmony and peace. How can we create a world that is a place of peace and harmony?

We rise.

עָלֵינוּ לְשַׁבֵּחַ לַאֲדוֹן הַכֹּל, לָתֵת גְּדֻלָּה לְיוֹצֵר בְּרֵאשִׁית, שֶׁלֹּא עָשָׂנוּ כְּגוֹיֵי הָאֲרָצוֹת, וְלֹא שָׂמָנוּ כְּמִשְׁפְּחוֹת הָאֲדָמָה, שֶׁלֹּא שָׂם חֶלְקֵנוּ כָּהֶם, וְגוֹרָלֵנוּ כְּכָל הֲמוֹנָם:
וַאֲנַחְנוּ כּוֹרְעִים וּמִשְׁתַּחֲוִים וּמוֹדִים,
לִפְנֵי מֶלֶךְ, מַלְכֵי הַמְּלָכִים, הַקָּדוֹשׁ בָּרוּךְ הוּא.
שֶׁהוּא נוֹטֶה שָׁמַיִם וְיֹסֵד אָרֶץ, וּמוֹשַׁב יְקָרוֹ בַּשָּׁמַיִם מִמַּעַל, וּשְׁכִינַת עֻזּוֹ בְּגָבְהֵי מְרוֹמִים, הוּא אֱלֹהֵינוּ אֵין עוֹד. אֱמֶת מַלְכֵּנוּ אֶפֶס זוּלָתוֹ, כַּכָּתוּב בְּתוֹרָתוֹ: וְיָדַעְתָּ הַיּוֹם וַהֲשֵׁבֹתָ אֶל לְבָבֶךָ, כִּי יְיָ הוּא הָאֱלֹהִים בַּשָּׁמַיִם מִמַּעַל, וְעַל הָאָרֶץ מִתָּחַת, אֵין עוֹד:

עַל כֵּן נְקַוֶּה לְךָ יְיָ אֱלֹהֵינוּ, לִרְאוֹת מְהֵרָה בְּתִפְאֶרֶת עֻזֶּךָ, לְהַעֲבִיר גִּלּוּלִים מִן הָאָרֶץ וְהָאֱלִילִים כָּרוֹת יִכָּרֵתוּן. לְתַקֵּן עוֹלָם בְּמַלְכוּת שַׁדַּי, וְכָל בְּנֵי בָשָׂר יִקְרְאוּ בִשְׁמֶךָ. לְהַפְנוֹת אֵלֶיךָ כָּל רִשְׁעֵי אָרֶץ. יַכִּירוּ וְיֵדְעוּ כָּל יוֹשְׁבֵי תֵבֵל, כִּי לְךָ תִּכְרַע כָּל בֶּרֶךְ, תִּשָּׁבַע כָּל לָשׁוֹן: לְפָנֶיךָ יְיָ אֱלֹהֵינוּ יִכְרְעוּ וְיִפֹּלוּ. וְלִכְבוֹד שִׁמְךָ יְקָר יִתֵּנוּ. וִיקַבְּלוּ כֻלָּם אֶת עֹל מַלְכוּתֶךָ, וְתִמְלֹךְ עֲלֵיהֶם מְהֵרָה לְעוֹלָם וָעֶד. כִּי הַמַּלְכוּת שֶׁלְּךָ הִיא, וּלְעוֹלְמֵי עַד תִּמְלוֹךְ בְּכָבוֹד:
❖ כַּכָּתוּב בְּתוֹרָתֶךָ, יְיָ יִמְלֹךְ לְעוֹלָם וָעֶד: וְנֶאֱמַר: וְהָיָה יְיָ לְמֶלֶךְ עַל כָּל הָאָרֶץ, בַּיּוֹם הַהוּא יִהְיֶה יְיָ אֶחָד, וּשְׁמוֹ אֶחָד:

We are seated.

Shabbat Musaf Prayers

Ein KEloheinu

No one is like our God.	Ein kEloheinu, ein kadoneinu,
No one is like our Master.	Ein k'mal'kenu, ein k'moshee-enu.
No one is like our Ruler.	
No one is like our Helper.	
Who can compare to our God?	Mee chEolheinu, mee chadoneinu,
Who can compare to our Master?	Mee ch'mal'kenu, mee ch'moshee-enu.
Who can compare to our Ruler?	
Who can compare to our Helper?	
Let us thank our God.	Nodeh lEloheinu, nodeh ladoneinu,
Let us thank our Master.	Nodeh l'mal'kenu, nodeh l'moshee-enu.
Let us thank our Ruler.	
Let us thank our Helper.	
Praised is our God.	Baruch Eloheinu, baruch adoneinu,
Praised is our Master.	Baruch mal'kenu, baruch moshee-enu.
Praised is our Ruler.	
Praised is our Helper.	
You are our God.	Atah hu Eloheinu, atah hu adoneinu,
You are our Master.	Atah hu mal'kenu, atah hu moshee-enu.
You are our Ruler.	
You are our Helper.	
You are the One to whom our ancestors offered fragrant incense.	Atah hu shehik'teeru avoteinu l'faneicha et k'toret hasameem.

אֵין כֵּאלֹהֵינוּ

אֵין כֵּאלֹהֵינוּ, אֵין כַּאדוֹנֵינוּ,
אֵין כְּמַלְכֵּנוּ, אֵין כְּמוֹשִׁיעֵנוּ.

מִי כֵאלֹהֵינוּ, מִי כַאדוֹנֵינוּ,
מִי כְמַלְכֵּנוּ, מִי כְמוֹשִׁיעֵנוּ.

נוֹדֶה לֵאלֹהֵינוּ, נוֹדֶה לַאדוֹנֵינוּ,
נוֹדֶה לְמַלְכֵּנוּ, נוֹדֶה לְמוֹשִׁיעֵנוּ.

בָּרוּךְ אֱלֹהֵינוּ, בָּרוּךְ אֲדוֹנֵינוּ,
בָּרוּךְ מַלְכֵּנוּ, בָּרוּךְ מוֹשִׁיעֵנוּ.

אַתָּה הוּא אֱלֹהֵינוּ, אַתָּה הוּא אֲדוֹנֵינוּ,
אַתָּה הוּא מַלְכֵּנוּ, אַתָּה הוּא מוֹשִׁיעֵנוּ.

אַתָּה הוּא שֶׁהִקְטִירוּ אֲבוֹתֵינוּ לְפָנֶיךָ אֶת קְטֹרֶת הַסַּמִּים.

Kaddish Shalem

Leader:

May God's great name be made great and holy in the world which God created according to God's will. May God establish Divine rule soon, in our days, quickly and in the near future, and let us say: Amen.

Yit'gadal v'yit'kadash sh'meh rabah. B'al'mah dee v'rah chir'utei, v'yam'leech mal'chutei b'chayeichon uv'yomeichon uv'chayei d'chol beit Yisra-el. Ba-agalah uviz'man kareev v'im'ru amen.

Everyone:

May God's great name be praised for ever and ever.

Y'heh sh'meh rabah m'varach l'alam ul'al'mei al'mayah.

Leader:

Blessed, praised, glorified and raised high, honored and elevated be the name of the Holy Blessed One, far beyond all blessings and songs, praises and words of comfort which people can say, and let us say: Amen.

Yit'barach v'yishtabach v'yitpa-ar v'yit'romam v'yit'naseh v'yit'hadar v'yit'aleh v'yit'halal sh'meh d'kud'shah b'reech hu l'elah min kol bir'chatah v'sheeratah tush'b'chatah v'nechematah, da-ameeran b'al'mah, v'im'ru amen.

May the prayers and pleas of the entire House of Israel be accepted before their Parent in heaven. And let us say: Amen.

Tit'kabal tz'lot'hon uva-ut'hon d'chol Yisra-el kadam avuhon dee vish'mayah v'im'ru amen.

May there be abundant peace from heaven and life for us and for all Israel, and let us say: Amen.

Y'hei sh'lamah rabah min sh'mayah v'chayeem aleinu v'al kol Yisra-el, v'im'ru amen.

May the One who makes peace in the high heavens make peace for us and for all Israel, and let us say: Amen.

Oseh shalom bim'romav, hu ya-aseh shalom aleinu, v'al kol Yisra-el v'im'ru amen.

קַדִּישׁ שָׁלֵם

Leader:

יִתְגַּדַּל וְיִתְקַדַּשׁ שְׁמֵהּ רַבָּא. בְּעָלְמָא דִּי בְרָא כִרְעוּתֵיהּ, וְיַמְלִיךְ מַלְכוּתֵהּ בְּחַיֵּיכוֹן וּבְיוֹמֵיכוֹן וּבְחַיֵּי דְכָל בֵּית יִשְׂרָאֵל. בַּעֲגָלָא וּבִזְמַן קָרִיב וְאִמְרוּ אָמֵן:

Everyone:

יְהֵא שְׁמֵהּ רַבָּא מְבָרַךְ לְעָלַם וּלְעָלְמֵי עָלְמַיָּא:

Leader:

יִתְבָּרַךְ וְיִשְׁתַּבַּח וְיִתְפָּאַר וְיִתְרוֹמַם וְיִתְנַשֵּׂא וְיִתְהַדָּר וְיִתְעַלֶּה וְיִתְהַלָּל שְׁמֵהּ דְּקֻדְשָׁא בְּרִיךְ הוּא לְעֵלָּא מִן כָּל בִּרְכָתָא וְשִׁירָתָא תֻּשְׁבְּחָתָא וְנֶחֱמָתָא, דַּאֲמִירָן בְּעָלְמָא, וְאִמְרוּ אָמֵן:

תִּתְקַבֵּל צְלוֹתְהוֹן וּבָעוּתְהוֹן דְּכָל יִשְׂרָאֵל קֳדָם אֲבוּהוֹן דִּי בִשְׁמַיָּא וְאִמְרוּ אָמֵן:

יְהֵא שְׁלָמָא רַבָּא מִן שְׁמַיָּא וְחַיִּים עָלֵינוּ וְעַל כָּל יִשְׂרָאֵל, וְאִמְרוּ אָמֵן:

עֹשֶׂה שָׁלוֹם בִּמְרוֹמָיו הוּא יַעֲשֶׂה שָׁלוֹם עָלֵינוּ וְעַל כָּל יִשְׂרָאֵל, וְאִמְרוּ אָמֵן:

Make peace in the world, with goodness, blessing, grace, lovingkindness and mercy for us and for all Your people Israel. Bless us, our Parent, all of us together, with Your light, by which You taught us Your Torah of life, love and kindness, justice and mercy, life and peace. May it be good in Your sight to bless Your people Israel at all times with peace.

Praised are You, Adonai, who blesses Your people Israel with peace.

My God, help me not to say bad things or to tell lies. Help me to ignore people who say bad things about me. Open my heart to Your Torah, so that I can do Your mitzvot. Quickly stop the ideas and spoil the plans of anyone who wants to hurt me. Do this because of Your love, Your holiness, and Your Torah: so that those You love will be free. May the words of my mouth and the thoughts of my heart find favor with You, my Rock and my Protector. May the One who makes peace up above give peace to us and to all the people of Israel. Amen.

Sim shalom tovah uv'racha, chen vachesed v'rachameem, aleinu v'al kol Yisra-el amecha. Bar'chenu, aveenu, kulanu k'echad b'or paneicha, kee v'or paneicha natata lanu, Adonai Eloheinu, Torat chayeem v'ahavat chesed, utz'dakah uv'racha v'rachameem v'chayeem v'shalom, v'tov b'eineicha l'varech et am'cha Yisra-el b'chol et uv'chol sha-ah bish'lomecha.

Baruch atah Adonai, ham'varech et amo Yisra-el bashalom.

Elohai, n'tzor l'shonee mera. Us'fatai midaber mir'mah. V'lim'kal'lai naf'shee tidom, v'naf'shee ke-afar lakol tih'yeh. P'tach libee b'Torahtecha, uv'mitzvoteicha tir'dof naf'shee. V'chol hachosh'veem alai ra-ah, m'herah hafer atzatam v'kal'kel macahshav'tam. Aseh l'ma-an Toratecha. Lama-an yechal'tzun y'deedeicha, hoshee-ah y'meen'cha va-anenee. Yih'yu l'ratzon im'rei fee v'heg'yon libee l'faneicha, Adonai tzuree v'go-alee. Oseh shalom bim'romav, hu ya-aseh shalom aleinu, v'al kol Yisra-el v'im'ru amen.

שִׂים שָׁלוֹם טוֹבָה וּבְרָכָה, חֵן וָחֶסֶד וְרַחֲמִים, עָלֵינוּ וְעַל כָּל יִשְׂרָאֵל עַמֶּךָ. בָּרְכֵנוּ, אָבִינוּ, כֻּלָּנוּ כְּאֶחָד בְּאוֹר פָּנֶיךָ, כִּי בְאוֹר פָּנֶיךָ נָתַתָּ לָּנוּ, יְיָ אֱלֹהֵינוּ, תּוֹרַת חַיִּים וְאַהֲבַת חֶסֶד, וּצְדָקָה וּבְרָכָה וְרַחֲמִים וְחַיִּים וְשָׁלוֹם, וְטוֹב בְּעֵינֶיךָ לְבָרֵךְ אֶת עַמְּךָ יִשְׂרָאֵל בְּכָל עֵת וּבְכָל שָׁעָה בִּשְׁלוֹמֶךָ.

בָּרוּךְ אַתָּה יְיָ, הַמְבָרֵךְ אֶת עַמּוֹ יִשְׂרָאֵל בַּשָּׁלוֹם.

אֱלֹהַי, נְצוֹר לְשׁוֹנִי מֵרָע. וּשְׂפָתַי מִדַּבֵּר מִרְמָה: וְלִמְקַלְלַי נַפְשִׁי תִדֹּם, וְנַפְשִׁי כֶּעָפָר לַכֹּל תִּהְיֶה. פְּתַח לִבִּי בְּתוֹרָתֶךָ, וּבְמִצְוֹתֶיךָ תִּרְדּוֹף נַפְשִׁי. וְכָל הַחוֹשְׁבִים עָלַי רָעָה, מְהֵרָה הָפֵר עֲצָתָם וְקַלְקֵל מַחֲשַׁבְתָּם. עֲשֵׂה לְמַעַן שְׁמֶךָ, עֲשֵׂה לְמַעַן יְמִינֶךָ, עֲשֵׂה לְמַעַן קְדֻשָּׁתֶךָ. עֲשֵׂה לְמַעַן תּוֹרָתֶךָ. לְמַעַן יֵחָלְצוּן יְדִידֶיךָ, הוֹשִׁיעָה יְמִינְךָ וַעֲנֵנִי. יִהְיוּ לְרָצוֹן אִמְרֵי פִי וְהֶגְיוֹן לִבִּי לְפָנֶיךָ, יְיָ צוּרִי וְגוֹאֲלִי. עֹשֶׂה שָׁלוֹם בִּמְרוֹמָיו, הוּא יַעֲשֶׂה שָׁלוֹם עָלֵינוּ, וְעַל כָּל יִשְׂרָאֵל וְאִמְרוּ: אָמֵן.

Our God and God of our ancestors, be pleased with our Shabbat rest, make us holy with Your mitzvot and let us share in Your Torah. Satisfy us with Your goodness and make us happy with Your help. Purify our hearts so that we can serve You truly. Adonai our God, let us receive Your holy Shabbat with love and favor, so that Your people Israel who make Your name holy will rest on it. Praised are You Adonai, who makes the Shabbat holy.

Adonai, be pleased with Your people Israel and with their prayer. Restore worship to Your Temple. May the prayer of Your people Israel always be accepted with love and favor.

May we see Your merciful return to Zion. Praised are You, Adonai, who restores Your presence to Zion.

We thank You for being our God and God of our ancestors for ever and ever. You are the Rock of our lives and our saving Shield. In every generation we will thank and praise You for our lives which are in Your power, for our souls which are in Your keeping, for Your miracles which are with us every day, and for Your wonders and good deeds that are with us at all times, evening, morning, and noon. O Good One, Your mercies have never stopped. O Merciful One, Your kindness has never stopped. We have always placed our hope in You.

For all these things, our Ruler, may Your name be blessed and honored forever.

May every living thing thank You and praise You sincerely, O God, our rescue and help. Praised are You, Your name is "the Good One," and it is good to thank You.

Eloheinu vElohei avoteinu, r'tzeh vim'nuchatenu, kad'shenu b'mitz'voteicha v'ten chel'kenu b'toratecha, sab'enu mituvecha v'sam'chenu beeshu-atecha, v'taher libenu l'ov'd'cha be-emet, v'han'cheelenu Adonai Eloheinu b'ahavah uv'ratzon Shabbat kod'shecha, v'yanuchu vah Yisra-el m'kad'shei sh'mecha. Baruch atah Adonai, m'kadesh haShabbat.

R'tzeh, Adonai Eloheinu, b'am'cha Yisra-el uvit'filatam, v'hashev et ha-avodah lid'veer beitecha, ut'filatam b'ahavah t'kabel b'ratzon, ut'hee l'ratzon tameed avodat Yisra-el amecha.

V'techezeinah eineinu b'shuv'cha l'tzee-on b'rachameem. Baruch atah Adonai, hamachazeer sh'cheenato l'tzee-on.

Modeem anach'nu lach, sha-atah hu, Adonai Eloheinu vElohei avoteinu, l'olam va-ed, tzur chayeinu, magen yish'enu, atah hu l'dor vador nodeh l'cha un'saper t'hilatecha. Al chayeinu ham'sureem b'yadecha, v'al nish'moteinu hap'kudot lach, v'al niseicha sheb'chol yom imanu, v'al nif'l'oteicha v'tovoteicha sheb'chol et, erev vavoker v'tzohorayim, hatov kee lo chalu rachameicha, v'ham'rachem kee lo tamu chasadeicha me-olam kiveenu lach.

V'al kulam yitbarach v'yit'romam shim'cha, mal'kenu, tameed l'olam va-ed.

V'chol hachayeem yoducha selah, veehal'lu et shim'cha be-emet, ha-El y'shu-atenu v'ez'ratenu selah. Baruch atah Adonai, hatov shim'cha ul'cha na-eh l'hodot.

אֱלֹהֵינוּ וֵאלֹהֵי אֲבוֹתֵינוּ, רְצֵה בִמְנוּחָתֵנוּ, קַדְּשֵׁנוּ בְּמִצְוֹתֶיךָ וְתֵן חֶלְקֵנוּ בְּתוֹרָתֶךָ, שַׂבְּעֵנוּ מִטּוּבֶךָ וְשַׂמְּחֵנוּ בִּישׁוּעָתֶךָ, וְטַהֵר לִבֵּנוּ לְעָבְדְּךָ בֶּאֱמֶת, וְהַנְחִילֵנוּ יְיָ אֱלֹהֵינוּ בְּאַהֲבָה וּבְרָצוֹן שַׁבַּת קָדְשֶׁךָ, וְיָנוּחוּ בָה יִשְׂרָאֵל מְקַדְּשֵׁי שְׁמֶךָ. בָּרוּךְ אַתָּה יְיָ, מְקַדֵּשׁ הַשַּׁבָּת:

רְצֵה, יְיָ אֱלֹהֵינוּ, בְּעַמְּךָ יִשְׂרָאֵל וּבִתְפִלָּתָם, וְהָשֵׁב אֶת הָעֲבוֹדָה לִדְבִיר בֵּיתֶךָ, וּתְפִלָּתָם בְּאַהֲבָה תְקַבֵּל בְּרָצוֹן, וּתְהִי לְרָצוֹן תָּמִיד עֲבוֹדַת יִשְׂרָאֵל עַמֶּךָ.

וְתֶחֱזֶינָה עֵינֵינוּ בְּשׁוּבְךָ לְצִיּוֹן בְּרַחֲמִים. בָּרוּךְ אַתָּה יְיָ, הַמַּחֲזִיר שְׁכִינָתוֹ לְצִיּוֹן.

מוֹדִים אֲנַחְנוּ לָךְ, שָׁאַתָּה הוּא, יְיָ אֱלֹהֵינוּ וֵאלֹהֵי אֲבוֹתֵינוּ, לְעוֹלָם וָעֶד, צוּר חַיֵּינוּ, מָגֵן יִשְׁעֵנוּ, אַתָּה הוּא לְדוֹר וָדוֹר נוֹדֶה לְךָ וּנְסַפֵּר תְּהִלָּתֶךָ. עַל חַיֵּינוּ הַמְּסוּרִים בְּיָדֶךָ, וְעַל נִשְׁמוֹתֵינוּ הַפְּקוּדוֹת לָךְ, וְעַל נִסֶּיךָ שֶׁבְּכָל יוֹם עִמָּנוּ, וְעַל נִפְלְאוֹתֶיךָ וְטוֹבוֹתֶיךָ שֶׁבְּכָל עֵת, עֶרֶב וָבֹקֶר וְצָהֳרָיִם, הַטּוֹב כִּי לֹא כָלוּ רַחֲמֶיךָ, וְהַמְרַחֵם כִּי לֹא תַמּוּ חֲסָדֶיךָ מֵעוֹלָם קִוִּינוּ לָךְ.

וְעַל כֻּלָּם יִתְבָּרַךְ וְיִתְרוֹמַם שִׁמְךָ, מַלְכֵּנוּ, תָּמִיד לְעוֹלָם וָעֶד.

וְכֹל הַחַיִּים יוֹדוּךָ סֶּלָה, וִיהַלְלוּ אֶת שִׁמְךָ בֶּאֱמֶת, הָאֵל יְשׁוּעָתֵנוּ וְעֶזְרָתֵנוּ סֶלָה. בָּרוּךְ אַתָּה יְיָ, הַטּוֹב שִׁמְךָ וּלְךָ נָאֶה לְהוֹדוֹת.

You established the Shabbat, accepted its sacrifices, commanded its special duties with its offerings. Those who delight in the Shabbat will always be honored. Those who taste Shabbat will merit life. Those who love its teachings have chosen greatness. At Sinai our ancestors were commanded about Shabbat, and You told them, Adonai our God, to offer an additional sacrifice on Shabbat. May it be Your will, Adonai our God and God of our ancestors, that You will return us to the borders of our land, bringing us up with joy to our land and planting us within our borders. For it was there that our ancestors presented the sacrifices to You: the daily offerings in proper order and the additional sacrifices as the law requires. There we will worship You with love and awe as in the days of old in former times. This additional sacrifice for Shabbat they offered to You with love, according to Your mitzvah, as is written in Your Torah, by Moses Your servant according to Your glory, saying:

Tikan'ta Shabbat ratzeeta kar'b'noteiha, tziveeta perusheiha im sidurei n'sacheiha. M'an'geiha l'olam kavod yin'chalu. To-ameiha chayeem zachu. V'gam ha-ohaveem d'vareiha g'dulah bacharu. Az miseenai nitz'tavu aleiha. Vat'tzavem Adonai Eloheinu, l'hak'reev bah kar'ban musaf Shabbat kara-uee. Y'hee ratzon mil'faneicha Adonai Eloheinu velohei avoteinu, hamesheev baneem lig'vulam, sheta-alenu v'sim'chah l'ar'tzenu, v'tita-enu big'vulenu. Shesham asu avoteinu l'faneicha et kar'b'not chovoteihem, t'meedeem k'sid'ram umusafeem k'hil'chatam, v'sham na-avad'cha b'ahavah uv'yir'ah keemei olam uch'shaneem kad'monee-ot. V'et musaf yom haShabbat hazeh, asu v'hik'reevu l'fanecha b'ahavah, k'mitz'vat r'tzonecha, kakatuv b'Toratecha, al y'dei Moshe av'decha, mipee ch'vodecha, ka-amur.

On the Shabbat day, two perfect year-old lambs, and two-tenths of an ephah of fine flour mixed with oil, and the proper drink-offering. A burnt-offering for the Shabbat in addition to the daily burnt-offering and its drink-offering.

Uv'yom haShabbat, sh'nei ch'vaseem b'nei shanah t'meemim, ush'nei es'roneem solet min'chah b'lulah vashemen v'nis'ko. Olat Shabbat b'Shabbato, al olat hatameed v'nis'ka.

Merciful Ruler, accept with mercy the prayer of Your people Israel wherever they live.

Melech rachaman, kabel b'rachameem et t'filat am'cha Yisra-el b'chol-m'komot mosh'voteihem.

Those who keep the Shabbat will be happy with Your rule, calling it a delight. The people who make the seventh day holy, will all be satisfied and delighted with Your goodness. For You were pleased with the seventh day and made it holy, calling it the most delightful of days, a reminder of Creation.

Yis'm'chu v'mal'chut'cha shomrei Shabbat v'kor'ei oneg, am m'kad'shei sh'vee-ee, kulam yis'b'u v'yit'an'gu mituvecha, uvash'vee-ee ratzeeta bo v'kidash'to, chem'dat yameem oto karata, zecher l'ma-aseh v'resheet.

תִּכַּנְתָּ שַׁבָּת רָצִיתָ קָרְבְּנוֹתֶיהָ, צִוִּיתָ פֵּרוּשֶׁיהָ עִם סִדּוּרֵי נְסָכֶיהָ. מְעַנְּגֶיהָ לְעוֹלָם כָּבוֹד יִנְחָלוּ. טוֹעֲמֶיהָ חַיִּים זָכוּ. וְגַם הָאוֹהֲבִים דְּבָרֶיהָ גְּדֻלָּה בָּחָרוּ. אָז מִסִּינַי נִצְטַוּוּ עָלֶיהָ: וַתְּצַוֵּנוּ יְיָ אֱלֹהֵינוּ, לְהַקְרִיב בָּהּ קָרְבַּן מוּסַף שַׁבָּת כָּרָאוּי: יְהִי רָצוֹן מִלְּפָנֶיךָ יְיָ אֱלֹהֵינוּ וֵאלֹהֵי אֲבוֹתֵינוּ, הַמֵּשִׁיב בָּנִים לִגְבוּלָם, שֶׁתַּעֲלֵנוּ בְשִׂמְחָה לְאַרְצֵנוּ, וְתִטָּעֵנוּ בִּגְבוּלֵנוּ. שָׁשָׁם עָשׂוּ אֲבוֹתֵינוּ לְפָנֶיךָ אֶת קָרְבְּנוֹת חוֹבוֹתֵיהֶם, תְּמִידִים כְּסִדְרָם וּמוּסָפִים כְּהִלְכָתָם, וְשָׁם נַעֲבָדְךָ בְּאַהֲבָה וּבְיִרְאָה כִּימֵי עוֹלָם וּכְשָׁנִים קַדְמוֹנִיּוֹת. וְאֶת מוּסַף יוֹם הַשַּׁבָּת הַזֶּה, עָשׂוּ וְהִקְרִיבוּ לְפָנֶיךָ בְּאַהֲבָה, כְּמִצְוַת רְצוֹנֶךָ, כַּכָּתוּב בְּתוֹרָתֶךָ, עַל יְדֵי מֹשֶׁה עַבְדֶּךָ, מִפִּי כְבוֹדֶךָ, כָּאָמוּר:

וּבְיוֹם הַשַּׁבָּת, שְׁנֵי כְבָשִׂים בְּנֵי שָׁנָה תְּמִימִם, וּשְׁנֵי עֶשְׂרֹנִים סֹלֶת מִנְחָה בְּלוּלָה בַשֶּׁמֶן וְנִסְכּוֹ. עֹלַת שַׁבַּת בְּשַׁבַּתּוֹ, עַל עֹלַת הַתָּמִיד וְנִסְכָּהּ.

מֶלֶךְ רַחֲמָן, קַבֵּל בְּרַחֲמִים אֶת תְּפִלַּת עַמְּךָ יִשְׂרָאֵל בְּכָל מְקוֹמוֹת מוֹשְׁבוֹתֵיהֶם:

יִשְׂמְחוּ בְמַלְכוּתְךָ שׁוֹמְרֵי שַׁבָּת וְקוֹרְאֵי עֹנֶג, עַם מְקַדְּשֵׁי שְׁבִיעִי, כֻּלָּם יִשְׂבְּעוּ וְיִתְעַנְּגוּ מִטּוּבֶךָ, וּבַשְּׁבִיעִי רָצִיתָ בּוֹ וְקִדַּשְׁתּוֹ, חֶמְדַּת יָמִים אוֹתוֹ קָרָאתָ, זֵכֶר לְמַעֲשֵׂה בְרֵאשִׁית:

K'dushah

When the Amidah is chanted out loud,
the K'dushah is substituted for "You are holy..." at the bottom of the page.

We shall tell of Your holiness on earth just as it is told in the heavens above. As Your prophet wrote, the angels called to one another, saying:	Na-areetz'cha v'nak'deesh'cha, k'sod see-ach sar'fei kodesh. Hamak'deesheem shim'cha bakodesh, kakatuv al yad n'vee-echa, v'kara zeh el zeh v'amar:
Holy, holy, holy is *Adonai Tzeva'ot*, the whole world is filled with God's glory.	Kadosh, kadosh, kadosh Adonai Tzeva-ot, m'lo chol ha-aretz k'vodo.
God's glory fills the world. One group of God's servants asks another: "Where is the place of God's glory?" They answer with praise:	K'vodo maleh olam, m'shar'tav sho-aleem zeh lazeh, ayeh m'kom k'vodo, l'umatam baruch yomeru:
Praised is God's glory from God's place.	Baruch k'vod Adonai mim'komo.
May God turn with mercy to show mercy to the People who proclaim God's oneness twice every day, lovingly saying the Shema:	Mim'komo hu yifen b'rachameem, v'yachon am ham'yachadeem sh'mo erev vavoker b'chol yom tameed, pa-amayim b'ahavah sh'ma om'reem:
Hear O Israel, Adonai is our God, Adonai is One.	Sh'ma Yisra-el, Adonai Eloheinu, Adonai Echad.
Adonai is our God, our Parent, our Ruler, our Rescuer. With mercy, God will say to us once again, before the world,	Hu Eloheinu hu aveenu, hu mal'kenu, hu moshee-enu, v'hu yash'mee-enu b'rachamav sheneet l'einei kol chai, lih'yot lachem leloheem:
I am Adonai your God.	Anee Adonai Eloheichem.
With Your holy words it is written:	Uv'div'rei kod'sh'cha katuv lemor:
Adonai will rule forever, your God, O Zion, for all generations. Halleluyah.	Yimloch Adonai l'olam, Elohayich tzee-on l'dor vador, hal'luyah.
For all generations we will tell Your greatness, and forever and ever we will add our holiness to Yours. We will never stop praising You, for You are a great and holy God. Praised are You Adonai, the holy God.	L'dor vador nageed god'lecha, ul'netzach n'tzacheem k'dushat'cha nakdeesh, v'shiv'chacha, Eloheinu, mipeenu lo yamush l'olam va-ed, kee El melech gadol v'kadosh atah. Baruch atah Adonai, ha-El hakadosh.

When the Amidah is recited silently:

You are holy and Your name is holy and holy beings praise You every day. Praised are You Adonai, the holy God.	Atah kadosh v'shim'cha kadosh uk'dosheem b'chol yom y'hal'lucha, selah. Baruch atah Adonai, ha-El hakadosh.

קְדוּשָׁה

When the עמידה *is chanted out loud,*
the קדושה *is substituted for* אתה קדוש *at the bottom of the page.*

נַעֲרִיצְךָ וְנַקְדִּישְׁךָ, כְּסוֹד שִׂיחַ שַׂרְפֵי קֹדֶשׁ. הַמַּקְדִּישִׁים שִׁמְךָ בַּקֹּדֶשׁ, כַּכָּתוּב עַל יַד נְבִיאֶךָ, וְקָרָא זֶה אֶל זֶה וְאָמַר:

קָדוֹשׁ, קָדוֹשׁ, קָדוֹשׁ יְיָ צְבָאוֹת, מְלֹא כָל הָאָרֶץ כְּבוֹדוֹ.

כְּבוֹדוֹ מָלֵא עוֹלָם, מְשָׁרְתָיו שׁוֹאֲלִים זֶה לָזֶה, אַיֵּה מְקוֹם כְּבוֹדוֹ, לְעֻמָּתָם בָּרוּךְ יֹאמֵרוּ:

בָּרוּךְ כְּבוֹד יְיָ מִמְּקוֹמוֹ.

מִמְּקוֹמוֹ הוּא יִפֶן בְּרַחֲמִים, וְיָחוֹן עַם הַמְיַחֲדִים שְׁמוֹ עֶרֶב וָבֹקֶר בְּכָל יוֹם תָּמִיד, פַּעֲמַיִם בְּאַהֲבָה שְׁמַע אוֹמְרִים:

שְׁמַע יִשְׂרָאֵל, יְיָ אֱלֹהֵינוּ, יְיָ אֶחָד:

הוּא אֱלֹהֵינוּ הוּא אָבִינוּ, הוּא מַלְכֵּנוּ, הוּא מוֹשִׁיעֵנוּ, וְהוּא יַשְׁמִיעֵנוּ בְּרַחֲמָיו שֵׁנִית לְעֵינֵי כָּל חָי, לִהְיוֹת לָכֶם לֵאלֹהִים:

אֲנִי יְיָ אֱלֹהֵיכֶם:

וּבְדִבְרֵי קָדְשְׁךָ כָּתוּב לֵאמֹר:

יִמְלֹךְ יְיָ לְעוֹלָם, אֱלֹהַיִךְ צִיּוֹן לְדֹר וָדֹר, הַלְלוּיָהּ.

לְדוֹר וָדוֹר נַגִּיד גָּדְלֶךָ, וּלְנֵצַח נְצָחִים קְדֻשָּׁתְךָ נַקְדִּישׁ, וְשִׁבְחֲךָ, אֱלֹהֵינוּ, מִפִּינוּ לֹא יָמוּשׁ לְעוֹלָם וָעֶד, כִּי אֵל מֶלֶךְ גָּדוֹל וְקָדוֹשׁ אָתָּה. בָּרוּךְ אַתָּה יְיָ, הָאֵל הַקָּדוֹשׁ.

When the עמידה *is recited silently:*

אַתָּה קָדוֹשׁ וְשִׁמְךָ קָדוֹשׁ וּקְדוֹשִׁים בְּכָל יוֹם יְהַלְלוּךָ, סֶּלָה. בָּרוּךְ אַתָּה יְיָ, הָאֵל הַקָּדוֹשׁ.

Shabbat Musaf Prayers

Shabbat Musaf Amidah

We rise and take three steps back and three steps forward as we say:

Adonai, open my lips so I may speak Your praise.

Adonai s'fatai tif'tach ufi yagid t'hilatecha.

Praised are You, Adonai our God and God of our ancestors, God of Abraham, God of Isaac, and God of Jacob, God of Sarah, God of Rebecca, God of Rachel, and God of Leah, the great, strong and awe-inspiring God, God on high. You act with lovingkindness and create everything. God remembers the loving deeds of our ancestors, and will bring a redeemer to their children's children because that is God's loving nature.

Baruch atah Adonai Eloheinu vElohei avoteinu, Elohei Av'raham, Elohei Yitz'chak, vElohei Ya-akov, Elohei Sarah, Elohei Riv'ka, Elohei Rachel, vElohei Le-ah. Ha-El hagadol hagibur v'hanora, El el'yon, gomel chasideem toveem, v'koneh hakol, v'zocher chasdei avot, umevee go-el liv'nei v'neihem l'ma-an sh'mo b'ahavah.

You are a helping, guarding, saving and shielding Ruler. Praised are You, Adonai, Shield of Abraham and Guardian of Sarah.

Melech ozer ufoked umoshee-a umagen. Baruch atah Adonai, magen Av'raham ufoked Sarah.

You are mighty forever, Adonai. You give life to the dead with Your great saving power.

Atah gibor l'olam Adonai, m'chayeh meteem atah rav l'hoshee-a.

From Shemini Atzeret until Pesach:
You cause the wind to blow and the rain to fall.   Masheev haru-ach umoreed hagashem.

You support the living with kindness. You give life to the dead with great mercy. You support the fallen, heal the sick and set free those in prison. You keep faith with those who sleep in the dust. Who is like You, mighty Ruler, and who can compare to You, Ruler of life and death who causes salvation to bloom.

M'chal'kel chayim b'chesed, m'chayeh meteem b'rachameem rabeem, somech nofleem, v'rofeh choleem, umateer asureem, um'kayem emunato leeshenei afar, mee chamocha ba-al g'vurot umee domeh lach, melech memeet um'chayeh umatz'mee-ach y'shu-ah.

You are trustworthy in giving life to the dead. Praised are You Adonai, who gives life to the dead.

V'ne-eman atah l'hachayot meteem. Baruch atah Adonai, m'chayeh hameteem.

עֲמִידָה שֶׁל מוּסָף לְשַׁבָּת

Just like in *Shacharit*, this *Amidah* has the same basic structure as the weekday version, but with one big difference. Instead of all of the usual blessings in the middle, we replace them with a special blessing that praises the holiness of Shabbat.

We rise and take three steps back and three steps forward as we say:

אֲדֹנָי שְׂפָתַי תִּפְתָּח וּפִי יַגִּיד תְּהִלָּתֶךָ:

בָּרוּךְ אַתָּה יְיָ אֱלֹהֵינוּ וֵאלֹהֵי אֲבוֹתֵינוּ, אֱלֹהֵי אַבְרָהָם, אֱלֹהֵי יִצְחָק, וֵאלֹהֵי יַעֲקֹב, אֱלֹהֵי שָׂרָה, אֱלֹהֵי רִבְקָה, אֱלֹהֵי רָחֵל וֵאלֹהֵי לֵאָה. הָאֵל הַגָּדוֹל הַגִּבּוֹר וְהַנּוֹרָא, אֵל עֶלְיוֹן, גּוֹמֵל חֲסָדִים טוֹבִים, וְקוֹנֵה הַכֹּל, וְזוֹכֵר חַסְדֵי אָבוֹת, וּמֵבִיא גוֹאֵל לִבְנֵי בְנֵיהֶם לְמַעַן שְׁמוֹ בְּאַהֲבָה.

מֶלֶךְ עוֹזֵר וּפוֹקֵד וּמוֹשִׁיעַ וּמָגֵן: בָּרוּךְ אַתָּה יְיָ, מָגֵן אַבְרָהָם וּפוֹקֵד שָׂרָה:

אַתָּה גִּבּוֹר לְעוֹלָם אֲדֹנָי, מְחַיֵּה מֵתִים אַתָּה, רַב לְהוֹשִׁיעַ:

From Shemini Atzeret until Pesach:
מַשִּׁיב הָרוּחַ וּמוֹרִיד הַגֶּשֶׁם:

מְכַלְכֵּל חַיִּים בְּחֶסֶד, מְחַיֵּה מֵתִים בְּרַחֲמִים רַבִּים, סוֹמֵךְ נוֹפְלִים, וְרוֹפֵא חוֹלִים, וּמַתִּיר אֲסוּרִים, וּמְקַיֵּם אֱמוּנָתוֹ לִישֵׁנֵי עָפָר, מִי כָמוֹךָ בַּעַל גְּבוּרוֹת וּמִי דּוֹמֶה לָּךְ, מֶלֶךְ מֵמִית וּמְחַיֶּה וּמַצְמִיחַ יְשׁוּעָה:

וְנֶאֱמָן אַתָּה לְהַחֲיוֹת מֵתִים. בָּרוּךְ אַתָּה יְיָ, מְחַיֵּה הַמֵּתִים:

Shabbat Musaf Prayers

Chatzi Kaddish

Leader:

May God's great name be made great and holy in the world which God created according to God's will. May God establish Divine rule soon, in our days, quickly and in the near future, and let us say, Amen.

Yit'gadal v'yit'kadash sh'meh rabah. B'al'mah dee v'rah chir'utei, v'yam'leech mal'chutei b'chayeichon uv'yomeichon uv'chayei d'chol beit Yisra-el. Ba-agalah uviz'man kareev v'im'ru amen.

Everyone:

May God's great name be praised for ever and ever.

Y'heh sh'meh rabah m'varach l'alam ul'al'mei al'mayah.

Leader:

Blessed, praised, glorified and raised high, honored and elevated be the name of the Blessed Holy One, far beyond all blessings and songs, praises and words of comfort which people can say, and let us say: Amen.

Yit'barach v'yishtabach v'yitpa-ar v'yit'romam v'yit'naseh v'yit'hadar v'yit'aleh v'yit'halal sh'meh d'kud'shah b'reech hu l'elah min kol bir'chatah v'sheeratah tush'b'chatah v'nechematah, da-ameeran b'al'mah, v'im'ru amen.

מוּסָף לְשַׁבָּת

> When the Temple was destroyed, prayers were made to replace the sacrifices made in the Temple. For every sacrifice that was made, we now have a version of the *Amidah*. On special days like Shabbat and Holidays, the Temple service included an extra sacrifice called *Musaf* (if you look on page 150, you can find what this sacrifice included). Today, in keeping with the *Musaf* tradition, we add an extra *Amidah* to our morning prayers on special days.

חֲצִי קַדִּישׁ

Leader:

יִתְגַּדַּל וְיִתְקַדַּשׁ שְׁמֵהּ רַבָּא. בְּעָלְמָא דִּי בְרָא כִרְעוּתֵיהּ, וְיַמְלִיךְ מַלְכוּתֵהּ בְּחַיֵּיכוֹן וּבְיוֹמֵיכוֹן וּבְחַיֵּי דְכָל בֵּית יִשְׂרָאֵל. בַּעֲגָלָא וּבִזְמַן קָרִיב וְאִמְרוּ אָמֵן:

Everyone:

יְהֵא שְׁמֵהּ רַבָּא מְבָרַךְ לְעָלַם וּלְעָלְמֵי עָלְמַיָּא:

Leader:

יִתְבָּרַךְ וְיִשְׁתַּבַּח וְיִתְפָּאַר וְיִתְרוֹמַם וְיִתְנַשֵּׂא וְיִתְהַדָּר וְיִתְעַלֶּה וְיִתְהַלָּל שְׁמֵהּ דְּקֻדְשָׁא בְּרִיךְ הוּא לְעֵלָּא מִן כָּל בִּרְכָתָא וְשִׁירָתָא תֻּשְׁבְּחָתָא וְנֶחֱמָתָא, דַּאֲמִירָן בְּעָלְמָא, וְאִמְרוּ אָמֵן:

Shabbat Musaf Prayers

We rise to return the Torah to the Ark. The leader chants:

Praise Adonai whose name alone is highly praised.

Y'hal'lu et shem Adonai, kee nis'gav sh'mo l'vado.

Everyone responds:

God's majesty is over the earth and the heavens.
God will increase the pride and the praise of the people of Israel, the people close to God. Halleluyah.

Hodo al eretz v'shamayim. Vayarem keren l'amo,
T'hilah l'chol chaseedav, liv'nei Yisra-el am k'rovo, hal'luyah.

The Torah is carried around in procession as we sing:

A psalm of David. Applaud Adonai, all the mighty. Praise Adonai's glory and might. Praise Adonai's glorious name. Bow down to Adonai's splendid holiness. Adonai's voice sounds over the waters, thunders over many waters. Adonai's voice is power. Adonai's voice is majestic. Adonai's voice shatters the cedars of Lebanon. God makes them leap like a calf, the hills of Sirion like a young wild ox. Adonai's voice carves out flames of fire. Adonai's voice makes the wilderness shake. Adonai's voice makes the trees dance, it strips the forests bare, while in God's Temple all say, "Glory!" Just as Adonai ruled at the time of the Flood, so Adonai will rule forever. Adonai will give strength to God's people. Adonai will bless God's people with peace.

Mizmor l'David.
Havu lAdonai b'nei eleem
Havu lAdonai kavod va-oz.
Havu lAdonai k'vod sh'mo
Hish'tachavu lAdonai b'had'rat kodesh.
Kol Adonai al hamayim
El hakavod hir'im
Adonai al mayim rabeem.
Kol Adonai bako-ach
Kol Adonai behadar.
Kol Adonai shover arazeem
Vay'shaber Adonai et ar'zei hal'vanon,
Vayar'keedem k'mo egel
L'vanon v'sir'yon k'mo ven r'emeem,
Kol Adonai chotzev lahavot esh,
Kol Adonai yacheel mid'bar,
Yachil Adonai midbar kadesh.
Kol Adonai y'cholel ayalot
Vayechsof y'arot
uv'heichalo kulo omer kavod.
Adonai lamabul yashav
Vayeshev Adonai melech l'olam.
Adonai oz l'amo yiten
Adonai y'varech et amo vashalom.

The Torah is returned to the Ark, and we sing:

It is a tree of life for those who hold fast to it,
And all its supporters are happy.
Its paths are pleasant and all its ways are peaceful.
Return us to You, Adonai, and we shall return.

Etz chayeem hee lamachazeekeem bah,
v'tomcheiha m'ushar.
D'racheiha dar'chei no-am, v'chol n'titvoteiha shalom.
Hasheevenu Adonai, eleicha v'nashuvah,
chadesh yameinu k'kedem.

We are seated.

We rise to return the Torah to the Ark. The leader chants:

יְהַלְלוּ אֶת שֵׁם יְיָ, כִּי נִשְׂגָּב שְׁמוֹ לְבַדּוֹ.

Everyone responds:

הוֹדוֹ עַל אֶרֶץ וְשָׁמָיִם. וַיָּרֶם קֶרֶן לְעַמּוֹ,
תְּהִלָּה לְכָל חֲסִידָיו, לִבְנֵי יִשְׂרָאֵל עַם קְרוֹבוֹ, הַלְלוּיָהּ.

The Torah is carried around in procession as we sing:

מִזְמוֹר לְדָוִד,
הָבוּ לַיְיָ בְּנֵי אֵלִים, הָבוּ לַיְיָ כָּבוֹד וָעֹז.
הָבוּ לַיְיָ כְּבוֹד שְׁמוֹ, הִשְׁתַּחֲווּ לַיְיָ בְּהַדְרַת קֹדֶשׁ.
קוֹל יְיָ עַל הַמָּיִם, אֵל הַכָּבוֹד הִרְעִים, יְיָ עַל מַיִם רַבִּים.
קוֹל יְיָ בַּכֹּחַ, קוֹל יְיָ בֶּהָדָר.
קוֹל יְיָ שֹׁבֵר אֲרָזִים, וַיְשַׁבֵּר יְיָ אֶת אַרְזֵי הַלְּבָנוֹן.
וַיַּרְקִידֵם כְּמוֹ עֵגֶל, לְבָנוֹן וְשִׂרְיוֹן כְּמוֹ בֶן רְאֵמִים.
קוֹל יְיָ חֹצֵב לַהֲבוֹת אֵשׁ. קוֹל יְיָ יָחִיל מִדְבָּר,
יָחִיל יְיָ מִדְבַּר קָדֵשׁ. קוֹל יְיָ יְחוֹלֵל אַיָּלוֹת,
וַיֶּחֱשֹׂף יְעָרוֹת, וּבְהֵיכָלוֹ, כֻּלּוֹ אֹמֵר כָּבוֹד.
יְיָ לַמַּבּוּל יָשָׁב, וַיֵּשֶׁב יְיָ מֶלֶךְ לְעוֹלָם.
יְיָ עֹז לְעַמּוֹ יִתֵּן, יְיָ יְבָרֵךְ אֶת עַמּוֹ בַשָּׁלוֹם.

PSALM 29

The Torah is returned to the Ark, and we sing:

עֵץ חַיִּים הִיא לַמַּחֲזִיקִים בָּהּ, וְתֹמְכֶיהָ מְאֻשָּׁר.
דְּרָכֶיהָ דַרְכֵי נֹעַם, וְכָל נְתִיבוֹתֶיהָ שָׁלוֹם.
הֲשִׁיבֵנוּ יְיָ, אֵלֶיךָ וְנָשׁוּבָה, חַדֵּשׁ יָמֵינוּ כְּקֶדֶם.

We are seated.

Shabbat Torah Service

Blessing Before the Haftarah

Praised are You, Adonai our God, Ruler of the universe, who chose good prophets, and was pleased with their words spoken in truth. Praised are You, Adonai, who chose the Torah, Moses, God's servant, and Israel, God's people, and the true and righteous prophets.

Baruch atah Adonai Eloheinu melech ha-olam, asher bachar bin'vee-eem toveem, v'ratzah v'div'reihem hane-emareem be-emet. Baruch atah Adonai, habocher baTorah uv'Moshe av'do, uv'Yisra-el amo, uvin'vee-ei ha-emet vatzedek.

Blessing After the Haftarah

Praised are You, Adonai our God, Ruler of the universe, everlasting Rock, righteous in every generation, dependable God who says and does, who speaks and fulfills, for all God's words are true and righteous. You, Adonai our God, are faithful and Your words are dependable. Not one of Your promises remains unkept, for You are a trustworthy and merciful Ruler. Praised are You, Adonai, God whose every word is dependable.

Baruch atah Adonai Eloheinu melech ha-olam, tzur kol ha-olameem, tzadeek b'chol hadorot, ha-el hane-eman ha-omer v'oseh, ham'daber um'kayem, shekol d'varav emet vatzedek. Ne-eman atah hu Adonai Eloheinu, v'ne-emaneem d'vareicha, v'davar echad mid'vareicha achor lo yashuv reikam, kee El melech ne-eman v'rachaman atah. Baruch atah Adonai, ha-El hane-eman b'chol d'varav.

Have mercy on Zion, Your city, for it is the source of our life. May You quickly save that unfortunate one, in our day. Praised are You, Adonai, who causes Zion to rejoice with her children.

Rachem al tzee-on kee hee beit chayeinu, v'la-aluvat nefesh toshee-a bim'herah v'yameinu. Baruch atah Adonai, m'same-ach tzee-on b'vaneiha.

Adonai our God, cause us to rejoice with Elijah the prophet, Your servant, and the rule of David, Your anointed one. May he come soon to make our hearts glad. May no stranger sit on his throne; may no others inherit his glory. For You promised by Your holy name that his light will never go out. Praised are You, Adonai, Shield of David.

Sam'chenu Adonai Eloheinu b'Elee-ahu hanavee av'decha, uv'mal'chut beit David m'sheechecha, bim'herah yavo v'yagel libenu, al kis'o lo yeshev zar v'lo yin'chalu od achereem ed k'vodo, kee b'shem kod'sh'cha nish'ba'ta lo, shelo yich'beh nero l'olam va-ed. Baruch atah Adonai, magen David.

For the Torah, and for worship, and for the prophets, and for this Shabbat day that You gave us, Adonai our God, for holiness and rest, for glory and beauty—for everything!—we thank and bless You. May Your name always be blessed by everything that lives. Praised are You, Adonai, who makes the Shabbat holy.

Al haTorah, v'al ha-avodah, v'al han'vee-eem, v'al yom haShabbat hazeh, shenatata lanu Adonai Eloheinu, lik'dushah v'lim'nuchah, l'chavod ul'tif'aret. Al hakol Adonai Eloheinu, anachnu modeem lach, um'var'cheem otach, yit'barach shim'cha b'fee kol chai tameed l'olam va-ed. Baruch atah Adonai, m'kadesh haShabbat.

DID YOU KNOW THAT... At one point in our history, we were forbidden to study Torah. At that time, people chose a section from the books of the Prophets with a similar theme to read instead of each week's Torah portion. Today, we keep that tradition alive by reading the *Haftarah* after the Torah reading every Shabbat.

בְּרָכוֹת לִפְנֵי הַהַפְטָרָה

בָּרוּךְ אַתָּה יְיָ אֱלֹהֵינוּ מֶלֶךְ הָעוֹלָם, אֲשֶׁר בָּחַר בִּנְבִיאִים טוֹבִים, וְרָצָה בְדִבְרֵיהֶם הַנֶּאֱמָרִים בֶּאֱמֶת. בָּרוּךְ אַתָּה יְיָ, הַבּוֹחֵר בַּתּוֹרָה וּבְמשֶׁה עַבְדּוֹ, וּבְיִשְׂרָאֵל עַמּוֹ, וּבִנְבִיאֵי הָאֱמֶת וָצֶדֶק.

בְּרָכוֹת אַחֲרֵי הַהַפְטָרָה

בָּרוּךְ אַתָּה יְיָ אֱלֹהֵינוּ מֶלֶךְ הָעוֹלָם, צוּר כָּל הָעוֹלָמִים, צַדִּיק בְּכָל הַדּוֹרוֹת, הָאֵל הַנֶּאֱמָן הָאוֹמֵר וְעֹשֶׂה, הַמְדַבֵּר וּמְקַיֵּם, שֶׁכָּל דְּבָרָיו אֱמֶת וָצֶדֶק. נֶאֱמָן אַתָּה הוּא יְיָ אֱלֹהֵינוּ, וְנֶאֱמָנִים דְּבָרֶיךָ, וְדָבָר אֶחָד מִדְּבָרֶיךָ אָחוֹר לֹא יָשׁוּב רֵיקָם, כִּי אֵל מֶלֶךְ נֶאֱמָן וְרַחֲמָן אָתָּה. בָּרוּךְ אַתָּה יְיָ, הָאֵל הַנֶּאֱמָן בְּכָל דְּבָרָיו.

רַחֵם עַל צִיּוֹן כִּי הִיא בֵּית חַיֵּינוּ, וְלַעֲלוּבַת נֶפֶשׁ תּוֹשִׁיעַ בִּמְהֵרָה בְיָמֵינוּ. בָּרוּךְ אַתָּה יְיָ, מְשַׂמֵּחַ צִיּוֹן בְּבָנֶיהָ.

שַׂמְּחֵנוּ יְיָ אֱלֹהֵינוּ בְּאֵלִיָּהוּ הַנָּבִיא עַבְדֶּךָ, וּבְמַלְכוּת בֵּית דָּוִד מְשִׁיחֶךָ, בִּמְהֵרָה יָבֹא וְיָגֵל לִבֵּנוּ, עַל כִּסְאוֹ לֹא יֵשֵׁב זָר וְלֹא יִנְחֲלוּ עוֹד אֲחֵרִים אֶת כְּבוֹדוֹ, כִּי בְשֵׁם קָדְשְׁךָ נִשְׁבַּעְתָּ לּוֹ, שֶׁלֹּא יִכְבֶּה נֵרוֹ לְעוֹלָם וָעֶד. בָּרוּךְ אַתָּה יְיָ, מָגֵן דָּוִד.

עַל הַתּוֹרָה, וְעַל הָעֲבוֹדָה, וְעַל הַנְּבִיאִים, וְעַל יוֹם הַשַּׁבָּת הַזֶּה, שֶׁנָּתַתָּ לָּנוּ יְיָ אֱלֹהֵינוּ, לִקְדֻשָּׁה וְלִמְנוּחָה, לְכָבוֹד וּלְתִפְאָרֶת. עַל הַכֹּל יְיָ אֱלֹהֵינוּ, אֲנַחְנוּ מוֹדִים לָךְ, וּמְבָרְכִים אוֹתָךְ, יִתְבָּרַךְ שִׁמְךָ בְּפִי כָּל חַי תָּמִיד לְעוֹלָם וָעֶד. בָּרוּךְ אַתָּה יְיָ, מְקַדֵּשׁ הַשַּׁבָּת.

Chatzi Kaddish

Leader:

May God's great name be made great and holy in the world which God created according to God's will. May God establish Divine rule soon, in our days, quickly and in the near future, and let us say, Amen.

Yit'gadal v'yit'kadash sh'meh rabah. B'al'mah dee v'rah chir'utei, v'yam'leech mal'chutei b'chayeichon uv'yomeichon uv'chayei d'chol beit Yisra-el. Ba-agalah uviz'man kareev v'im'ru amen.

Everyone:

May God's great name be praised for ever and ever.

Y'heh sh'meh rabah m'varach l'alam ul'al'mei al'mayah.

Leader:

Blessed, praised, glorified and raised high, honored and elevated be the name of the Blessed Holy One, far beyond all blessings and songs, praises and words of comfort which people can say, and let us say: Amen.

Yit'barach v'yishtabach v'yitpa-ar v'yit'romam v'yit'naseh v'yit'hadar v'yit'aleh v'yit'halal sh'meh d'kud'shah b'reech hu l'elah min kol bir'chatah v'sheeratah tush'b'chatah v'nechematah, da-ameeran b'al'mah, v'im'ru amen.

We rise as the Hagbah lifts up the Torah and shows its written side to us and chant:

This is the Torah that Moses placed before the Israelites, by God's authority, through Moses.

V'zot haTorah asher sam Moshe lif'nei b'nei Yisra-el al pee Adonai b'yad Moshe.

The Torah which Moses handed down to us is the heritage of the community of Jacob.

Torah tzivah lanu Moshe, Morasha k'hilat Ya-akov.

סדר הוצאת התורה לשבת

חֲצִי קַדִּישׁ

Leader:

יִתְגַּדַּל וְיִתְקַדַּשׁ שְׁמֵהּ רַבָּא. בְּעָלְמָא דִּי בְרָא כִרְעוּתֵיהּ, וְיַמְלִיךְ מַלְכוּתֵהּ בְּחַיֵּיכוֹן וּבְיוֹמֵיכוֹן וּבְחַיֵּי דְכָל בֵּית יִשְׂרָאֵל. בַּעֲגָלָא וּבִזְמַן קָרִיב וְאִמְרוּ אָמֵן:

Everyone:

יְהֵא שְׁמֵהּ רַבָּא מְבָרַךְ לְעָלַם וּלְעָלְמֵי עָלְמַיָּא:

Leader:

יִתְבָּרַךְ וְיִשְׁתַּבַּח וְיִתְפָּאַר וְיִתְרוֹמַם וְיִתְנַשֵּׂא וְיִתְהַדָּר וְיִתְעַלֶּה וְיִתְהַלָּל שְׁמֵהּ דְּקֻדְשָׁא בְּרִיךְ הוּא לְעֵלָּא מִן כָּל בִּרְכָתָא וְשִׁירָתָא תֻּשְׁבְּחָתָא וְנֶחָמָתָא, דַּאֲמִירָן בְּעָלְמָא, וְאִמְרוּ אָמֵן:

We rise as the Hagbah lifts up the Torah and shows its written side to us and chant:

וְזֹאת הַתּוֹרָה אֲשֶׁר שָׂם מֹשֶׁה לִפְנֵי בְּנֵי יִשְׂרָאֵל, עַל פִּי יְיָ בְּיַד מֹשֶׁה:

תּוֹרָה צִוָּה לָנוּ מֹשֶׁה, מוֹרָשָׁה קְהִלַּת יַעֲקֹב:

Torah Blessings

The leader sings:

Praise Adonai, who is to be praised.   Bar'chu et Adonai ham'vorach.

Everyone replies, then the leader repeats:

Praised be Adonai who is to be praised for ever and ever.   Baruch Adonai ham'vorach l'olam va-ed.

Praised are You, Adonai our God, Ruler of the universe, who chose us from among all peoples by giving us God's Torah. Praised are You, Adonai, who gives the Torah.   Baruch atah Adonai, Eloheinu melech ha-olam, asher bachar banu mikol ha-ameem v'natan lanu et Torato. Baruch atah Adonai, noten haTorah.

After the Torah is read:

Praised are You, Adonai our God, Ruler of the universe, who gave us a Torah of truth and planted within us lasting life. Praised are You, Adonai, who gives the Torah.   Baruch atah Adonai, Eloheinu melech ha-olam, asher natan lanu Torat emet, v'chayei olam nata b'tochenu. Baruch atah Adonai, noten haTorah.

Prayer For The Sick

May God who blessed our ancestors; Abraham, Isaac, and Jacob, Sarah, Rebecea, Rachel, and Leah, bring blessing and healing to (____ and) all those who suffer illness within our community. May the Holy One mercifully restore them to health and vigor, granting them physical and spiritual well-being, together with all others who are ill. And let us say: Amen.   Mee sheberach avoteinu Av'raham Yitz'chak v'Ya-akov, Sarah Riv'kah Rachel v'Le-ah, hu y'varech veerapeh (et _____ ben/bat _____ v') et-kol hacholeem. Hakadosh baruch hu yimaleh rachameem aleihem l'hachazeekam ul'rap'otam, v'yish'lach lahem m'herah r'fu-ah sh'lemah l'chol-evarav v'geedav b'toch sh'ar cholei Yisra-el, r'fu-at hanefesh ur'fu-at haguf. V'nomar amen.

סדר הוצאת התורה לשבת

בִּרְכוֹת הַתּוֹרָה

The leader sings:

בָּרְכוּ אֶת יְיָ הַמְבֹרָךְ:

Everyone replies, then the leader repeats:

בָּרוּךְ יְיָ הַמְבֹרָךְ לְעוֹלָם וָעֶד:

בָּרוּךְ אַתָּה יְיָ אֱלֹהֵינוּ מֶלֶךְ הָעוֹלָם, אֲשֶׁר בָּחַר בָּנוּ מִכָּל הָעַמִּים וְנָתַן לָנוּ אֶת תּוֹרָתוֹ: בָּרוּךְ אַתָּה יְיָ, נוֹתֵן הַתּוֹרָה:

After the Torah is read:

בָּרוּךְ אַתָּה יְיָ אֱלֹהֵינוּ מֶלֶךְ הָעוֹלָם, אֲשֶׁר נָתַן לָנוּ תּוֹרַת אֱמֶת, וְחַיֵּי עוֹלָם נָטַע בְּתוֹכֵנוּ: בָּרוּךְ אַתָּה יְיָ, נוֹתֵן הַתּוֹרָה:

מִי שֶׁבֵּרַךְ לַחוֹלִים

In our tradition we stop to pray for loved ones and community members who are ill. By saying their names out loud or thinking of them in our minds, we pray for their health to be restored.

מִי שֶׁבֵּרַךְ אֲבוֹתֵינוּ אַבְרָהָם יִצְחָק וְיַעֲקֹב, שָׂרָה רִבְקָה רָחֵל וְלֵאָה, הוּא יְבָרֵךְ וִירַפֵּא (אֶת־_____ בֶּן/בַּת _____) וְאֶת־כָּל הַחוֹלִים. הַקָּדוֹשׁ בָּרוּךְ הוּא יִמָּלֵא רַחֲמִים עֲלֵיהֶם לְהַחֲזִיקָם וּלְרַפְּאוֹתָם, וְיִשְׁלַח לָהֶם מְהֵרָה רְפוּאָה שְׁלֵמָה לְכָל־אֲבָרָיו וְגִידָיו בְּתוֹךְ שְׁאָר חוֹלֵי יִשְׂרָאֵל, רְפוּאַת הַנֶּפֶשׁ וּרְפוּאַת הַגּוּף. וְנֹאמַר אָמֵן.

Shabbat Torah Service

The Torah is taken from the Ark.
The leader sings each of the following two lines, then everyone repeats them:

Hear O Israel, Adonai is our God, Adonai is One.	Sh'ma Yisra-el, Adonai Eloheinu, Adonai echad.
One is our God, great is our Master, whose name is holy and awe-inspiring.	Echad Eloheinu, gadol adonenu, kadosh sh'mo.

The leader faces the Ark, bows, and chants:

Declare Adonai's greatness with me; let us praise God together.	Gad'lu lAdonai itee, un'rom'mah sh'mo yach'dav.

The Torah is carried around in procession as we sing:

Greatness, might, wonder, triumph, and majesty are Yours, Adonai—yes, all that is in heaven and on earth; to You, Adonai, belong kingship and rule over all.	L'cha Adonai hag'dulah v'hag'vurah v'hatif'eret v'hanetzach v'hahod, kee chol bashamayim uva-aretz. L'cha Adonai hamam'lacha v'hamit'naseh l'chol l'rosh:
Praise Adonai and bow down to God's presence; God is holy!	Rom'mu Adonai Eloheinu, v'hishtachavu lahadom rag'lav kadosh hu.
Praise Adonai, our God, bow to God's holy mountain. Adonai our God is holy.	Rom'mu Adonai Eloheinu, v'hishtachavu l'har kod'sho, kee kadosh Adonai Eloheinu.

Once the Torah is set down, we are seated.

The Gabbai calls up the first person to have an aliyah:

May God help, save, and shield all who trust in God. And let us say: Amen. Let us all declare the greatness of our God and give honor to the Torah.	V'ya-azor v'yagen v'yoshee-a l'chol hachoseem bo, v'nomar amen. Hakol havu godel lEloheinu ut'nu chavod laTorah.
Let the first to be honored come forward.	Kohen, k'rav. Ya-amod _____ ben _____ hakohen.
	Bat kohen, kir'vee. Ta-amod _____ bat _____ hakohen.
	Ya-amod _____ ben _____ harishon.
	Ta-amod _____ bat _____ harishonah.
Praised is God who in holiness gave the Torah to God's people Israel.	Baruch shenatan Torah l'amo Yisra-el bik'dushto.

Everyone:

You who remain steadfast to Adonai your God have been sustained to this day.	V'atem had'vekeem bAdonai Eloheichem, chayeem kul'chem hayom.

סדר הוצאת התורה לשבת

The Torah is taken from the Ark.
The leader sings each of the following two lines, then everyone repeats them:

שְׁמַע יִשְׂרָאֵל, יְיָ אֱלֹהֵינוּ, יְיָ אֶחָד.

אֶחָד אֱלֹהֵינוּ, גָּדוֹל אֲדוֹנֵנוּ, קָדוֹשׁ שְׁמוֹ.

The leader faces the Ark, bows, and chants:

גַּדְּלוּ לַייָ אִתִּי, וּנְרוֹמְמָה שְׁמוֹ יַחְדָּו:

The Torah is carried around in procession as we sing:

לְךָ יְיָ הַגְּדֻלָּה וְהַגְּבוּרָה וְהַתִּפְאֶרֶת וְהַנֵּצַח וְהַהוֹד,
כִּי כֹל בַּשָּׁמַיִם וּבָאָרֶץ: לְךָ יְיָ הַמַּמְלָכָה וְהַמִּתְנַשֵּׂא לְכֹל לְרֹאשׁ:
רוֹמְמוּ יְיָ אֱלֹהֵינוּ, וְהִשְׁתַּחֲווּ לַהֲדֹם רַגְלָיו קָדוֹשׁ הוּא:
רוֹמְמוּ יְיָ אֱלֹהֵינוּ, וְהִשְׁתַּחֲווּ לְהַר קָדְשׁוֹ, כִּי קָדוֹשׁ יְיָ אֱלֹהֵינוּ:

Once the Torah is set down, we are seated.

The Gabbai calls up the first person to have an aliyah:

וְיַעֲזוֹר וְיָגֵן וְיוֹשִׁיעַ לְכָל הַחוֹסִים בּוֹ, וְנֹאמַר אָמֵן.
הַכֹּל הָבוּ גֹדֶל לֵאלֹהֵינוּ וּתְנוּ כָבוֹד לַתּוֹרָה.
כֹּהֵן, קְרָב. יַעֲמֹד _____ בֶּן _____ הַכֹּהֵן.
בַּת כֹּהֵן, קִרְבִי. תַּעֲמֹד _____ בַּת _____ הַכֹּהֵן.
יַעֲמֹד _____ בֶּן _____ הָרִאשׁוֹן.
תַּעֲמֹד _____ בַּת _____ הָרִאשׁוֹנָה.
בָּרוּךְ שֶׁנָּתַן תּוֹרָה לְעַמּוֹ יִשְׂרָאֵל בִּקְדֻשָּׁתוֹ.

Everyone:

וְאַתֶּם הַדְּבֵקִים בַּייָ אֱלֹהֵיכֶם, חַיִּים כֻּלְּכֶם הַיּוֹם:

Shabbat Torah Service

Shabbat Torah Service

There is none like You, Adonai,
And there is nothing like Your deeds.
God, You rule eternally,
Your rule lasts for all generations.

Adonai rules, Adonai ruled,
Adonai will rule for ever and ever.
Adonai will give strength to God's people,
Adonai will bless God's people with peace.

Merciful Parent,
Favor Zion with Your goodness.
Rebuild the walls of Jerusalem.
For we trust only You, Ruler, God on high,
Master of worlds.

Ein kamocha va-Eloheem, Adonai,
v'ein k'ma-seicha.
Malchut'cha mal'chut kol olameem,
Umem'shal't'cha b'chol dor vador.

Adonai melech, Adonai malach,
Adonai yim'loch l'olam va-ed.
Adonai oz l'amo yiten
Adonai y'varech et amo vashalom.

Av harachameem, heiteevah vir'tzon'cha
et tzee-on, tiv'neh chomot Y'rushalayim.
Kee v'cha l'vad batach'nu, melech El ram
v'nisa, adon olameem.

We rise as the Ark is opened and sing:

Whenever the Ark would travel,
Moses would say,
Arise, Adonai, and scatter Your enemies;
May those that hate You flee from You.
For Torah shall come from Zion,
The word of Adonai from Jerusalem.
Blessed is the One who in holiness gave the Torah to Israel.

Vay'hee bin'so-a ha-aron vayomer Moshe,
Kuma Adonai v'yafutzu oy'vecha,
V'yanusu m'san'eicha mipaneicha.
Kee mitzee-on tetzeh Torah,
ud'var Adonai mirushalayim.
Baruch shenatan Torah l'amo Yisra-el bik'dushato.

סֵדֶר הוֹצָאַת הַתּוֹרָה לְשַׁבָּת

> On Mondays and Thursdays we get a preview of the week's Torah portion. On Shabbat, we get a chance to take a closer look at it. Since the Torah is such a holy book, we don't just take it out and read from it, but we ceremoniously move closer to it step by step. First, we open the ark and look at it, then the leader takes it out and holds it in front of us. After that, it is paraded around the entire camp. Then, we unwrap it and begin to read it once we have been brought closer to it.

אֵין כָּמוֹךָ בָאֱלֹהִים, יְיָ, וְאֵין כְּמַעֲשֶׂיךָ.
מַלְכוּתְךָ מַלְכוּת כָּל עֹלָמִים, וּמֶמְשַׁלְתְּךָ בְּכָל דּוֹר וָדוֹר.

יְיָ מֶלֶךְ, יְיָ מָלָךְ, יְיָ יִמְלֹךְ לְעֹלָם וָעֶד.
יְיָ עֹז לְעַמּוֹ יִתֵּן יְיָ יְבָרֵךְ אֶת עַמּוֹ בַשָּׁלוֹם.

אַב הָרַחֲמִים, הֵיטִיבָה בִרְצוֹנְךָ אֶת צִיּוֹן, תִּבְנֶה חוֹמוֹת יְרוּשָׁלָיִם.
כִּי בְךָ לְבַד בָּטָחְנוּ, מֶלֶךְ אֵל רָם וְנִשָּׂא, אֲדוֹן עוֹלָמִים.

We rise as the Ark is opened and sing:

וַיְהִי בִּנְסֹעַ הָאָרֹן וַיֹּאמֶר מֹשֶׁה:
קוּמָה יְיָ, וְיָפֻצוּ אֹיְבֶיךָ, וְיָנֻסוּ מְשַׂנְאֶיךָ מִפָּנֶיךָ.
כִּי מִצִּיּוֹן תֵּצֵא תוֹרָה, וּדְבַר יְיָ מִירוּשָׁלָיִם.
בָּרוּךְ שֶׁנָּתַן תּוֹרָה לְעַמּוֹ יִשְׂרָאֵל בִּקְדֻשָּׁתוֹ.

Shabbat Torah Service

Kaddish Shalem

Leader:

May God's great name be made great and holy in the world which God created according to God's will. May God establish Divine rule soon, in our days, quickly and in the near future, and let us say: Amen.	Yit'gadal v'yit'kadash sh'meh rabah. B'al'mah dee v'rah chir'utei, v'yam'leech mal'chutei b'chayeichon uv'yomeichon uv'chayei d'chol beit Yisra-el. Ba-agalah uviz'man kareev v'im'ru amen.

Everyone:

May God's great name be praised for ever and ever.	Y'heh sh'meh rabah m'varach l'alam ul'al'mei al'mayah.

Leader:

Blessed, praised, glorified and raised high, honored and elevated be the name of the Holy Blessed One, far beyond all blessings and songs, praises and words of comfort which people can say, and let us say: Amen.	Yit'barach v'yishtabach v'yitpa-ar v'yit'romam v'yit'naseh v'yit'hadar v'yit'aleh v'yit'halal sh'meh d'kud'shah b'reech hu l'elah min kol bir'chatah v'sheeratah tush'b'chatah v'nechematah, da-ameeran b'al'mah, v'im'ru amen.
May the prayers and pleas of the entire House of Israel be accepted before their Parent in heaven. And let us say: Amen.	Tit'kabal tz'lot'hon uva-ut'hon d'chol Yisra-el kadam avuhon dee vish'mayah v'im'ru amen.
May there be abundant peace from heaven and life for us and for all Israel, and let us say: Amen.	Y'hei sh'lamah rabah min sh'mayah v'chayeem aleinu v'al kol Yisra-el, v'im'ru amen.
May the One who makes peace in the high heavens make peace for us and for all Israel, and let us say: Amen.	Oseh shalom bim'romav, hu ya-aseh shalom aleinu, v'al kol Yisra-el v'im'ru amen.

שחרית לשבת

קַדִישׁ שָׁלֵם

Leader:

יִתְגַדַּל וְיִתְקַדַּשׁ שְׁמֵהּ רַבָּא. בְּעָלְמָא דִי בְרָא כִרְעוּתֵיהּ, וְיַמְלִיךְ מַלְכוּתֵהּ בְּחַיֵּיכוֹן וּבְיוֹמֵיכוֹן וּבְחַיֵּי דְכָל בֵּית יִשְׂרָאֵל. בַּעֲגָלָא וּבִזְמַן קָרִיב וְאִמְרוּ אָמֵן:

Everyone:

יְהֵא שְׁמֵהּ רַבָּא מְבָרַךְ לְעָלַם וּלְעָלְמֵי עָלְמַיָּא:

Leader:

יִתְבָּרַךְ וְיִשְׁתַּבַּח וְיִתְפָּאַר וְיִתְרוֹמַם וְיִתְנַשֵּׂא וְיִתְהַדָּר וְיִתְעַלֶּה וְיִתְהַלָּל שְׁמֵהּ דְּקֻדְשָׁא בְּרִיךְ הוּא לְעֵלָּא מִן כָּל בִּרְכָתָא וְשִׁירָתָא תֻּשְׁבְּחָתָא וְנֶחֱמָתָא, דַּאֲמִירָן בְּעָלְמָא, וְאִמְרוּ אָמֵן:

תִּתְקַבֵּל צְלוֹתְהוֹן וּבָעוּתְהוֹן דְּכָל יִשְׂרָאֵל קֳדָם אֲבוּהוֹן דִּי בִשְׁמַיָּא וְאִמְרוּ אָמֵן:

יְהֵא שְׁלָמָא רַבָּא מִן שְׁמַיָּא וְחַיִּים עָלֵינוּ וְעַל כָּל יִשְׂרָאֵל, וְאִמְרוּ אָמֵן:

עֹשֶׂה שָׁלוֹם בִּמְרוֹמָיו הוּא יַעֲשֶׂה שָׁלוֹם עָלֵינוּ וְעַל כָּל יִשְׂרָאֵל, וְאִמְרוּ אָמֵן:

Make peace in the world, with goodness, blessing, grace, lovingkindness and mercy for us and for all Your people Israel. Bless us, our Parent, all of us together, with Your light, by which You taught us Your Torah of life, love and kindness, justice and mercy, life and peace. May it be good in Your sight to bless Your people Israel at all times with peace.

Praised are You, Adonai, who blesses Your people Israel with peace.

My God, help me not to say bad things or to tell lies. Help me to ignore people who say bad things about me. Open my heart to Your Torah, so that I can do Your mitzvot. Quickly stop the ideas and spoil the plans of anyone who wants to hurt me. Do this because of Your love, Your holiness, and Your Torah: so that those You love will be free. May the words of my mouth and the thoughts of my heart find favor with You, my Rock and my Protector. May the One who makes peace up above give peace to us and to all the people of Israel. Amen.

Sim shalom tovah uv'racha, chen vachesed v'rachameem, aleinu v'al kol Yisra-el amecha. Bar'chenu, aveenu, kulanu k'echad b'or paneicha, kee v'or paneicha natata lanu, Adonai Eloheinu, Torat chayeem v'ahavat chesed, utz'dakah uv'racha v'rachameem v'chayeem v'shalom, v'tov b'eineicha l'varech et am'cha Yisra-el b'chol et uv'chol sha-ah bish'lomecha.

Baruch atah Adonai, ham'varech et amo Yisra-el bashalom.

Elohai, n'tzor l'shonee mera. Us'fatai midaber mir'mah. V'lim'kal'lai naf'shee tidom, v'naf'shee ke-afar lakol tih'yeh. P'tach libee b'Torahtecha, uv'mitzvoteicha tir'dof naf'shee. V'chol hachosh'veem alai ra-ah, m'herah hafer atzatam v'kal'kel macahshav'tam. Aseh l'ma-an Toratecha. Lama-an yechal'tzun y'deedeicha, hoshee-ah y'meen'cha va-anenee. Yih'yu l'ratzon im'rei fee v'heg'yon libee l'faneicha, Adonai tzuree v'go-alee. Oseh shalom bim'romav, hu ya-aseh shalom aleinu, v'al kol Yisra-el v'im'ru amen.

> "When the world was created, God made everything a little bit incomplete. Rather than making bread grow out of the earth, God made wheat grow so that we might bake it into bread. Rather than making the earth of bricks, God made it of clay, so that we might make the clay into bricks. Why? So that we might become partners in completing the work of creation."
> —Midrash

שִׂים שָׁלוֹם טוֹבָה וּבְרָכָה, חֵן וָחֶסֶד וְרַחֲמִים, עָלֵינוּ וְעַל כָּל יִשְׂרָאֵל עַמֶּךָ. בָּרְכֵנוּ, אָבִינוּ, כֻּלָּנוּ כְּאֶחָד בְּאוֹר פָּנֶיךָ, כִּי בְאוֹר פָּנֶיךָ נָתַתָּ לָּנוּ, יְיָ אֱלֹהֵינוּ, תּוֹרַת חַיִּים וְאַהֲבַת חֶסֶד, וּצְדָקָה וּבְרָכָה וְרַחֲמִים וְחַיִּים וְשָׁלוֹם, וְטוֹב בְּעֵינֶיךָ לְבָרֵךְ אֶת עַמְּךָ יִשְׂרָאֵל בְּכָל עֵת וּבְכָל שָׁעָה בִּשְׁלוֹמֶךָ.

בָּרוּךְ אַתָּה יְיָ, הַמְבָרֵךְ אֶת עַמּוֹ יִשְׂרָאֵל בַּשָּׁלוֹם.

אֱלֹהַי, נְצוֹר לְשׁוֹנִי מֵרָע. וּשְׂפָתַי מִדַּבֵּר מִרְמָה: וְלִמְקַלְלַי נַפְשִׁי תִדֹּם, וְנַפְשִׁי כֶּעָפָר לַכֹּל תִּהְיֶה. פְּתַח לִבִּי בְּתוֹרָתֶךָ, וּבְמִצְוֹתֶיךָ תִּרְדּוֹף נַפְשִׁי. וְכָל הַחוֹשְׁבִים עָלַי רָעָה, מְהֵרָה הָפֵר עֲצָתָם וְקַלְקֵל מַחֲשַׁבְתָּם. עֲשֵׂה לְמַעַן שְׁמֶךָ, עֲשֵׂה לְמַעַן יְמִינֶךָ, עֲשֵׂה לְמַעַן קְדֻשָּׁתֶךָ. עֲשֵׂה לְמַעַן תּוֹרָתֶךָ. לְמַעַן יֵחָלְצוּן יְדִידֶיךָ, הוֹשִׁיעָה יְמִינְךָ וַעֲנֵנִי. יִהְיוּ לְרָצוֹן אִמְרֵי פִי וְהֶגְיוֹן לִבִּי לְפָנֶיךָ, יְיָ צוּרִי וְגוֹאֲלִי. עֹשֶׂה שָׁלוֹם בִּמְרוֹמָיו, הוּא יַעֲשֶׂה שָׁלוֹם עָלֵינוּ, וְעַל כָּל יִשְׂרָאֵל וְאִמְרוּ: אָמֵן.

On Rosh Chodesh, add the following:

Our God and God of our ancestors, please remember us, our ancestors, the Messiah, Your holy city Jerusalem, and Your people Israel. Remember them for good, with mercy and lovingkindness, for life and peace on this day of the New Moon.

Remember us, Adonai our God; keep us in mind for blessing, and give us life. You promised to protect and save us, have mercy on us and save us, for our eyes turn to You, for You are a kind and merciful Ruler.

Eloheinu vElohei avoteinu, ya-aleh v'yavo, v'yagee-a, v'yera-eh, v'yeratzeh, v'yishama, v'yipaked, v'yizacher zich'ronenu ufikdonenu, v'zich'ron avoteinu mashiach ben David av'decha, v'zich'ron Y'rushalayim eer kod'shecha, v'zich'ron kol am'cha beit Yisra-el l'faneicha, lif'leitah, l'tovah, l'chen ul'chesed ul'rachameem, l'chayim ul'shalom, b'yom Rosh Hachodesh hazeh.

Zochrenu, Adonai, Eloheinu, bo l'tovah, ufok'denu vo liv'rachah, v'hoshee-enu vo l'chayim, uvid'var y'shu-ah v'rachameem, chus v'chonenu, v'rachem aleinu v'hoshee-enu, kee eleicha eineinu, kee El melech chanun v'rachum atah.

May we see Your merciful return to Zion. Praised are You, Adonai, who restores Your presence to Zion.

V'techezeinah eineinu b'shuv'cha l'tzee-on b'rachameem. Baruch atah Adonai, hamachazeer sh'cheenato l'tzee-on.

We thank You for being our God and God of our ancestors for ever and ever. You are the Rock of our lives and our saving Shield. In every generation we will thank and praise You for our lives which are in Your power, for our souls which are in Your keeping, for Your miracles which are with us every day, and for Your wonders and good deeds that are with us at all times, evening, morning, and noon. O Good One, Your mercies have never stopped. O Merciful One, Your kindness has never stopped. We have always placed our hope in You.

Modeem anach'nu lach, sha-atah hu, Adonai Eloheinu vElohei avoteinu, l'olam va-ed, tzur chayeinu, magen yish'enu, atah hu l'dor vador nodeh l'cha un'saper t'hilatecha. Al chayeinu ham'sureem b'yadecha, v'al nish'moteinu hap'kudot lach, v'al niseicha sheb'chol yom imanu, v'al nif'l'oteicha v'tovoteicha sheb'chol et, erev vavoker v'tzohorayim, hatov kee lo chalu rachameicha, v'ham'rachem kee lo tamu chasadeicha me-olam kiveenu lach.

For all these things, our Ruler, may Your name be blessed and honored forever.

V'al kulam yitbarach v'yit'romam shim'cha, mal'kenu, tameed l'olam va-ed.

May every living thing thank You and praise You sincerely, O God, our rescue and help. Praised are You, Your name is "the Good One," and it is good to thank You.

V'chol hachayeem yoducha selah, veehal'lu et shim'cha be-emet, ha-El y'shu-atenu v'ez'ratenu selah. Baruch atah Adonai, hatov shim'cha ul'cha na-eh l'hodot.

On ראש חדש, add the following:

אֱלֹהֵינוּ וֵאלֹהֵי אֲבוֹתֵינוּ, יַעֲלֶה וְיָבֹא, וְיַגִּיעַ, וְיֵרָאֶה, וְיֵרָצֶה, וְיִשָּׁמַע, וְיִפָּקֵד, וְיִזָּכֵר זִכְרוֹנֵנוּ וּפִקְדּוֹנֵנוּ, וְזִכְרוֹן אֲבוֹתֵינוּ, וְזִכְרוֹן מָשִׁיחַ בֶּן דָּוִד עַבְדֶּךָ, וְזִכְרוֹן יְרוּשָׁלַיִם עִיר קָדְשֶׁךָ, וְזִכְרוֹן כָּל עַמְּךָ בֵּית יִשְׂרָאֵל לְפָנֶיךָ, לִפְלֵיטָה, לְטוֹבָה, לְחֵן וּלְחֶסֶד וּלְרַחֲמִים, לְחַיִּים וּלְשָׁלוֹם, בְּיוֹם רֹאשׁ הַחֹדֶשׁ הַזֶּה.

זָכְרֵנוּ, יְיָ, אֱלֹהֵינוּ, בּוֹ לְטוֹבָה, וּפָקְדֵנוּ בוֹ לִבְרָכָה, וְהוֹשִׁיעֵנוּ בוֹ לְחַיִּים. וּבִדְבַר יְשׁוּעָה וְרַחֲמִים, חוּס וְחָנֵּנוּ, וְרַחֵם עָלֵינוּ וְהוֹשִׁיעֵנוּ, כִּי אֵלֶיךָ עֵינֵינוּ, כִּי אֵל מֶלֶךְ חַנּוּן וְרַחוּם אָתָּה.

וְתֶחֱזֶינָה עֵינֵינוּ בְּשׁוּבְךָ לְצִיּוֹן בְּרַחֲמִים. בָּרוּךְ אַתָּה יְיָ, הַמַּחֲזִיר שְׁכִינָתוֹ לְצִיּוֹן.

מוֹדִים אֲנַחְנוּ לָךְ, שָׁאַתָּה הוּא, יְיָ אֱלֹהֵינוּ וֵאלֹהֵי אֲבוֹתֵינוּ, לְעוֹלָם וָעֶד, צוּר חַיֵּינוּ, מָגֵן יִשְׁעֵנוּ, אַתָּה הוּא לְדוֹר וָדוֹר נוֹדֶה לְךָ וּנְסַפֵּר תְּהִלָּתֶךָ. עַל חַיֵּינוּ הַמְּסוּרִים בְּיָדֶךָ, וְעַל נִשְׁמוֹתֵינוּ הַפְּקוּדוֹת לָךְ, וְעַל נִסֶּיךָ שֶׁבְּכָל יוֹם עִמָּנוּ, וְעַל נִפְלְאוֹתֶיךָ וְטוֹבוֹתֶיךָ שֶׁבְּכָל עֵת, עֶרֶב וָבֹקֶר וְצָהֳרָיִם, הַטּוֹב כִּי לֹא כָלוּ רַחֲמֶיךָ, וְהַמְרַחֵם כִּי לֹא תַמּוּ חֲסָדֶיךָ מֵעוֹלָם קִוִּינוּ לָךְ.

וְעַל כֻּלָּם יִתְבָּרַךְ וְיִתְרוֹמַם שִׁמְךָ, מַלְכֵּנוּ, תָּמִיד לְעוֹלָם וָעֶד.

וְכֹל הַחַיִּים יוֹדוּךָ סֶּלָה, וִיהַלְלוּ אֶת שִׁמְךָ בֶּאֱמֶת, הָאֵל יְשׁוּעָתֵנוּ וְעֶזְרָתֵנוּ סֶלָה. בָּרוּךְ אַתָּה יְיָ, הַטּוֹב שִׁמְךָ וּלְךָ נָאֶה לְהוֹדוֹת.

Shabbat Morning Service

Moses was happy because You, God, gave him a gift: You called him a faithful servant; You crowned him with glory as he stood before You on Mount Sinai. He brought down two stone tablets, with the command to observe the Shabbat written on them. So it is written in Your Torah:

The people of Israel shall keep the Shabbat, to make Shabbat in every generation as a forever covenant. It is a sign between Me and the people of Israel forever, that in six days Adonai made the heavens and the earth, and on the seventh day God stopped working and rested.

Adonai our God, You did not give the Shabbat to other peoples and nations, but You lovingly gave it to Your people Israel, Jacob's children, whom You chose. May all the people who make the seventh day holy be satisfied and delighted by Your goodness. You favored the seventh day and made it holy, calling it the most desirable of days, a day to remember the Creation of the world.

Our God and God of our ancestors, be pleased with our Shabbat rest, make us holy with Your mitzvot and let us share in Your Torah. Satisfy us with Your goodness and make us happy with Your help. Purify our hearts so that we can serve You truly. Adonai our God, let us receive Your holy Shabbat with love and favor, so that Your people Israel who make Your name holy will rest on it. Praised are You Adonai, who makes the Shabbat holy.

Adonai, be pleased with Your people Israel and with their prayer. Restore worship to Your Temple. May the prayer of Your people Israel always be accepted with love and favor.

Yis'mach Moshe b'mat'nat chelko, kee eved ne-eman karata lo. K'leel tif'eret b'rosho natata b'am'do l'faneicha al har seenai. Ush'nei luchot avaneem horeed b'yado, v'chatuv bahem sh'meerat Shabbat. V'chen katuv b'toratecha:

V'sham'ru v'nei Yisra-el et haShabbat, la-asot et haShabbat l'dorotam b'reet olam. Beinee uvein b'nei Yisra-el ot hee l'olam, kee sheshet yameem asah Adonai et hashamayim v'et ha-aretz, uvayom hash'vee'ee shavat vayinafash.

V'lo n'tato Adonai Eloheinu l'goyei ha-aratzot, v'lo hin'chal'to mal'keinu l'ov'dei f'seeleem, v'gam bim'nuchato lo yish'k'nu areleem. Kee l'Yisra-el am'cha n'tato b'ahava, l'zera Ya-akov asher bam bachar'ta. Am m'kadshei sh'vee-ee kulam yis'b'u v'yit'an'gu mituvecha, uvash'vee-ee ratzeeta bo v'keedash'to, chem'dat yameem oto karata, zecher l'ma-aseh v'resheet.

Eloheinu vElohei avoteinu, r'tzeh vim'nuchatenu, kad'shenu b'mitz'voteicha v'ten chel'kenu b'toratecha, sab'enu mituvecha v'sam'chenu beeshu-atecha, v'taher libenu l'ov'd'cha be-emet, v'han'cheelenu Adonai Eloheinu b'ahavah uv'ratzon Shabbat kod'shecha, v'yanuchu vah Yisra-el m'kad'shei sh'mecha. Baruch atah Adonai, m'kadesh haShabbat.

R'tzeh, Adonai Eloheinu, b'am'cha Yisra-el uvit'filatam, v'hashev et ha-avodah lid'veer beitecha, ut'filatam b'ahavah t'kabel b'ratzon, ut'hee l'ratzon tameed avodat Yisra-el amecha.

יִשְׂמַח מֹשֶׁה בְּמַתְּנַת חֶלְקוֹ, כִּי עֶבֶד נֶאֱמָן קָרָאתָ לּוֹ. כְּלִיל תִּפְאֶרֶת בְּרֹאשׁוֹ נָתַתָּ בְּעָמְדוֹ לְפָנֶיךָ עַל הַר סִינָי. וּשְׁנֵי לוּחוֹת אֲבָנִים הוֹרִיד בְּיָדוֹ, וְכָתוּב בָּהֶם שְׁמִירַת שַׁבָּת. וְכֵן כָּתוּב בְּתוֹרָתֶךָ:

וְשָׁמְרוּ בְנֵי יִשְׂרָאֵל אֶת הַשַּׁבָּת, לַעֲשׂוֹת אֶת הַשַּׁבָּת לְדֹרֹתָם בְּרִית עוֹלָם. בֵּינִי וּבֵין בְּנֵי יִשְׂרָאֵל אוֹת הִיא לְעֹלָם, כִּי שֵׁשֶׁת יָמִים עָשָׂה יְיָ אֶת הַשָּׁמַיִם וְאֶת הָאָרֶץ, וּבַיוֹם הַשְּׁבִיעִי שָׁבַת וַיִּנָּפַשׁ.

וְלֹא נְתַתּוֹ יְיָ אֱלֹהֵינוּ לְגוֹיֵי הָאֲרָצוֹת, וְלֹא הִנְחַלְתּוֹ מַלְכֵּנוּ לְעוֹבְדֵי פְסִילִים, וְגַם בִּמְנוּחָתוֹ לֹא יִשְׁכְּנוּ עֲרֵלִים. כִּי לְיִשְׂרָאֵל עַמְּךָ נְתַתּוֹ בְּאַהֲבָה, לְזֶרַע יַעֲקֹב אֲשֶׁר בָּם בָּחָרְתָּ. עַם מְקַדְּשֵׁי שְׁבִיעִי, כֻּלָּם יִשְׂבְּעוּ וְיִתְעַנְּגוּ מִטּוּבֶךָ, וּבַשְּׁבִיעִי רָצִיתָ בּוֹ וְקִדַּשְׁתּוֹ, חֶמְדַּת יָמִים אוֹתוֹ קָרָאתָ, זֵכֶר לְמַעֲשֵׂה בְרֵאשִׁית.

אֱלֹהֵינוּ וֵאלֹהֵי אֲבוֹתֵינוּ, רְצֵה בִמְנוּחָתֵנוּ, קַדְּשֵׁנוּ בְּמִצְוֹתֶיךָ וְתֵן חֶלְקֵנוּ בְּתוֹרָתֶךָ, שַׂבְּעֵנוּ מִטּוּבֶךָ וְשַׂמְּחֵנוּ בִּישׁוּעָתֶךָ, וְטַהֵר לִבֵּנוּ לְעָבְדְּךָ בֶּאֱמֶת, וְהַנְחִילֵנוּ יְיָ אֱלֹהֵינוּ בְּאַהֲבָה וּבְרָצוֹן שַׁבַּת קָדְשֶׁךָ, וְיָנוּחוּ בָהּ יִשְׂרָאֵל מְקַדְּשֵׁי שְׁמֶךָ. בָּרוּךְ אַתָּה יְיָ, מְקַדֵּשׁ הַשַּׁבָּת:

רְצֵה, יְיָ אֱלֹהֵינוּ, בְּעַמְּךָ יִשְׂרָאֵל וּבִתְפִלָּתָם, וְהָשֵׁב אֶת הָעֲבוֹדָה לִדְבִיר בֵּיתֶךָ, וּתְפִלָּתָם בְּאַהֲבָה תְקַבֵּל בְּרָצוֹן, וּתְהִי לְרָצוֹן תָּמִיד עֲבוֹדַת יִשְׂרָאֵל עַמֶּךָ.

K'dushah

*When the Amidah is chanted out loud,
the K'dushah is substituted for "You are holy..." at the bottom of the page.*

We shall tell of Your holiness on earth just as it is told in the heavens above. As Your prophet wrote, the angels called to one another, saying:

> Holy, holy, holy is *Adonai Tzeva'ot*, the whole world is filled with God's glory.

Then the Serafim responded in a mighty chorus:

> Praised is God's glory from God's place.

Our Ruler, show Yourself to us from Your place, and rule over us for we are waiting for You. When will You rule in Zion? Soon, in our days, may You establish Yourself there forever. May You be made great and holy in Jerusalem, Your city, for all generations and forever. May our eyes see Your kingdom as described in righteous David's psalms of Your might:

> Adonai will rule forever, your God, O Zion, for all generations. Halleluyah.

For all generations we will tell Your greatness, and forever and ever we will add our holiness to Yours. We will never stop praising You, for You are a great and holy God. Praised are You Adonai, the holy God.

N'kadesh et shim'cha ba-olam, k'shem shemakdisheem oto bish'mei marom, kakatuv al yad n'vee-echa, v'kara zeh el zeh v'amar:

> Kadosh, kadosh, kadosh Adonai Tzeva-ot, m'lo chol ha-aretz k'vodo.

Az b'kol ra-ash gadol adeer v'chazak mash'mee-eem kol, mit'nas'eem l'umat s'rafeem, l'umatam baruch yomeru:

> Baruch k'vod Adonai mim'komo.

Mim'kom'cha mal'kenu tofee-a, v'tim'loch aleinu, kee m'chakeem anach'nu lach. Matai tim'loch b'tzee-on, b'karov b'yameinu, l'olam va-ed tish'kon. Tit'gadal v'tit'kadash b'toch y'rushalayim eer'cha, l'dor vador ul'netzach n'tachim. V'eineinu tir'einah mal'chutecha, kadavar ha-amur b'sheerei uzecha, al y'dei David m'shee-ach tzid'kecha:

> Yimloch Adonai l'olam, Elohayich Tzion l'dor vador, hal'luyah.

L'dor vador nageed god'lecha, ul'netzach n'tzacheem k'dushat'cha nakdeesh, v'shiv'chacha, Eloheinu, mipeenu lo yamush l'olam va-ed, kee El melech gadol v'kadosh atah. Baruch atah Adonai, ha-El hakadosh.

When the Amidah is recited silently:

You are holy and Your name is holy and holy beings praise You every day. Praised are You Adonai, the holy God.

Atah kadosh v'shim'cha kadosh uk'dosheem b'chol yom y'hal'lucha, selah. Baruch atah Adonai, ha-El hakadosh.

קְדוּשָׁה

When the עמידה *is chanted out loud,*
the קדושה *is substituted for* אתה קדוש *at the bottom of the page.*

נְקַדֵּשׁ אֶת שִׁמְךָ בָּעוֹלָם, כְּשֵׁם שֶׁמַּקְדִּישִׁים אוֹתוֹ בִּשְׁמֵי מָרוֹם, כַּכָּתוּב עַל יַד נְבִיאֶךָ: וְקָרָא זֶה אֶל זֶה וְאָמַר:

קָדוֹשׁ, קָדוֹשׁ, קָדוֹשׁ יְיָ צְבָאוֹת, מְלֹא כָל הָאָרֶץ כְּבוֹדוֹ.

אָז בְּקוֹל רַעַשׁ גָּדוֹל אַדִּיר וְחָזָק מַשְׁמִיעִים קוֹל, מִתְנַשְּׂאִים לְעֻמַּת שְׂרָפִים, לְעֻמָּתָם בָּרוּךְ יֹאמֵרוּ:

בָּרוּךְ כְּבוֹד יְיָ מִמְּקוֹמוֹ.

מִמְּקוֹמְךָ מַלְכֵּנוּ תוֹפִיעַ, וְתִמְלֹךְ עָלֵינוּ, כִּי מְחַכִּים אֲנַחְנוּ לָךְ. מָתַי תִּמְלֹךְ בְּצִיּוֹן, בְּקָרוֹב בְּיָמֵינוּ, לְעוֹלָם וָעֶד תִּשְׁכּוֹן. תִּתְגַּדַּל וְתִתְקַדַּשׁ בְּתוֹךְ יְרוּשָׁלַיִם עִירְךָ, לְדוֹר וָדוֹר וּלְנֵצַח נְצָחִים. וְעֵינֵינוּ תִרְאֶינָה מַלְכוּתֶךָ, כַּדָּבָר הָאָמוּר בְּשִׁירֵי עֻזֶּךָ, עַל יְדֵי דָוִד מְשִׁיחַ צִדְקֶךָ:

יִמְלֹךְ יְיָ לְעוֹלָם, אֱלֹהַיִךְ צִיּוֹן לְדֹר וָדֹר, הַלְלוּיָהּ.

לְדוֹר וָדוֹר נַגִּיד גָּדְלֶךָ, וּלְנֵצַח נְצָחִים קְדֻשָּׁתְךָ נַקְדִּישׁ, וְשִׁבְחֲךָ, אֱלֹהֵינוּ, מִפִּינוּ לֹא יָמוּשׁ לְעוֹלָם וָעֶד, כִּי אֵל מֶלֶךְ גָּדוֹל וְקָדוֹשׁ אָתָּה. בָּרוּךְ אַתָּה יְיָ, הָאֵל הַקָּדוֹשׁ.

When the עמידה *is recited silently:*

אַתָּה קָדוֹשׁ וְשִׁמְךָ קָדוֹשׁ וּקְדוֹשִׁים בְּכָל יוֹם יְהַלְלוּךָ, סֶּלָה. בָּרוּךְ אַתָּה יְיָ, הָאֵל הַקָּדוֹשׁ.

Shabbat Morning Service

Shabbat Morning Amidah

> "Adonai, open my lips
> so I may speak Your praise."

We take three steps back and three steps forward as we say:

Adonai, open my lips so I may speak Your praise.	Adonai s'fatai tif'tach ufi yagid t'hilatecha.
Praised are You, Adonai our God and God of our ancestors, God of Abraham, God of Isaac, and God of Jacob, God of Sarah, God of Rebecca, God of Rachel, and God of Leah, the great, strong and awe-inspiring God, God on high. You act with lovingkindness and create everything. God remembers the loving deeds of our ancestors, and will bring a redeemer to their children's children because that is God's loving nature.	Baruch atah Adonai Eloheinu vElohei avoteinu, Elohei Av'raham, Elohei Yitz'chak, vElohei Ya-akov, Elohei Sarah, Elohei Riv'ka, Elohei Rachel, vElohei Le-ah. Ha-El hagadol hagibur v'hanora, El el'yon, gomel chasideem toveem, v'koneh hakol, v'zocher chasdei avot, umevee go-el liv'nei v'neihem l'ma-an sh'mo b'ahavah.
You are a helping, guarding, saving and shielding Ruler. Praised are You, Adonai, Shield of Abraham and Guardian of Sarah.	Melech ozer ufoked umoshee-a umagen. Baruch atah Adonai, magen Av'raham ufoked Sarah.
You are mighty forever, Adonai. You give life to the dead with Your great saving power.	Atah gibor l'olam Adonai, m'chayeh meteem atah rav l'hoshee-a.

From Shemini Atzeret until Pesach:	
You cause the wind to blow and the rain to fall.	Masheev haru-ach umoreed hagashem.

You support the living with kindness. You give life to the dead with great mercy. You support the fallen, heal the sick and set free those in prison. You keep faith with those who sleep in the dust. Who is like You, mighty Ruler, and who can compare to You, Ruler of life and death who causes salvation to bloom.	M'chal'kel chayim b'chesed, m'chayeh meteem b'rachameem rabeem, somech nofleem, v'rofeh choleem, umateer asureem, um'kayem emunato leeshenei afar, mee chamocha ba-al g'vurot umee domeh lach, melech memeet um'chayeh umatz'mee-ach y'shu-ah.
You are trustworthy in giving life to the dead. Praised are You Adonai, who gives life to the dead.	V'ne-eman atah l'hachayot meteem. Baruch atah Adonai, m'chayeh hameteem.

עֲמִידָה שֶׁל שַׁחֲרִית לְשַׁבָּת

On Shabbat, the Amidah has the same basic structure as the weekday version, with one big difference. Instead of all of the usual blessings in the middle, we replace them with a special blessing that praises the holiness of Shabbat.

We take three steps back and three steps forward as we say:

אֲדֹנָי שְׂפָתַי תִּפְתָּח וּפִי יַגִּיד תְּהִלָּתֶךָ:

בָּרוּךְ אַתָּה יְיָ אֱלֹהֵינוּ וֵאלֹהֵי אֲבוֹתֵינוּ, אֱלֹהֵי אַבְרָהָם, אֱלֹהֵי יִצְחָק, וֵאלֹהֵי יַעֲקֹב, אֱלֹהֵי שָׂרָה, אֱלֹהֵי רִבְקָה, אֱלֹהֵי רָחֵל וֵאלֹהֵי לֵאָה. הָאֵל הַגָּדוֹל הַגִּבּוֹר וְהַנּוֹרָא, אֵל עֶלְיוֹן, גּוֹמֵל חֲסָדִים טוֹבִים, וְקוֹנֵה הַכֹּל, וְזוֹכֵר חַסְדֵי אָבוֹת, וּמֵבִיא גוֹאֵל לִבְנֵי בְנֵיהֶם לְמַעַן שְׁמוֹ בְּאַהֲבָה.

מֶלֶךְ עוֹזֵר וּפוֹקֵד וּמוֹשִׁיעַ וּמָגֵן: בָּרוּךְ אַתָּה יְיָ, מָגֵן אַבְרָהָם וּפוֹקֵד שָׂרָה:

אַתָּה גִּבּוֹר לְעוֹלָם אֲדֹנָי, מְחַיֵּה מֵתִים אַתָּה, רַב לְהוֹשִׁיעַ:

From Shemini Atzeret until Pesach:
מַשִּׁיב הָרוּחַ וּמוֹרִיד הַגֶּשֶׁם:

מְכַלְכֵּל חַיִּים בְּחֶסֶד, מְחַיֵּה מֵתִים בְּרַחֲמִים רַבִּים, סוֹמֵךְ נוֹפְלִים, וְרוֹפֵא חוֹלִים, וּמַתִּיר אֲסוּרִים, וּמְקַיֵּם אֱמוּנָתוֹ לִישֵׁנֵי עָפָר, מִי כָמוֹךָ בַּעַל גְּבוּרוֹת וּמִי דוֹמֶה לָּךְ, מֶלֶךְ מֵמִית וּמְחַיֶּה וּמַצְמִיחַ יְשׁוּעָה:

וְנֶאֱמָן אַתָּה לְהַחֲיוֹת מֵתִים. בָּרוּךְ אַתָּה יְיָ, מְחַיֵּה הַמֵּתִים:

Shabbat Morning Service 120

Mee Chamocha

Praises to God supreme, who is ever praised. Moses and the Israelites sang a song to You with great joy, as they all said:

Who is like You, Adonai, among the mighty?
Who is like You, glorious in holiness,
Awesome in praises, doing wonders.

Those who were rescued sang a new song at the shore of the sea. Together they thanked You and announced Your power:

Adonai will rule for ever and ever.

❖ T'hilot l'el el'yon, baruch hu um'vorach. Moshe uv'nei Yisra-el l'cha anu sheera b'sim'chah rabah v'am'ru chulam:

Mee chamocha ba-elim Adonai,
Mee kamocha ne'dar bakodesh,
Nora t'hilot oseh fele.

❖ Sheerah chadashah Shib'chu g'uleem l'shim'cha al s'fat hayam, yachad kulam hodu v'him'leechu v'am'ru:

Adonai yimloch l'olam va-ed.

Tzur Yisrael

We rise.

Rock of Israel, rise up to help Israel, and rescue Judah and Israel as You promised. Your are our Savior, *Adonai Tz'vaot* is Your name.
Praised are you, Adonai, who rescues Israel.

Tzur Yisra-el, kuma b'ezrat Yisra-el,
uf'deh chin'umecha Y'hudah v'Yisra-el.
Go-alenu Adonai tz'va-ot sh'mo, K'dosh Yisra-el.
Baruch atah Adonai ga-al Yisra-el.

שחרית לשבת

מִי כָמְכָה

❖ תְּהִלּוֹת לְאֵל עֶלְיוֹן, בָּרוּךְ הוּא וּמְבוֹרָךְ. מֹשֶׁה וּבְנֵי יִשְׂרָאֵל לְךָ
עָנוּ שִׁירָה בְּשִׂמְחָה רַבָּה וְאָמְרוּ כֻלָּם:

מִי כָמְכָה בָּאֵלִם יְיָ,
מִי כָּמְכָה נֶאְדָּר בַּקֹּדֶשׁ,
נוֹרָא תְהִלֹּת עֹשֵׂה פֶלֶא.
EXODUS 15:11

❖ שִׁירָה חֲדָשָׁה שִׁבְּחוּ גְאוּלִים לְשִׁמְךָ עַל שְׂפַת הַיָּם, יַחַד כֻּלָּם
הוֹדוּ וְהִמְלִיכוּ וְאָמְרוּ:

יְיָ יִמְלֹךְ לְעֹלָם וָעֶד:
EXODUS 15:18

צוּר יִשְׂרָאֵל

We rise.

צוּר יִשְׂרָאֵל, קוּמָה בְּעֶזְרַת יִשְׂרָאֵל, וּפְדֵה כִנְאֻמֶךָ יְהוּדָה וְיִשְׂרָאֵל.
גֹּאֲלֵנוּ יְיָ צְבָאוֹת שְׁמוֹ, קְדוֹשׁ יִשְׂרָאֵל.
בָּרוּךְ אַתָּה יְיָ גָּאַל יִשְׂרָאֵל:

If you will really listen to My commandments which I command you today, to love Adonai your God and to serve God with all your heart and soul, then I will give your land rain at the proper season—rain in autumn and rain in spring—and you will gather in your grain and wine and oil. I will give grass in the fields for your cattle, and you will eat your fill. Beware that you are not tempted to turn aside and worship other gods. For then God will be angry at you and will shut up the skies and there will be no rain, and the earth will not give you its produce, and you will quickly disappear from the good land which God is giving to you. So keep these words in mind and take them to heart, and bind them as a sign on your hand, and let them be a symbol between your eyes. Teach them to your children, speaking of them at home and away, when you lie down and when you get up. Write them upon the doorposts of your house and upon your gates, so that your days and the days of your children will last long on the land which Adonai promised to your ancestors, to give to them for as long as the heavens and earth last.

V'haya im-shamo-a tish'm'u el-mitzvotai asher anochi m'tzaveh et'chem hayom l'ahavah et-Adonai Eloheichem ul'av'do b'chol-l'vav'chem uv'chol-naf'sh'chem. V'natatee m'tar-ar'tz'chem b'ito yoreh umal'kosh v'asaf'ta d'gonecha v'teerosh'cha v'yitz'harecha. V'natatee esev b'sad'cha liv'hem'techa v'achal'ta v'sava'ta. Hisham'ru lachem pen-yif'teh l'vav'chem v'sar'tem v-avad'tem Eloheem achereem v'hish'tachaveetem lahem. V'chara af-Adonai bachem v'atzar et-hashamayim v'lo-yih'yeh matar v'ha-adamah lo titen et-y'vulah va-avad'tem m'herah me-al ha-aretz hatovah asher Adonai noten lachem. V'sam'tem et-d'varai eleh al-l'vav'chem v'al-naf'sh'chem uk'shar'tem otam l'ot al-yedchem v'hayu l'totafot bein eineichem. V'limad'tem otam et-b'neichem l'daber bam b'shiv't'cha b'veitecha uv'lech't'cha baderech uv'shoch'b'cha uv'kumecha. Uch'tav'tam al-m'zuzot beitecha uvish'areicha. L'ma-an yirbu y'meichem veemei v'neichem al ha-adamah asher nish'ba Adonai la-avoteichem latet lahem keemei hashamayim al-ha-aretz.

Adonai said to Moses: Speak to the people Israel and tell them to make fringes for the corners of their clothes in all future generations. They shall put a blue thread in the fringe of each corner. When they look at them they will remember all of Adonai's mitzvot, and do them, and they won't be led astray by their hearts or their eyes. Do this so that you will remember and do all My mitzvot, and you will be holy for your God. I am Adonai your God, who took you out of the land of Egypt to be your God. I, Adonai, am your God.

Vayomer Adonai el-Mosheh lemor. Daber el-b'nei Yisra-el v'amar'ta alehem v'asu lahem tzeetzit al-can'fei vig'deihem l'dorotam v'nat'nu al-tzeetzit hakanaf p'til t'chelet. V'haya lachem l'tzeetzit ur'eetem oto uz'char'tem et-kol-mitzvot Adonai va-aseetem otam v'lo taturu acharei l'vav'chem v'acharei eineichem asher-atem zoneem achareihem. L'ma'an tiz'k'ru va-aseetem et-kol mitz'votai vih'yeetem k'dosheem leloheichem. Ani Adonai Eloheichem asher hotzetee et'chem me-eretz mitz'rayim lih'yot lachem lEloheem ani Adonai Eloheichem.

Adonai, your God, is truth.

❖ Adonai Eloheichem emet.

וְהָיָה אִם־שָׁמֹעַ תִּשְׁמְעוּ אֶל־מִצְוֹתַי אֲשֶׁר אָנֹכִי מְצַוֶּה אֶתְכֶם הַיּוֹם לְאַהֲבָה אֶת־יְהֹוָה אֱלֹהֵיכֶם וּלְעָבְדוֹ בְּכָל־לְבַבְכֶם וּבְכָל־נַפְשְׁכֶם: וְנָתַתִּי מְטַר־אַרְצְכֶם בְּעִתּוֹ יוֹרֶה וּמַלְקוֹשׁ וְאָסַפְתָּ דְגָנֶךָ וְתִירֹשְׁךָ וְיִצְהָרֶךָ: וְנָתַתִּי עֵשֶׂב בְּשָׂדְךָ לִבְהֶמְתֶּךָ וְאָכַלְתָּ וְשָׂבָעְתָּ: הִשָּׁמְרוּ לָכֶם פֶּן־יִפְתֶּה לְבַבְכֶם וְסַרְתֶּם וַעֲבַדְתֶּם אֱלֹהִים אֲחֵרִים וְהִשְׁתַּחֲוִיתֶם לָהֶם: וְחָרָה אַף־יְהֹוָה בָּכֶם וְעָצַר אֶת־הַשָּׁמַיִם וְלֹא־יִהְיֶה מָטָר וְהָאֲדָמָה לֹא תִתֵּן אֶת־יְבוּלָהּ וַאֲבַדְתֶּם מְהֵרָה מֵעַל הָאָרֶץ הַטֹּבָה אֲשֶׁר יְהֹוָה נֹתֵן לָכֶם: וְשַׂמְתֶּם אֶת־דְּבָרַי אֵלֶּה עַל־לְבַבְכֶם וְעַל־נַפְשְׁכֶם וּקְשַׁרְתֶּם אֹתָם לְאוֹת עַל־יֶדְכֶם וְהָיוּ לְטוֹטָפֹת בֵּין עֵינֵיכֶם: וְלִמַּדְתֶּם אֹתָם אֶת־בְּנֵיכֶם לְדַבֵּר בָּם בְּשִׁבְתְּךָ בְּבֵיתֶךָ וּבְלֶכְתְּךָ בַדֶּרֶךְ וּבְשָׁכְבְּךָ וּבְקוּמֶךָ: וּכְתַבְתָּם עַל־מְזוּזוֹת בֵּיתֶךָ וּבִשְׁעָרֶיךָ: לְמַעַן יִרְבּוּ יְמֵיכֶם וִימֵי בְנֵיכֶם עַל הָאֲדָמָה אֲשֶׁר נִשְׁבַּע יְהֹוָה לַאֲבֹתֵיכֶם לָתֵת לָהֶם כִּימֵי הַשָּׁמַיִם עַל־הָאָרֶץ:

DEUTERONOMY 11:13–21

וַיֹּאמֶר יְהֹוָה אֶל־מֹשֶׁה לֵּאמֹר: דַּבֵּר אֶל־בְּנֵי יִשְׂרָאֵל וְאָמַרְתָּ אֲלֵהֶם וְעָשׂוּ לָהֶם צִיצִת עַל־כַּנְפֵי בִגְדֵיהֶם לְדֹרֹתָם וְנָתְנוּ עַל־צִיצִת הַכָּנָף פְּתִיל תְּכֵלֶת: וְהָיָה לָכֶם לְצִיצִת וּרְאִיתֶם אֹתוֹ וּזְכַרְתֶּם אֶת־כָּל־מִצְוֹת יְהֹוָה וַעֲשִׂיתֶם אֹתָם וְלֹא תָתוּרוּ אַחֲרֵי לְבַבְכֶם וְאַחֲרֵי עֵינֵיכֶם אֲשֶׁר־אַתֶּם זֹנִים אַחֲרֵיהֶם: לְמַעַן תִּזְכְּרוּ וַעֲשִׂיתֶם אֶת־כָּל־מִצְוֹתָי וִהְיִיתֶם קְדֹשִׁים לֵאלֹהֵיכֶם: אֲנִי יְהֹוָה אֱלֹהֵיכֶם אֲשֶׁר הוֹצֵאתִי אֶתְכֶם מֵאֶרֶץ מִצְרַיִם לִהְיוֹת לָכֶם לֵאלֹהִים אֲנִי יְהֹוָה אֱלֹהֵיכֶם:

NUMBERS 15:37–41

❖ יְיָ אֱלֹהֵיכֶם אֱמֶת.

Shabbat Morning Service 116

Ahavah Rabah

With great love have You loved us, Adonai our God; with great and extra tenderness You have cared for us. Our Parent, our Ruler, for the sake of our ancestors who trusted in You, and whom You taught for life-giving laws, be kind to us, too, and teach us. Our merciful Parent, treat us with mercy, and help our minds to understand Your Torah, teaching us to listen, to learn and to teach, to observe, to do, and to fulfill all its words with love. Light up our eyes with Your Torah and cause our hearts to hold tight to Your commandments. Unify our hearts to love and respect Your name so that we will never be ashamed. For we trust in Your holy, great, and awe-inspiring name—may we rejoice in Your saving power. Gather us in peace from the four corners of the earth, and lead us to our land with our heads held high, for You are a God who is able to rescue. You have chosen us from among all peoples and brought us near to You, to thank You sincerely, and to announce with love that You are One. Praised are You, Adonai, who lovingly chooses the people of Israel.

Ahavah rabah ahav'tanu, Adonai Eloheinu, chem'lah g'dolah veeterah chamal'ta aleinu. Aveenu mal'keinu, ba-avur avoteinu shebat'chu v'cha, vat'lam'dem chukei chayim, ken t'chonenu ut'lam'denu. Aveenu, ha-av harachaman, ham'rachem, rachem aleinu, v'ten b'libenu l'haveen ul'haskeel, lish'mo-ah, lil'mod ul'lamed, lish'mor v'la-asot ul'kayem et kol divrei tal'mud toratecha b'ahavah. V'ha-er eineinu b'Toratecha, v'dabek libenu b'mitz'voteicha, v'yached l'vavenu l'ahavah ul'yir'ah et sh'mecha, v'lo nevosh l'olam va-ed. Kee v'shem kod'sh'cha hagadol v'honora batach'nu, nageelah v'nis'm'cha beeshu-atecha. Vahavee-enu l'shalom me-ar'ba can'fot ha-aretz, v'tolichenu kom'mee-ut l'ar'tzenu, kee El po-el y'shu-ot atah, uvanu vachar'ta mikol am v'lashon. ❖ V'kerav'tanu l'shim'cha hagadol selah be-emet l'hodot l'cha ul'yached'cha b'ahava. Baruch atah Adonai, habocher b'amo Yisra-el b'ahavah.

Shema

If there is no minyan, add:

God is a faithful ruler.   El melech ne-eman.

Hear O Israel, Adonai is our God, Adonai is One.

Sh'ma Yisra-el, Adonai Eloheinu, Adonai echad.

Silently:

Praised be God's glorious name forever.

Baruch shem k'vod mal'chuto l'olam va-ed.

You will love Adonai your God with all your mind, soul, and might. Take to heart these words which I command you today. Teach them carefully to your children. Repeat them at home and away, morning and night. Bind them as a sign on your hand, and let them be a symbol above your eyes. Write them on the doorposts of your homes and on your gates.

V'ahav'ta et Adonai Eloheicha b'chol-l'vav'cha uv'chol-naf'sh'cha uv'chol-m'odecha. V'hayu had'vareem ha-eleh ahser anochi m'tzav'cha hayom al-l'vavecha. V'shinan'tam l'vaneicha v'dibar'ta bam b'shiv't'cha b'veitecha uv'lech't'cha baderech uv'shoch'b'cha uv'kumecha. Uk'shar'tam l'ot al-yadecha v'hayu l'totafot bein eineicha. Uch'tav'tam al m'zuzot beitecha uvish'areicha.

אַהֲבָה רַבָּה

אַהֲבָה רַבָּה אֲהַבְתָּנוּ, יְיָ אֱלֹהֵינוּ, חֶמְלָה גְדוֹלָה וִיתֵרָה חָמַלְתָּ עָלֵינוּ. אָבִינוּ מַלְכֵּנוּ, בַּעֲבוּר אֲבוֹתֵינוּ שֶׁבָּטְחוּ בְךָ, וַתְּלַמְּדֵם חֻקֵּי חַיִּים, כֵּן תְּחָנֵּנוּ וּתְלַמְּדֵנוּ. אָבִינוּ, הָאָב הָרַחֲמָן, הַמְרַחֵם, רַחֵם עָלֵינוּ, וְתֵן בְּלִבֵּנוּ לְהָבִין וּלְהַשְׂכִּיל, לִשְׁמֹעַ, לִלְמֹד וּלְלַמֵּד, לִשְׁמֹר וְלַעֲשׂוֹת וּלְקַיֵּם אֶת כָּל דִּבְרֵי תַלְמוּד תּוֹרָתֶךָ בְּאַהֲבָה. וְהָאֵר עֵינֵינוּ בְּתוֹרָתֶךָ, וְדַבֵּק לִבֵּנוּ בְּמִצְוֹתֶיךָ, וְיַחֵד לְבָבֵנוּ לְאַהֲבָה וּלְיִרְאָה אֶת שְׁמֶךָ, וְלֹא נֵבוֹשׁ לְעוֹלָם וָעֶד: כִּי בְשֵׁם קָדְשְׁךָ הַגָּדוֹל וְהַנּוֹרָא בָּטָחְנוּ, נָגִילָה וְנִשְׂמְחָה בִּישׁוּעָתֶךָ. וַהֲבִיאֵנוּ לְשָׁלוֹם מֵאַרְבַּע כַּנְפוֹת הָאָרֶץ, וְתוֹלִיכֵנוּ קוֹמְמִיּוּת לְאַרְצֵנוּ, כִּי אֵל פּוֹעֵל יְשׁוּעוֹת אָתָּה, וּבָנוּ בָחַרְתָּ מִכָּל עַם וְלָשׁוֹן. ✷ וְקֵרַבְתָּנוּ לְשִׁמְךָ הַגָּדוֹל סֶלָה בֶּאֱמֶת לְהוֹדוֹת לְךָ וּלְיַחֶדְךָ בְּאַהֲבָה. בָּרוּךְ אַתָּה יְיָ, הַבּוֹחֵר בְּעַמּוֹ יִשְׂרָאֵל בְּאַהֲבָה.

קְרִיאַת שְׁמַע

If there is no minyan, add: אֵל מֶלֶךְ נֶאֱמָן

שְׁמַע יִשְׂרָאֵל, יְיָ אֱלֹהֵינוּ, יְיָ אֶחָד:

Silently:
בָּרוּךְ שֵׁם כְּבוֹד מַלְכוּתוֹ לְעוֹלָם וָעֶד.

וְאָהַבְתָּ אֵת יְהוָה אֱלֹהֶיךָ בְּכָל־לְבָבְךָ וּבְכָל־נַפְשְׁךָ וּבְכָל־מְאֹדֶךָ: וְהָיוּ הַדְּבָרִים הָאֵלֶּה אֲשֶׁר אָנֹכִי מְצַוְּךָ הַיּוֹם עַל־לְבָבֶךָ: וְשִׁנַּנְתָּם לְבָנֶיךָ וְדִבַּרְתָּ בָּם בְּשִׁבְתְּךָ בְּבֵיתֶךָ וּבְלֶכְתְּךָ בַדֶּרֶךְ וּבְשָׁכְבְּךָ וּבְקוּמֶךָ: וּקְשַׁרְתָּם לְאוֹת עַל־יָדֶךָ וְהָיוּ לְטֹטָפֹת בֵּין עֵינֶיךָ: וּכְתַבְתָּם עַל־מְזֻזוֹת בֵּיתֶךָ וּבִשְׁעָרֶיךָ:

DEUTERONOMY 6:4–9

Shabbat Morning Service

El Adon

God, Master over all creation, is blessed, and praised by all that breathes. God's greatness and goodness fill the world. Knowledge and understanding surround God. God is above the heavenly beings, and wonderful in glory. Goodness and uprightness stand before God's throne; kindness and mercy before God's glory. The heavenly lights that our God created are good. God made them wisely, putting strength and power into them to oversee the earth. They shine brightly, their glow is beautiful throughout the world. They rise with joy and set with happiness, faithfully doing God's will. They bring glory and honor to God's name, causing rejoicing and joyous song at the mention of God's rule. God called to the sun and it shone with light; God set the phases of the moon. All the heavenly beings praise God's glory and greatness.

El adon al kol hama-asim,
Baruch um'vorach b'fee kol n'shama.
Gad'lo v'tuvo malei olam,
Da-at ut'vunah sov'veem oto.
Hamit'ga-eh al chayot hakodesh,
V'neh'dar b'chavod al hamer'kavah.
Z'chut umeeshor lif'nei chis'o,
Chesed v'rachameem lif'nei ch'vodo.
Toveem m'orot shebara Eloheinu,
Y'tzaram b'da-at b'veenah uv'has'kel.
Ko-ach ug'vurah natan bahem,
Lih'yot mosh'leem bekerev tevel.
M'le-eem zeev um'feekeem nogah,
Na-eh zeevam b'chol ha-olam.
S'mecheem b'tzetam v'saseem b'vo-am,
Oseem b'eimah r'tzon konam.
P'er v'chavod not'neem lish'mo,
Tzahalah v'rinah l'zecher malchuto.
Kara lashemesh vayiz'rach or,
Ra-ah, v'hit'keen tzurat hal'vanah.
Shevach not'nim lo kol tz'va marom,
Tif'eret ug'dulah, s'rafeem v'ofaneem v'chayot hakodesh.

Or Chadash

Cause a new light to shine upon Zion, and may we all soon be able to enjoy its light, Praised are You, Adonai, Creator of the heavenly lights.

Or chadash al tzee-on ta-eer v'niz'keh chulanu m'herah l'oro. Baruch atah Adonai yotzer ham'orot.

אֵל אָדוֹן

אֵל אָדוֹן עַל כָּל הַמַּעֲשִׂים, בָּרוּךְ וּמְבֹרָךְ בְּפִי כָּל נְשָׁמָה.
גָּדְלוֹ וְטוּבוֹ מָלֵא עוֹלָם, דַּעַת וּתְבוּנָה סֹבְבִים אוֹתוֹ:
הַמִּתְגָּאֶה עַל חַיּוֹת הַקֹּדֶשׁ, וְנֶהְדָּר בְּכָבוֹד עַל הַמֶּרְכָּבָה.
זְכוּת וּמִישׁוֹר לִפְנֵי כִסְאוֹ, חֶסֶד וְרַחֲמִים לִפְנֵי כְבוֹדוֹ:
טוֹבִים מְאוֹרוֹת שֶׁבָּרָא אֱלֹהֵינוּ, יְצָרָם בְּדַעַת בְּבִינָה וּבְהַשְׂכֵּל.
כֹּחַ וּגְבוּרָה נָתַן בָּהֶם, לִהְיוֹת מוֹשְׁלִים בְּקֶרֶב תֵּבֵל:
מְלֵאִים זִיו וּמְפִיקִים נֹגַהּ, נָאֶה זִיוָם בְּכָל הָעוֹלָם.
שְׂמֵחִים בְּצֵאתָם וְשָׂשִׂים בְּבוֹאָם, עֹשִׂים בְּאֵימָה רְצוֹן קוֹנָם:
פְּאֵר וְכָבוֹד נוֹתְנִים לִשְׁמוֹ, צָהֳלָה וְרִנָּה לְזֵכֶר מַלְכוּתוֹ.
קָרָא לַשֶּׁמֶשׁ וַיִּזְרַח אוֹר, רָאָה, וְהִתְקִין צוּרַת הַלְּבָנָה:
שֶׁבַח נוֹתְנִים לוֹ כָּל צְבָא מָרוֹם,
תִּפְאֶרֶת וּגְדֻלָּה, שְׂרָפִים וְאוֹפַנִּים וְחַיּוֹת הַקֹּדֶשׁ:

אוֹר חָדָשׁ

אוֹר חָדָשׁ עַל צִיּוֹן תָּאִיר וְנִזְכֶּה כֻלָּנוּ מְהֵרָה לְאוֹרוֹ: בָּרוּךְ אַתָּה יְיָ יוֹצֵר הַמְּאוֹרוֹת:

Chatzi Kaddish

Leader:

May God's great name be made great and holy in the world which God created according to God's will. May God establish Divine rule soon, in our days, quickly and in the near future, and let us say, Amen.

Yit'gadal v'yit'kadash sh'meh rabah. B'al'mah dee v'rah chir'utei, v'yam'leech mal'chutei b'chayeichon uv'yomeichon uv'chayei d'chol beit Yisra-el. Ba-agalah uviz'man kareev v'im'ru amen.

Everyone:

May God's great name be praised for ever and ever.

Y'heh sh'meh rabah m'varach l'alam ul'al'mei al'mayah.

Leader:

Blessed, praised, glorified and raised high, honored and elevated be the name of the Blessed Holy One, far beyond all blessings and songs, praises and words of comfort which people can say, and let us say: Amen.

Yit'barach v'yishtabach v'yitpa-ar v'yit'romam v'yit'naseh v'yit'hadar v'yit'aleh v'yit'halal sh'meh d'kud'shah b'reech hu l'elah min kol bir'chatah v'sheeratah tush'b'chatah v'nechematah, da-ameeran b'al'mah, v'im'ru amen.

Barchu

We rise and the leader sings:

Praise Adonai, who is to be praised.

Bar'chu et Adonai ham'vorach.

Everyone replies, then the leader repeats:

Praised be Adonai who is to be praised for ever and ever.

Baruch Adonai ham'vorach l'olam va-ed.

Praised are You, Adonai our God, Ruler of the universe, who forms light and creates darkness, who makes peace and creates everything.

Baruch atah Adonai, Eloheinu melech ha-olam, yotzeir or, uvoreh choshech, oseh shalom uvoreh et hakol.

We are seated.

חֲצִי קַדִישׁ

Leader:

יִתְגַּדַּל וְיִתְקַדַּשׁ שְׁמֵהּ רַבָּא. בְּעָלְמָא דִּי בְרָא כִרְעוּתֵיהּ, וְיַמְלִיךְ מַלְכוּתֵהּ בְּחַיֵּיכוֹן וּבְיוֹמֵיכוֹן וּבְחַיֵּי דְכָל בֵּית יִשְׂרָאֵל. בַּעֲגָלָא וּבִזְמַן קָרִיב וְאִמְרוּ אָמֵן:

Everyone:

יְהֵא שְׁמֵהּ רַבָּא מְבָרַךְ לְעָלַם וּלְעָלְמֵי עָלְמַיָּא:

Leader:

יִתְבָּרַךְ וְיִשְׁתַּבַּח וְיִתְפָּאַר וְיִתְרוֹמַם וְיִתְנַשֵּׂא וְיִתְהַדָּר וְיִתְעַלֶּה וְיִתְהַלָּל שְׁמֵהּ דְּקֻדְשָׁא בְּרִיךְ הוּא לְעֵלָּא מִן כָּל בִּרְכָתָא וְשִׁירָתָא תֻּשְׁבְּחָתָא וְנֶחֱמָתָא, דַּאֲמִירָן בְּעָלְמָא, וְאִמְרוּ אָמֵן:

בָּרְכוּ

We rise and the leader sings:

בָּרְכוּ אֶת יְיָ הַמְבֹרָךְ:

Everyone replies, then the leader repeats:

בָּרוּךְ יְיָ הַמְבֹרָךְ לְעוֹלָם וָעֶד:

בָּרוּךְ אַתָּה יְיָ, אֱלֹהֵינוּ מֶלֶךְ הָעוֹלָם, יוֹצֵר אוֹר, וּבוֹרֵא חֹשֶׁךְ, עֹשֶׂה שָׁלוֹם וּבוֹרֵא אֶת הַכֹּל:

We are seated.

Shochein Ad

God dwells forever-high and holy is God's name.	Shochein ad, marom v'kadosh sh'mo: V'chatuv, ran'nu tzadeekeem bAdonai, lai'shareem navah t'hilah.
As the Psalmist wrote: "Good people, rejoice in Adonai; it is right for the honest to praise God."	
You are honored by the mouths of the upright.	B'fee y'shareem tit'halal.
You are praised by the words of the righteous.	Uv'div'rei tzadeekeem tit'barach.
Your are acclaimed by the tongue of the faithful.	Uvil'shon chaseedeem tit'romam.
In the soul of the holy, You are made holy.	Uv'kerev k'dosheem tit'kadash.

Yishtabach

We rise.

May Your name be praised forever, our Ruler, great and holy God, in heaven and on earth. Adonai our God and God of our ancestors, it is proper to sing songs of glory to You, songs of praise, of strength and rule, victory and greatness, power, praise and splendor, holiness and mastery; singing praises and thanks now and forever. Praised are You, Adonai, God and Ruler, great in praises, Master of wonders, who chooses songs of praise, Ruler, God, Life-giver of the universe.

Yishtabach shim'cha la-ad mal'kenu, ha-el hamelech hagadol v'hakadosh bashamayim uva-aretz. Kee l'cha na-eh, Adonai Eloheinu vElohei avoteinu: Sheer ush'vacha, halel v'zim'rah, oz umem'shala, netzach, g'dulah ug'vurah, t'hilah v'tif'eret, k'dushah umal'chut. ❖ B'rachot v'hoda-ot me-atah v'ad olam. Baruch atah Adonai, El melech gadol batish'bachot, El hahoda-ot, adon hanif'la-ot, habocher b'sheerei zim'rah, melech, El, chei ha-olameem.

שׁוֹכֵן עַד

שׁוֹכֵן עַד, מָרוֹם וְקָדוֹשׁ שְׁמוֹ:
וְכָתוּב, רַנְּנוּ צַדִּיקִים בַּיְיָ, לַיְשָׁרִים נָאוָה תְהִלָּה.
בְּפִי יְשָׁרִים תִּתְהַלָּל.
וּבְדִבְרֵי צַדִּיקִים תִּתְבָּרַךְ.
וּבִלְשׁוֹן חֲסִידִים תִּתְרוֹמָם.
וּבְקֶרֶב קְדוֹשִׁים תִּתְקַדָּשׁ:

יִשְׁתַּבַּח

We rise.

יִשְׁתַּבַּח שִׁמְךָ לָעַד מַלְכֵּנוּ, הָאֵל הַמֶּלֶךְ הַגָּדוֹל וְהַקָּדוֹשׁ בַּשָּׁמַיִם וּבָאָרֶץ. כִּי לְךָ נָאֶה, יְיָ אֱלֹהֵינוּ וֵאלֹהֵי אֲבוֹתֵינוּ: שִׁיר וּשְׁבָחָה, הַלֵּל וְזִמְרָה, עֹז וּמֶמְשָׁלָה, נֶצַח, גְּדֻלָּה וּגְבוּרָה, תְּהִלָּה וְתִפְאֶרֶת, קְדֻשָּׁה וּמַלְכוּת. ❖ בְּרָכוֹת וְהוֹדָאוֹת מֵעַתָּה וְעַד עוֹלָם. בָּרוּךְ אַתָּה יְיָ, אֵל מֶלֶךְ גָּדוֹל בַּתִּשְׁבָּחוֹת, אֵל הַהוֹדָאוֹת, אֲדוֹן הַנִּפְלָאוֹת, הַבּוֹחֵר בְּשִׁירֵי זִמְרָה, מֶלֶךְ, אֵל, חֵי הָעוֹלָמִים.

צ Adonai is righteous in every way, and kind in every deed.

ק Adonai is near to all who call, to all who call to God's sincerity.

ר God does the wishes of those who respect God, God hears their cry and saves them.

ש Adonai protects all who love God, but God will destroy the wicked.

ת My mouth shall speak praises of God, and all beings shall bless God's holy name forever and ever.

We shall praise God, now and forever. Halleluyah.

Tzadeek Adonai b'chol d'rachav,
v'chaseed b'chol ma-asav.

Karov Adonai l'chol kor'av,
l'chol asher yik'ra-uhu ve-emet.

R'tzon y're-av ya-aseh,
v'et shav'atam yish'ma v'yoshee-em.

Shomer Adonai et kol ohavav,
v'et kol har'sha-im yash'meed.

❖ T'hilat Adonai y'daber pee,
Veevarech kol basar shem kod'sho, l'olam va-ed.

Va-anach'nu n'varech Yah, me-atah v'ad olam, hal'luyah.

Halleluyah

Halleluyah! Praise God in God's holy place.
Praise God in the heavens.
Praise God for mighty deeds,
Praise God for endless greatness.
Praise God with the sound of the Shofar.
Praise God with harp and lyre.
Praise God with drum and dance,
Praise God with lute and pipe.
Praise God with loud cymbals,
Praise God with clashing cymbals.
Let everything the breathes praise God.
Halleluyah!
Let everything the breathes praise God.
Halleluyah!

Hal'luyah,
Hal'lu El b'kod'sho,
Hal'luhu bir'kee-a uzo.
Hal'luhu big'vurotav,
Hal'luhu b'nevel k'rov gud'lo.
Hal'luhu b'teka shofar,
Hal'luhu b'nevel v'chinor.
Hal'luhu b'tof umachol,
Hal'luhu b'mineem v'ugav.
Hal'luhu v'tzil'tz'lei shama,
Hal'luhu b'tzil'tz'lei t'ruah.
❖ Kol han'shamah t'halel Yah hal'luyah.
Kol han'shamah t'halel Yah hal'luyah.

> **"As long as one keeps searching, the answers will come."**
> —Joan Baez

צַדִּיק יְיָ בְּכָל דְּרָכָיו, וְחָסִיד בְּכָל מַעֲשָׂיו:
קָרוֹב יְיָ לְכָל קֹרְאָיו, לְכֹל אֲשֶׁר יִקְרָאֻהוּ בֶאֱמֶת:
רְצוֹן יְרֵאָיו יַעֲשֶׂה, וְאֶת שַׁוְעָתָם יִשְׁמַע וְיוֹשִׁיעֵם:
שׁוֹמֵר יְיָ אֶת כָּל אֹהֲבָיו, וְאֵת כָּל הָרְשָׁעִים יַשְׁמִיד:
❖ תְּהִלַּת יְיָ יְדַבֶּר פִּי,
וִיבָרֵךְ כָּל בָּשָׂר שֵׁם קָדְשׁוֹ, לְעוֹלָם וָעֶד:

PSALM 145

וַאֲנַחְנוּ נְבָרֵךְ יָהּ, מֵעַתָּה וְעַד עוֹלָם, הַלְלוּיָהּ:

PSALM 115:18

הַלְלוּיָהּ

הַלְלוּיָהּ,
הַלְלוּ אֵל בְּקָדְשׁוֹ, הַלְלוּהוּ בִּרְקִיעַ עֻזּוֹ:
הַלְלוּהוּ בִגְבוּרֹתָיו, הַלְלוּהוּ כְּרֹב גֻּדְלוֹ:
הַלְלוּהוּ בְּתֵקַע שׁוֹפָר, הַלְלוּהוּ בְּנֵבֶל וְכִנּוֹר:
הַלְלוּהוּ בְּתֹף וּמָחוֹל, הַלְלוּהוּ בְּמִנִּים וְעֻגָב:
הַלְלוּהוּ בְצִלְצְלֵי שָׁמַע, הַלְלוּהוּ בְּצִלְצְלֵי תְרוּעָה:
❖ כֹּל הַנְּשָׁמָה תְּהַלֵּל יָהּ הַלְלוּיָהּ.
כֹּל הַנְּשָׁמָה תְּהַלֵּל יָהּ הַלְלוּיָהּ:

PSALM 150

Ashrei

Happy are they who live in Your house;
They shall continue to praise You.

Happy are the people for whom this is so;
Happy are the people whose God is Adonai.

A Psalm of David.

א I will honor You, my God and Ruler, I will praise Your name forever and ever.

ב Every day I will praise You, and sing praises to Your name forever and ever.

ג Great is Adonai and greatly praised; there is no limit to God's greatness.

ד One generation shall praise Your deeds to another, and tell about Your mighty deeds.

ה I will speak about Your majesty, splendor and glory, and Your wonderful deeds.

ו They will talk about the power of Your mighty acts; and I will tell of Your greatness.

ז They recall Your great goodness, and sing of Your righteousness.

ח Adonai is gracious and caring, patient and very kind.

ט Adonai is good to all, and merciful to everything God made.

י All Your work shall praise You, Adonai, and Your faithful ones shall bless You.

כ They shall speak of the glory of Your rule, and talk of Your might.

ל To announce to humanity God's greatness, the splendor and glory of God's rule.

מ God, You rule eternally, Your kingdom is for all generations.

ס God holds up all who fall, and helps all who are bent over to stand straight.

ע The eyes of all look to You with hope, and You give them their food at the right time.

פ You open Your hand, and feed everything alive to its heart's content.

Ashrei yosh'vei veitecha,
od y'hal'lucha selah.

Ashrei ha-am shekacha lo,
ashrei ha-am she-Adonai elohav.

T'hilah l'David,

Aromim'cha elohai hamelech,
va-aver'chah shim'cha l'olam va-ed.

B'chol yom avar'checha,
va-ahal'lah shim'cha l'olam va-ed.

Gadol Adonai um'hulal m'od,
v'lig'dulato ein cheker.

Dor l'dor y'shabach ma-aseicha,
ug'vuroteicha yageedu.

Hadar k'vod hodecha,
v'div'rei nif'l'oteicha aseechah.

Ve-ezuz noroteicha yomeru,
ug'dulat'cha asap'renah.

Zecher rav tuv'cha yabee-u,
v'tzid'kat'cha y'ranenu.

Chanun v'rachum Adonai,
erech apayim ug'dal chased.

Tov Adonai lakol,
v'rachamav al kol ma-asav.

Yoducha Adonai kol ma-aseicha,
v'chaseedeicha y'varchucha.

K'vod mal'chut'cha yomeru,
ug'vurat'cha y'daberu.

L'hodee-ah liv'nei ha-adam g'vurotav,
uch'vod hadar mal'chuto.

Mal'chut'cha mal'chut kol olameem,
umem'shal't'cha b'chol dor vador.

Somech Adonai l'chol hanof'leem,
v'zokef l'chol hak'fufeem.

Einei chol eleicha y'saberu,
v'atah noten lahem et ach'lam b'ito.

Pote-ach et yadecha,
umas'bee-a l'chol chai ratzon.

אַשְׁרֵי

אַשְׁרֵי יוֹשְׁבֵי בֵיתֶךָ, עוֹד יְהַלְלוּךָ סֶּלָה:
PSALM 84:5

אַשְׁרֵי הָעָם שֶׁכָּכָה לּוֹ, אַשְׁרֵי הָעָם שֶׁיְיָ אֱלֹהָיו:
PSALM 144:15

תְּהִלָּה לְדָוִד,
אֲרוֹמִמְךָ אֱלוֹהַי הַמֶּלֶךְ, וַאֲבָרְכָה שִׁמְךָ לְעוֹלָם וָעֶד:
בְּכָל יוֹם אֲבָרְכֶךָּ, וַאֲהַלְלָה שִׁמְךָ לְעוֹלָם וָעֶד:

גָּדוֹל יְיָ וּמְהֻלָּל מְאֹד, וְלִגְדֻלָּתוֹ אֵין חֵקֶר:
דּוֹר לְדוֹר יְשַׁבַּח מַעֲשֶׂיךָ, וּגְבוּרֹתֶיךָ יַגִּידוּ:

הֲדַר כְּבוֹד הוֹדֶךָ, וְדִבְרֵי נִפְלְאֹתֶיךָ אָשִׂיחָה:
וֶעֱזוּז נוֹרְאוֹתֶיךָ יֹאמֵרוּ, וּגְדֻלָּתְךָ אֲסַפְּרֶנָּה:

זֵכֶר רַב טוּבְךָ יַבִּיעוּ, וְצִדְקָתְךָ יְרַנֵּנוּ:
חַנּוּן וְרַחוּם יְיָ, אֶרֶךְ אַפַּיִם וּגְדָל חָסֶד:

טוֹב יְיָ לַכֹּל, וְרַחֲמָיו עַל כָּל מַעֲשָׂיו:
יוֹדוּךָ יְיָ כָּל מַעֲשֶׂיךָ, וַחֲסִידֶיךָ יְבָרְכוּכָה:

כְּבוֹד מַלְכוּתְךָ יֹאמֵרוּ, וּגְבוּרָתְךָ יְדַבֵּרוּ:
לְהוֹדִיעַ לִבְנֵי הָאָדָם גְּבוּרֹתָיו, וּכְבוֹד הֲדַר מַלְכוּתוֹ:

מַלְכוּתְךָ מַלְכוּת כָּל עוֹלָמִים, וּמֶמְשַׁלְתְּךָ בְּכָל דּוֹר וָדֹר:
סוֹמֵךְ יְיָ לְכָל הַנֹּפְלִים, וְזוֹקֵף לְכָל הַכְּפוּפִים:

עֵינֵי כֹל אֵלֶיךָ יְשַׂבֵּרוּ, וְאַתָּה נוֹתֵן לָהֶם אֶת אָכְלָם בְּעִתּוֹ:
פּוֹתֵחַ אֶת יָדֶךָ, וּמַשְׂבִּיעַ לְכָל חַי רָצוֹן:

Shabbat Morning Service

Baruch Sheamar

We rise.

Praised is the One who spoke— and the world was! Praised is God.	Baruch she-amar v'hayah ha-olam, Baruch hu,
Praised is the One who... ...made Creation. ...speaks and it is done.	Baruch oseh v'resheet, Baruch omer v'oseh,
...decides and it happens. ...has mercy on the world.	Baruch gozer um'kayem, Baruch m'rachem al ha-aretz,
...has mercy on all creatures. ...rewards those who respect God.	Baruch m'rachem al hab'reeyot, Baruch m'shalem sachar tov leere-av,
...lives for ever and exists eternally. ...redeems and rescues. Praised be God's name.	Baruch chai la-ad v'kayam lanetzach, Baruch podeh umatzeel, Baruch sh'mo.

Praised are You, Adonai our God, Ruler of the universe, God, merciful Parent, Your people sing Your praises. Your loyal servants glorify You. We will sing to You, Adonai our God, with the songs written by Your servant David. We will tell how great You are with praises and Psalms. Unique One, Who lives forever, You are the Ruler whom we praise, whose great name is wonderful forever. Praised are You, Adonai, Ruler whom we praise with songs.

Baruch atah Adonai Eloheinu melech ha-olam, ha-el ha-av harachaman, ham'hulal b'fee amo, m'shubach um'fo-ar bil'shon chasidav, va-avadav, uv'shirei david av'decha. N'halel'cha Adonai Eloheinu bish'vachot uviz'meerot, un'gadel'cha un'shabechacha un'fa-er'cha v'naz'keer shim'cha, v'nam'leech'cha, mal'keinu Eloheinu, ❖ yachid, chei ha-olameem, melech m'shubach um'fo-ar adei ad sh'mo hagadol. Baruch atah Adonai, melech m'hulal batish'bachot.

We are seated.

> "As often as you can, take a trip out to the fields to pray. All the grasses will join you. They will enter your prayers and give you strength to sing praises to God."
> —Rav Nachman, LM 2:11

שחרית לשבת

בָּרוּךְ שֶׁאָמַר

We rise.

בָּרוּךְ שֶׁאָמַר וְהָיָה הָעוֹלָם,
בָּרוּךְ הוּא,

בָּרוּךְ עֹשֶׂה בְרֵאשִׁית,
בָּרוּךְ אוֹמֵר וְעוֹשֶׂה,

בָּרוּךְ גּוֹזֵר וּמְקַיֵּם,
בָּרוּךְ מְרַחֵם עַל הָאָרֶץ,

בָּרוּךְ מְרַחֵם עַל הַבְּרִיּוֹת,
בָּרוּךְ מְשַׁלֵּם שָׂכָר טוֹב לִירֵאָיו,

בָּרוּךְ חַי לָעַד וְקַיָּם לָנֶצַח,
בָּרוּךְ פּוֹדֶה וּמַצִּיל,
בָּרוּךְ שְׁמוֹ.

בָּרוּךְ אַתָּה יְיָ אֱלֹהֵינוּ מֶלֶךְ הָעוֹלָם, הָאֵל הָאָב הָרַחֲמָן, הַמְהֻלָּל בְּפִי עַמּוֹ, מְשֻׁבָּח וּמְפֹאָר בִּלְשׁוֹן חֲסִידָיו וַעֲבָדָיו, וּבְשִׁירֵי דָוִד עַבְדֶּךָ. נְהַלֶּלְךָ יְיָ אֱלֹהֵינוּ בִּשְׁבָחוֹת וּבִזְמִירוֹת, וּנְגַדֶּלְךָ וּנְשַׁבֵּחֲךָ וּנְפָאֶרְךָ וְנַזְכִּיר שִׁמְךָ, וְנַמְלִיכְךָ, מַלְכֵּנוּ אֱלֹהֵינוּ, ❖ יָחִיד, חֵי הָעוֹלָמִים, מֶלֶךְ מְשֻׁבָּח וּמְפֹאָר עֲדֵי עַד שְׁמוֹ הַגָּדוֹל: בָּרוּךְ אַתָּה יְיָ, מֶלֶךְ מְהֻלָּל בַּתִּשְׁבָּחוֹת:

We are seated.

Shabbat Morning Service

Shabbat Morning Prayers

Blessing for putting on the tallit

Praised are You, Adonai our God, Ruler of the universe, who made us holy with mitzvot, and who gave us the mitzvah to wrap ourselves in tzitzit.

Baruch atah Adonai Eloheinu melech ha-olam asher kidshanu b'mitzvotav, v'tzivanu l'hit'atef batzitzit.

Mah Tovu

How beautiful are your tents, O Jacob, your houses, O Israel.
Your great love inspires me to enter Your house, to worship in Your holy sanctuary, filled with awe for You.

Mah tovu ohalecha ya-akov, mish'k'notecha yisra-el.
Va-ani b'rov chas'd'cha avo veitecha, Esh'tachaveh el heichal kod'sh'cha b'yir'atecha.

The Morning Blessings

Praised are you Adonai our God, Ruler of the universe...
- ...who gave us the ability to tell day from night.
- ...who made me in God's image.
- ...who made me a Jew.
- ...who made me free.
- ...who opens the eyes of the blind.
- ...who clothes the unclothed.
- ...who frees the bound.
- ...who helps those who are bent over by trouble stand straight.
- ...who spreads out the earth over the waters.
- ...who made for me everything I need.
- ...who prepares the way for our footsteps.
- ...who gives the people of Israel strength.
- ...who crowns the people Israel with glory.
- ...who gives strength to the weary.
- ...who removes sleep from my eyes and slumber from my eyelids.

Baruch atah Adonai Eloheinu melech ha-olam...
- ...asher natan lasech'vee vina, l'hav'cheen bein yom uvein lai'la.
- ...she-asanee b'tzalmo.
- ...she-asanee Yisra-el
- ...she-asanee ben/bat choreen.
- ...poke-ach iv'reem.
- ...malbeesh arumeem.
- ...mateer asureem.
- ...zokef k'fufeem.

- ...roka ha-aretz al hamayim.

- ...she-asah lee kol tzor'kee.
- ...hamecheen mitz'adei gaver.

- ...ozer Yisra-el bigvurah.

- ...oter Yisra-el b'tif'arah.

- ...hanoten laya-ef ko-ach.
- ...hama-aveer shenah me-einai ut'numah me-af'apai.

שחרית לשבת

שַׁחֲרִית לְשַׁבָּת

> Just like during the week, we begin our day on Shabbat with *Shacharit*. We follow the same structure as we do on weekdays, but we add in some extra prayers to celebrate the holiness of Shabbat.

Blessing for putting on the תלית

בָּרוּךְ אַתָּה יְיָ אֱלֹהֵינוּ מֶלֶךְ הָעוֹלָם, אֲשֶׁר קִדְּשָׁנוּ בְּמִצְוֹתָיו, וְצִוָּנוּ לְהִתְעַטֵּף בַּצִּיצִת.

מַה טֹּבוּ

מַה טֹּבוּ אֹהָלֶיךָ יַעֲקֹב, מִשְׁכְּנֹתֶיךָ יִשְׂרָאֵל.
וַאֲנִי בְּרֹב חַסְדְּךָ אָבוֹא בֵיתֶךָ,
אֶשְׁתַּחֲוֶה אֶל הֵיכַל קָדְשְׁךָ בְּיִרְאָתֶךָ.

בִּרְכוֹת הַשַּׁחַר

בָּרוּךְ אַתָּה יְיָ אֱלֹהֵינוּ מֶלֶךְ הָעוֹלָם, אֲשֶׁר נָתַן לַשֶּׂכְוִי בִינָה, לְהַבְחִין בֵּין יוֹם וּבֵין לָיְלָה:

בָּרוּךְ אַתָּה יְיָ אֱלֹהֵינוּ מֶלֶךְ הָעוֹלָם, שֶׁעָשַׂנִי בְּצַלְמוֹ:
בָּרוּךְ אַתָּה יְיָ אֱלֹהֵינוּ מֶלֶךְ הָעוֹלָם, שֶׁעָשַׂנִי יִשְׂרָאֵל:
בָּרוּךְ אַתָּה יְיָ אֱלֹהֵינוּ מֶלֶךְ הָעוֹלָם, שֶׁעָשַׂנִי בֶּן־/בַּת־חוֹרִין:
בָּרוּךְ אַתָּה יְיָ אֱלֹהֵינוּ מֶלֶךְ הָעוֹלָם, פּוֹקֵחַ עִוְרִים:
בָּרוּךְ אַתָּה יְיָ אֱלֹהֵינוּ מֶלֶךְ הָעוֹלָם, מַלְבִּישׁ עֲרֻמִּים:
בָּרוּךְ אַתָּה יְיָ אֱלֹהֵינוּ מֶלֶךְ הָעוֹלָם, מַתִּיר אֲסוּרִים:
בָּרוּךְ אַתָּה יְיָ אֱלֹהֵינוּ מֶלֶךְ הָעוֹלָם, זוֹקֵף כְּפוּפִים:
בָּרוּךְ אַתָּה יְיָ אֱלֹהֵינוּ מֶלֶךְ הָעוֹלָם, רוֹקַע הָאָרֶץ עַל הַמָּיִם:
בָּרוּךְ אַתָּה יְיָ אֱלֹהֵינוּ מֶלֶךְ הָעוֹלָם, שֶׁעָשָׂה לִי כָּל צָרְכִּי:
בָּרוּךְ אַתָּה יְיָ אֱלֹהֵינוּ מֶלֶךְ הָעוֹלָם, הַמֵּכִין מִצְעֲדֵי גָבֶר:
בָּרוּךְ אַתָּה יְיָ אֱלֹהֵינוּ מֶלֶךְ הָעוֹלָם, אוֹזֵר יִשְׂרָאֵל בִּגְבוּרָה:
בָּרוּךְ אַתָּה יְיָ אֱלֹהֵינוּ מֶלֶךְ הָעוֹלָם, עוֹטֵר יִשְׂרָאֵל בְּתִפְאָרָה:
בָּרוּךְ אַתָּה יְיָ אֱלֹהֵינוּ מֶלֶךְ הָעוֹלָם, הַנּוֹתֵן לַיָּעֵף כֹּחַ:
בָּרוּךְ אַתָּה יְיָ אֱלֹהֵינוּ מֶלֶךְ הָעוֹלָם, הַמַּעֲבִיר שֵׁנָה מֵעֵינַי וּתְנוּמָה מֵעַפְעַפָּי:

Yigdal

Revere the living God, sing praises to God's name, both immanent and timeless, through eternity.	Yig'dal Eloheem chai v'yish'tabach, Nim'tza, v'ein et el m'tzee-uto.
God's oneness is unique, no other can compare, unlimited and boundless is God's majesty.	Echad v'ein yacheed k'yichudo, Ne'lam, v'gam ein sof l'ach'duto.
No image can be seen, no form or body known, no mortal mind can fathom God's totality.	Ein lo d'mut haguf v'eino guf, Lo na-aroch elav k'dushato.
Before creation's start, the world as yet unformed, the living God endured in endless mystery.	Kad'mon l'chol davar asher niv'ra, Rishon v'ein resheet l'resheeto.
The Ruler of the world! Whose creatures all declare the glory and the greatness of God's sovereignty.	Hino adon olam, v'chol notzar. Yoreh g'dulato umal'chuto.
God chose devoted servants, wise and faithful seers and showered on each one the gift of prophecy.	Shefa n'vu-ato n'tano, El an'shei s'gulato v'tif'ar'to.
In Israel none arose like Moses, touched by God, whose visions probed the limits of humanity.	Lo kam b'Yisra-el k'moshe od, Navee umabeet et t'munato.
The Torah, in its truth, God granted to us all, which loyal servant Moses taught us faithfully.	Torat emet natan l'amo, El, Al yad n'vee-o ne-eman beito.
Our God will neither change nor modify God's law, its place remains established for eternity.	Lo yachaleef ha-El v'lo yameer dato. L'olameem, l'zulato.
God penetrates our minds, the promptings of our hearts, anticipating actions that are yet to be.	Tzofeh v'yode-ah s'tareinu, Mabeet l'sof davar b'kad'mato.
God grants reward to those who lead a noble life, while punishing transgressors sinning wantonly.	Gomel l'eesh chesed k'meef'alo, Noten l'rasha ra k'rish'ato.
Messiah, God will send, to greet the end of days, redeeming all who long for God to make them free.	Yish'lach l'ketz yameem m'sheechenu, Lif'dot m'chakei ketz y'shuato.
In love our God restores the life of all our souls, may God be ever praised until eternity.	Meteem y'chayeh El b'rov chasdo, Baruch adei ad shem t'hilato.

יִגְדַּל

יִגְדַּל אֱלֹהִים חַי וְיִשְׁתַּבַּח, נִמְצָא, וְאֵין עֵת אֶל מְצִיאוּתוֹ:
אֶחָד וְאֵין יָחִיד כְּיִחוּדוֹ, נֶעְלָם, וְגַם אֵין סוֹף לְאַחְדוּתוֹ:
אֵין לוֹ דְמוּת הַגּוּף וְאֵינוֹ גוּף, לֹא נַעֲרוֹךְ אֵלָיו קְדֻשָּׁתוֹ:
קַדְמוֹן לְכָל דָּבָר אֲשֶׁר נִבְרָא, רִאשׁוֹן וְאֵין רֵאשִׁית לְרֵאשִׁיתוֹ:
הִנּוֹ אֲדוֹן עוֹלָם, וְכָל נוֹצָר. יוֹרֶה גְדֻלָּתוֹ וּמַלְכוּתוֹ:
שֶׁפַע נְבוּאָתוֹ נְתָנוֹ, אֶל אַנְשֵׁי סְגֻלָּתוֹ וְתִפְאַרְתּוֹ:
לֹא קָם בְּיִשְׂרָאֵל כְּמֹשֶׁה עוֹד, נָבִיא וּמַבִּיט אֶת תְּמוּנָתוֹ:
תּוֹרַת אֱמֶת נָתַן לְעַמּוֹ, אֵל, עַל יַד נְבִיאוֹ נֶאֱמַן בֵּיתוֹ:
לֹא יַחֲלִיף הָאֵל וְלֹא יָמִיר דָּתוֹ, לְעוֹלָמִים, לְזוּלָתוֹ:
צוֹפֶה וְיוֹדֵעַ סְתָרֵינוּ, מַבִּיט לְסוֹף דָּבָר בְּקַדְמָתוֹ:
גּוֹמֵל לְאִישׁ חֶסֶד כְּמִפְעָלוֹ, נוֹתֵן לְרָשָׁע רָע כְּרִשְׁעָתוֹ:
יִשְׁלַח לְקֵץ יָמִין מְשִׁיחֵנוּ, לִפְדּוֹת מְחַכֵּי קֵץ יְשׁוּעָתוֹ:
מֵתִים יְחַיֶּה אֵל בְּרֹב חַסְדּוֹ, בָּרוּךְ עֲדֵי עַד שֵׁם תְּהִלָּתוֹ:

Shabbat Evening Prayers

Mourner's Kaddish

Mourners:

May God's great name be made great and holy in the world which God created according to God's will. May God establish Divine rule soon, in our days, quickly and in the near future, and let us say: Amen.

Yit'gadal v'yit'kadash sh'meh rabah. B'al'mah dee v'rah chir'utei, v'yam'leech mal'chutei b'chayeichon uv'yomeichon uv'chayei d'chol beit Yisra-el. Ba-agalah uviz'man kareev v'im'ru amen.

Everyone:

May God's great name be praised for ever and ever.

Y'heh sh'meh rabah m'varach l'alam ul'al'mei al'mayah.

Mourners:

Blessed, praised, glorified and raised high, honored and elevated be the name of the Holy Blessed One, far beyond all blessings and songs, praises and words of comfort which people can say, and let us say: Amen.

Yit'barach v'yishtabach v'yitpa-ar v'yit'romam v'yit'naseh v'yit'hadar v'yit'aleh v'yit'halal sh'meh d'kud'shah b'reech hu l'elah min kol bir'chatah v'sheeratah tush'b'chatah v'nechematah, da-ameeran b'al'mah, v'im'ru amen.

May there be abundant peace from heaven and life for us and for all Israel, and let us say: Amen.

Y'hei sh'lamah rabah min sh'mayah v'chayeem aleinu v'al kol Yisra-el, v'im'ru amen.

May the One who makes peace in the high heavens make peace for us and for all Israel, and let us say: Amen.

Oseh shalom bim'romav, hu ya-aseh shalom aleinu, v'al kol Yisra-el v'im'ru amen.

מעריב לשבת

קַדִּישׁ יָתוֹם

DID YOU KNOW THAT... The Mourner's Kaddish is a prayer for us to recite in honor of those loved ones who are no longer with us physically in this world. Out of respect for the memories of our loved ones and the millions of Jews that died in the Holocaust we say the Mourner's Kaddish.

Mourners:

יִתְגַּדַּל וְיִתְקַדַּשׁ שְׁמֵהּ רַבָּא. בְּעָלְמָא דִּי בְרָא כִרְעוּתֵיהּ, וְיַמְלִיךְ מַלְכוּתֵהּ בְּחַיֵּיכוֹן וּבְיוֹמֵיכוֹן וּבְחַיֵּי דְכָל בֵּית יִשְׂרָאֵל. בַּעֲגָלָא וּבִזְמַן קָרִיב וְאִמְרוּ אָמֵן:

Everyone:

יְהֵא שְׁמֵהּ רַבָּא מְבָרַךְ לְעָלַם וּלְעָלְמֵי עָלְמַיָּא:

Mourners:

יִתְבָּרַךְ וְיִשְׁתַּבַּח וְיִתְפָּאַר וְיִתְרוֹמַם וְיִתְנַשֵּׂא וְיִתְהַדָּר וְיִתְעַלֶּה וְיִתְהַלָּל שְׁמֵהּ דְּקֻדְשָׁא בְּרִיךְ הוּא לְעֵלָּא מִן כָּל בִּרְכָתָא וְשִׁירָתָא תֻּשְׁבְּחָתָא וְנֶחֱמָתָא, דַּאֲמִירָן בְּעָלְמָא, וְאִמְרוּ אָמֵן:

יְהֵא שְׁלָמָא רַבָּא מִן שְׁמַיָּא וְחַיִּים עָלֵינוּ וְעַל כָּל יִשְׂרָאֵל, וְאִמְרוּ אָמֵן:

עֹשֶׂה שָׁלוֹם בִּמְרוֹמָיו הוּא יַעֲשֶׂה שָׁלוֹם עָלֵינוּ וְעַל כָּל יִשְׂרָאֵל, וְאִמְרוּ אָמֵן:

Aleinu

We should praise God for not making us like the other peoples and families of the earth. We bend the knee and bow and give thanks to the Ruler of all earthly rulers, the Blessed Holy One. God spread out the heavens and built the earth's foundations. God's mighty presence is in the highest heights. God is our God—no one else. Our Ruler is true. There is nothing besides God, as it is written in God's Torah: "You shall know therefore this day and keep in mind that Adonai alone is God in heaven above and on earth below; there is no other."

And so we hope in You, Adonai our God, soon to see Your power used in a wonderful way: removing false gods from the earth, fixing the brokenness of the world so that it will be a world truly ruled by God. All humanity will call Your name, and all the wicked of the earth will turn toward You. All who live in the world will know and understand that everyone should accept You as their God. They will bow to You, Adonai our God, honoring the glory of Your name. For You will rule the world, and You will always rule over it in glory, as it is written in the Torah: "Adonai will rule for ever and ever." And as the prophet Zechariah said: "Then God will be Ruler over all the earth. On that day Adonai will be One and God's name will be One."

Aleinu l'shabe-ach la-adon hakol, latet g'dulah l'yotzer b'resheet, shelo asanu k'goyei ha-aratzot, v'lo samanu k'mish'p'chot ha-adamah, shelo sam chel'kenu kahem, v'goralenu k'chol hamonam. Va-anachnu kor'eem umish'tachaveem umodeem, lifnei melech, malchei ham'lacheem, hakadosh baruch hu. Shehu noteh shamayeem v'yosed aretz, umoshav y'karo bashamayim mima-al, ush'cheenat uzo b'gav'hei m'romeem, hu Eloheinu ein od. Emet malkenu efes zulato, kakatuv b'Torato: V'yada'ta hayom vahashevota El l'vavecha, kee Adonai hu haEloheem bashamayim mima-al, v'al ha-aretz mitachat, ein od.

Al ken n'kaveh l'cha Adonai Eloheinu, lir'ot m'hera b'tif'eret uzecha, l'ha-aveer giluleem min ha-aretz v'ha-eleeleem karot yikaretun. L'taken olam b'mal'chut shadai, v'chol b'nei vasar yik'r'u vish'mecha. L'haf'not eleicha kol rish'ei aretz. Yakeeru v'yed'u kol yosh'vei tevel, kee l'cha tich'ra kol berech, tishava kol lashon. L'faneicha Adonai Eloheinu yich'r'u v'yipolu. V'lich'vod shim'cha y'kar yitenu. Veekab'lu chulam et ol mal'chutecha. V'tim'loch aleihem m'herah l'olam va-ed.

❖ Kakatuv b'toratecha, Adonai yim'loch l'olam va-ed. V'ne-emar, v'haya Adonai l'melech al kol ha-aretz, bayom hahu yih'yeh Adonai echad, ush'mo echad.

עָלֵינוּ

DID YOU KNOW THAT... The first paragraph of *Aleinu* praises God for our uniqueness as Jews, while the second looks to the future, hoping for the day when the world will belong to God and be a place of harmony and peace. How can we create a world that is a place of peace and harmony?

We rise.

עָלֵינוּ לְשַׁבֵּחַ לַאֲדוֹן הַכֹּל, לָתֵת גְּדֻלָּה לְיוֹצֵר בְּרֵאשִׁית, שֶׁלֹּא עָשָׂנוּ כְּגוֹיֵי הָאֲרָצוֹת, וְלֹא שָׂמָנוּ כְּמִשְׁפְּחוֹת הָאֲדָמָה, שֶׁלֹּא שָׂם חֶלְקֵנוּ כָּהֶם, וְגוֹרָלֵנוּ כְּכָל הֲמוֹנָם:
וַאֲנַחְנוּ כּוֹרְעִים וּמִשְׁתַּחֲוִים וּמוֹדִים,
לִפְנֵי מֶלֶךְ, מַלְכֵי הַמְּלָכִים, הַקָּדוֹשׁ בָּרוּךְ הוּא.
שֶׁהוּא נוֹטֶה שָׁמַיִם וְיֹסֵד אָרֶץ, וּמוֹשַׁב יְקָרוֹ בַּשָּׁמַיִם מִמַּעַל, וּשְׁכִינַת עֻזּוֹ בְּגָבְהֵי מְרוֹמִים, הוּא אֱלֹהֵינוּ אֵין עוֹד. אֱמֶת מַלְכֵּנוּ אֶפֶס זוּלָתוֹ, כַּכָּתוּב בְּתוֹרָתוֹ: וְיָדַעְתָּ הַיּוֹם וַהֲשֵׁבֹתָ אֶל לְבָבֶךָ, כִּי יְיָ הוּא הָאֱלֹהִים בַּשָּׁמַיִם מִמַּעַל, וְעַל הָאָרֶץ מִתָּחַת, אֵין עוֹד:

עַל כֵּן נְקַוֶּה לְךָ יְיָ אֱלֹהֵינוּ, לִרְאוֹת מְהֵרָה בְּתִפְאֶרֶת עֻזֶּךָ, לְהַעֲבִיר גִּלּוּלִים מִן הָאָרֶץ וְהָאֱלִילִים כָּרוֹת יִכָּרֵתוּן. לְתַקֵּן עוֹלָם בְּמַלְכוּת שַׁדַּי, וְכָל בְּנֵי בָשָׂר יִקְרְאוּ בִשְׁמֶךָ. לְהַפְנוֹת אֵלֶיךָ כָּל רִשְׁעֵי אָרֶץ. יַכִּירוּ וְיֵדְעוּ כָּל יוֹשְׁבֵי תֵבֵל, כִּי לְךָ תִּכְרַע כָּל בֶּרֶךְ, תִּשָּׁבַע כָּל לָשׁוֹן: לְפָנֶיךָ יְיָ אֱלֹהֵינוּ יִכְרְעוּ וְיִפֹּלוּ. וְלִכְבוֹד שִׁמְךָ יְקָר יִתֵּנוּ. וִיקַבְּלוּ כֻלָּם אֶת עֹל מַלְכוּתֶךָ. וְתִמְלֹךְ עֲלֵיהֶם מְהֵרָה לְעוֹלָם וָעֶד. כִּי הַמַּלְכוּת שֶׁלְּךָ הִיא, וּלְעוֹלְמֵי עַד תִּמְלוֹךְ בְּכָבוֹד:
❖ כַּכָּתוּב בְּתוֹרָתֶךָ, יְיָ יִמְלֹךְ לְעוֹלָם וָעֶד: וְנֶאֱמַר: וְהָיָה יְיָ לְמֶלֶךְ עַל כָּל הָאָרֶץ, בַּיּוֹם הַהוּא יִהְיֶה יְיָ אֶחָד, וּשְׁמוֹ אֶחָד:

We are seated.

Magen Avot

Shield of our ancestors by God's promised word, Guarantor of life to the dead, Holy God beyond compare, who bestows rest to God's people on the holy Shabbat, who takes pleasure in them, and invites them to rest. We will honor God with reverence and awe, and offer our thanks day after day. The Source of blessings, God worthy of acclaim, the Master of peace, hallows Shabbat, the seventh day—granting Shabbat in holiness to a people overflowing with joy—this day that recalls the act of Creation.

Magen avot bid'varo, m'chayeh meteem b'ma-amaro, ha-El hakadosh she-ein kamohu, hamenee-ach l'amo b'yom Shabbat kod'sho, kee vam ratzah l'hanee-ach lahem. L'fanav na-avod b'yir'ah vafachad, v'nodeh lish'mo b'chol yom tameed, me-ein hab'rachot. El hahoda-ot adon hashalom, m'kadesh haShabbat, um'varech sh'vee-ee, umenee-ach bik'dushah l'am m'dush'nei oneg, zecher l'ma-aseh v'resheet.

Kaddish Shalem

Leader:

May God's great name be made great and holy in the world which God created according to God's will. May God establish Divine rule soon, in our days, quickly and in the near future, and let us say: Amen.

Yit'gadal v'yit'kadash sh'meh rabah. B'al'mah dee v'rah chir'utei, v'yam'leech mal'chutei b'chayeichon uv'yomeichon uv'chayei d'chol beit Yisra-el. Ba-agalah uviz'man kareev v'im'ru amen.

Everyone:

May God's great name be praised for ever and ever.

Y'heh sh'meh rabah m'varach l'alam ul'al'mei al'mayah.

Leader:

Blessed, praised, glorified and raised high, honored and elevated be the name of the Holy Blessed One, far beyond all blessings and songs, praises and words of comfort which people can say, and let us say: Amen.

Yit'barach v'yishtabach v'yitpa-ar v'yit'romam v'yit'naseh v'yit'hadar v'yit'aleh v'yit'halal sh'meh d'kud'shah b'reech hu l'elah min kol bir'chatah v'sheeratah tush'b'chatah v'nechematah, da-ameeran b'al'mah, v'im'ru amen.

May the prayers and pleas of the entire House of Israel be accepted before their Parent in heaven. And let us say: Amen.

Tit'kabal tz'lot'hon uva-ut'hon d'chol Yisra-el kadam avuhon dee vish'mayah v'im'ru amen.

May there be abundant peace from heaven and life for us and for all Israel, and let us say: Amen.

Y'hei sh'lamah rabah min sh'mayah v'chayeem aleinu v'al kol Yisra-el, v'im'ru amen.

May the One who makes peace in the high heavens make peace for us and for all Israel, and let us say: Amen.

Oseh shalom bim'romav, hu ya-aseh shalom aleinu, v'al kol Yisra-el v'im'ru amen.

מָגֵן אָבוֹת

מָגֵן אָבוֹת בִּדְבָרוֹ, מְחַיֶּה מֵתִים בְּמַאֲמָרוֹ, הָאֵל הַקָּדוֹשׁ שֶׁאֵין כָּמוֹהוּ, הַמֵּנִיחַ לְעַמּוֹ בְּיוֹם שַׁבַּת קָדְשׁוֹ, כִּי בָם רָצָה לְהָנִיחַ לָהֶם. לְפָנָיו נַעֲבוֹד בְּיִרְאָה וָפַחַד, וְנוֹדֶה לִשְׁמוֹ בְּכָל יוֹם תָּמִיד, מֵעֵין הַבְּרָכוֹת. אֵל הַהוֹדָאוֹת אֲדוֹן הַשָּׁלוֹם, מְקַדֵּשׁ הַשַּׁבָּת, וּמְבָרֵךְ שְׁבִיעִי, וּמֵנִיחַ בִּקְדֻשָּׁה לְעַם מְדֻשְּׁנֵי עֹנֶג, זֵכֶר לְמַעֲשֵׂה בְרֵאשִׁית:

קַדִּישׁ שָׁלֵם

Leader:

יִתְגַּדַּל וְיִתְקַדַּשׁ שְׁמֵהּ רַבָּא. בְּעָלְמָא דִּי בְרָא כִרְעוּתֵיהּ, וְיַמְלִיךְ מַלְכוּתֵהּ בְּחַיֵּיכוֹן וּבְיוֹמֵיכוֹן וּבְחַיֵּי דְכָל בֵּית יִשְׂרָאֵל. בַּעֲגָלָא וּבִזְמַן קָרִיב וְאִמְרוּ אָמֵן:

Everyone:

יְהֵא שְׁמֵהּ רַבָּא מְבָרַךְ לְעָלַם וּלְעָלְמֵי עָלְמַיָּא:

Leader:

יִתְבָּרַךְ וְיִשְׁתַּבַּח וְיִתְפָּאַר וְיִתְרוֹמַם וְיִתְנַשֵּׂא וְיִתְהַדָּר וְיִתְעַלֶּה וְיִתְהַלָּל שְׁמֵהּ דְּקֻדְשָׁא בְּרִיךְ הוּא לְעֵלָּא מִן כָּל בִּרְכָתָא וְשִׁירָתָא תֻּשְׁבְּחָתָא וְנֶחֱמָתָא, דַּאֲמִירָן בְּעָלְמָא, וְאִמְרוּ אָמֵן:

תִּתְקַבַּל צְלוֹתְהוֹן וּבָעוּתְהוֹן דְּכָל יִשְׂרָאֵל קֳדָם אֲבוּהוֹן דִּי בִשְׁמַיָּא וְאִמְרוּ אָמֵן:

יְהֵא שְׁלָמָא רַבָּא מִן שְׁמַיָּא וְחַיִּים עָלֵינוּ וְעַל כָּל יִשְׂרָאֵל, וְאִמְרוּ אָמֵן:

עֹשֶׂה שָׁלוֹם בִּמְרוֹמָיו הוּא יַעֲשֶׂה שָׁלוֹם עָלֵינוּ וְעַל כָּל יִשְׂרָאֵל, וְאִמְרוּ אָמֵן:

May we see Your merciful return to Zion. Praised are You, Adonai, who restores Your presence to Zion.

We thank You for being our God and God of our ancestors for ever and ever. You are the Rock of our lives and our saving Shield. In every generation we will thank and praise You for our lives which are in Your power, for our souls which are in Your keeping, for Your miracles which are with us every day, and for Your wonders and good deeds that are with us at all times, evening, morning, and noon. O Good One, Your mercies have never stopped. O Merciful One, Your kindness has never stopped. We have always placed our hope in You.

For all these things, our Ruler, may Your name be blessed and honored forever.

May every living thing thank You and praise You sincerely, O God, our rescue and help. Praised are You, Your name is the Good One, and it is good to thank You.

Give peace to Your people Israel and to the whole world forever, for You are the Ruler of peace. May it please You always to bless Your people Israel with Your peace.

Praised are You, Adonai, who blesses Your people Israel with peace.

My God, help me not to say bad things or to tell lies. Help me to ignore people who say bad things about me. Open my heart to Your Torah, so that I can do Your mitzvot. Quickly stop the ideas and spoil the plans of anyone who wants to hurt me. Do this because of Your love, Your holiness, and Your Torah: so that those You love will be free. May the words of my mouth and the thoughts of my heart find favor with You, my Rock and my Protector. May the One who makes peace up above give peace to us and to all the people of Israel. Amen.

V'techezeinah eineinu b'shuv'cha l'tzee-on b'rachameem. Baruch atah Adonai, hamachazeer sh'cheenato l'tzee-on.

Modeem anach'nu lach, sha-atah hu, Adonai Eloheinu vElohei avoteinu, l'olam va-ed, tzur chayeinu, magen yish'enu, atah hu l'dor vador nodeh l'cha un'saper t'hilatecha. Al chayeinu ham'sureem b'yadecha, v'al nish'moteinu hap'kudot lach, v'al niseicha sheb'chol yom imanu, v'al nif'l'oteicha v'tovoteicha sheb'chol et, erev vavoker v'tzohorayim, hatov kee lo chalu rachameicha, v'ham'rachem kee lo tamu chasadeicha me-olam kiveenu lach.

V'al kulam yitbarach v'yit'romam shim'cha, mal'kenu, tameed l'olam va-ed.

V'chol hachayeem yoducha selah, veehal'lu et shim'cha be-emet, ha-El y'shu-atenu v'ez'ratenu selah. Baruch atah Adonai, hatov shim'cha ul'cha na-eh l'hodot.

Shalom rav al Yisra-el am'cha taseem l'olam, kee atah hu melech adon l'chol hashalom. V'tov b'eineicha l'varech et am'cha Yisra-el b'chol et uv'chol sha-ah bish'lomecha.

Baruch atah Adonai, ham'varech et amo Yisra-el bashalom.

Elohai, n'tzor l'shonee mera. Us'fatai midaber mir'mah. V'lim'kal'lai naf'shee tidom, v'naf'shee ke-afar lakol tih'yeh. P'tach libee b'Torahtecha, uv'mitzvoteicha tir'dof naf'shee. V'chol hachosh'veem alai ra-ah, m'herah hafer atzatam v'kal'kel macahshav'tam. Aseh l'ma-an Toratecha. Lama-an yechal'tzun y'deedeicha, hoshee-ah y'meen'cha va-anenee. Yih'yu l'ratzon im'rei fee v'heg'yon libee l'faneicha, Adonai tzuree v'go-alee. Oseh shalom bim'romav, hu ya-aseh shalom aleinu, v'al kol Yisra-el v'im'ru amen.

We are seated.

וְתֶחֱזֶינָה עֵינֵינוּ בְּשׁוּבְךָ לְצִיּוֹן בְּרַחֲמִים. בָּרוּךְ אַתָּה יְיָ, הַמַּחֲזִיר שְׁכִינָתוֹ לְצִיּוֹן.

מוֹדִים אֲנַחְנוּ לָךְ, שָׁאַתָּה הוּא, יְיָ אֱלֹהֵינוּ וֵאלֹהֵי אֲבוֹתֵינוּ, לְעוֹלָם וָעֶד, צוּר חַיֵּינוּ, מָגֵן יִשְׁעֵנוּ, אַתָּה הוּא לְדוֹר וָדוֹר נוֹדֶה לְּךָ וּנְסַפֵּר תְּהִלָּתֶךָ. עַל חַיֵּינוּ הַמְּסוּרִים בְּיָדֶךָ, וְעַל נִשְׁמוֹתֵינוּ הַפְּקוּדוֹת לָךְ, וְעַל נִסֶּיךָ שֶׁבְּכָל יוֹם עִמָּנוּ, וְעַל נִפְלְאוֹתֶיךָ וְטוֹבוֹתֶיךָ שֶׁבְּכָל עֵת, עֶרֶב וָבֹקֶר וְצָהֳרָיִם, הַטּוֹב כִּי לֹא כָלוּ רַחֲמֶיךָ, וְהַמְרַחֵם כִּי לֹא תַמּוּ חֲסָדֶיךָ מֵעוֹלָם קִוִּינוּ לָךְ.

וְעַל כֻּלָּם יִתְבָּרַךְ וְיִתְרוֹמַם שִׁמְךָ, מַלְכֵּנוּ, תָּמִיד לְעוֹלָם וָעֶד.

וְכֹל הַחַיִּים יוֹדוּךָ סֶּלָה, וִיהַלְלוּ אֶת שִׁמְךָ בֶּאֱמֶת, הָאֵל יְשׁוּעָתֵנוּ וְעֶזְרָתֵנוּ סֶלָה. בָּרוּךְ אַתָּה יְיָ, הַטּוֹב שִׁמְךָ וּלְךָ נָאֶה לְהוֹדוֹת.

שָׁלוֹם רָב עַל יִשְׂרָאֵל עַמְּךָ תָּשִׂים לְעוֹלָם, כִּי אַתָּה הוּא מֶלֶךְ אָדוֹן לְכָל הַשָּׁלוֹם. וְטוֹב בְּעֵינֶיךָ לְבָרֵךְ אֶת עַמְּךָ יִשְׂרָאֵל בְּכָל עֵת וּבְכָל שָׁעָה בִּשְׁלוֹמֶךָ.

בָּרוּךְ אַתָּה יְיָ, הַמְבָרֵךְ אֶת עַמּוֹ יִשְׂרָאֵל בַּשָּׁלוֹם.

אֱלֹהַי, נְצוֹר לְשׁוֹנִי מֵרָע. וּשְׂפָתַי מִדַּבֵּר מִרְמָה: וְלִמְקַלְלַי נַפְשִׁי תִדֹּם, וְנַפְשִׁי כֶּעָפָר לַכֹּל תִּהְיֶה. פְּתַח לִבִּי בְּתוֹרָתֶךָ, וּבְמִצְוֹתֶיךָ תִּרְדּוֹף נַפְשִׁי. וְכָל הַחוֹשְׁבִים עָלַי רָעָה, מְהֵרָה הָפֵר עֲצָתָם וְקַלְקֵל מַחֲשַׁבְתָּם. עֲשֵׂה לְמַעַן שְׁמֶךָ, עֲשֵׂה לְמַעַן יְמִינֶךָ, עֲשֵׂה לְמַעַן קְדֻשָּׁתֶךָ. עֲשֵׂה לְמַעַן תּוֹרָתֶךָ. לְמַעַן יֵחָלְצוּן יְדִידֶיךָ, הוֹשִׁיעָה יְמִינְךָ וַעֲנֵנִי. יִהְיוּ לְרָצוֹן אִמְרֵי פִי וְהֶגְיוֹן לִבִּי לְפָנֶיךָ, יְיָ צוּרִי וְגוֹאֲלִי. עֹשֶׂה שָׁלוֹם בִּמְרוֹמָיו, הוּא יַעֲשֶׂה שָׁלוֹם עָלֵינוּ, וְעַל כָּל יִשְׂרָאֵל וְאִמְרוּ: אָמֵן.

We are seated.

Shabbat Evening Prayers

You are holy and Your name is holy and holy beings praise You every day. Praised are You Adonai, the holy God.

Atah kidash'ta et yom hash'vee-ee lish'mecha. Tach'leet ma-aseh shamayim va-aretz. Uverach'to mikol hayameem, v'kidash'to mikol haz'maneem v'chen katuv b'toratecha.

The heavens and earth and all that is in them were finished. On the seventh day God finished the work that had been done, and stopped working on the seventh day. God blessed the seventh day and made it holy, because God ceased from all the work of creation.

Vay'chulu hashamayim v'ha-aretz v'chol tz'va-am. Vay'chal Eloheem bayom hash'vee-ee, m'lach'to asher asah, vayish'bot bayom hash'vee-ee, mikol m'lachto asher asah. Vay'varech Eloheem et yom hash'vee-ee vay'kadesh oto kee vo shavat mikol m'lach'to, asher bara Eloheem la-asot.

Our God and God of our ancestors, be pleased with our Shabbat rest, make us holy with Your mitzvot and let us share in Your Torah. Satisfy us with Your goodness and make us happy with Your help. Purify our hearts so that we can serve You truly. Adonai our God, let us receive Your holy Shabbat with love and favor, so that Your people Israel who make Your name holy will rest on it. Praised are You Adonai, who makes the Shabbat holy.

Eloheinu vElohei avoteinu, r'tzeh vim'nuchatenu, kad'shenu b'mitz'voteicha v'ten chel'kenu b'toratecha, sab'enu mituvecha v'sam'chenu beeshu-atecha, v'taher libenu l'ov'd'cha be-emet, v'han'cheelenu Adonai Eloheinu b'ahavah uv'ratzon Shabbat kod'shecha, v'yanuchu vah Yisra-el m'kad'shei sh'mecha. Baruch atah Adonai, m'kadesh haShabbat.

Adonai, be pleased with Your people Israel and with their prayer. Restore worship to Your Temple. May the prayer of Your people Israel always be accepted with love and favor.

R'tzeh, Adonai Eloheinu, b'am'cha Yisra-el uvit'filatam, v'hashev et ha-avodah lid'veer beitecha, ut'filatam b'ahavah t'kabel b'ratzon, ut'hee l'ratzon tameed avodat Yisra-el amecha.

On Rosh Chodesh, add the following:

Our God and God of our ancestors, please remember us, our ancestors, the Messiah, Your holy city Jerusalem, and Your people Israel. Remember them for good, with mercy and lovingkindness, for life and peace on this day of the New Moon.
Remember us, Adonai our God; keep us in mind for blessing, and give us life. You promised to protect and save us, have mercy on us and save us, for our eyes turn to You, for You are a kind and merciful Ruler.

Eloheinu vElohei avoteinu, ya-aleh v'yavo, v'yagee-a, v'yera-eh, v'yeratzeh, v'yishama, v'yipaked, v'yizacher zich'ronenu ufikdonenu, v'zich'ron avoteinu mashiach ben David av'decha, v'zich'ron Y'rushalayim eer kod'shecha, v'zich'ron kol am'cha beit Yisra-el l'faneicha, lif'leitah, l'tovah, l'chen ul'chesed ul'rachameem, l'chayim ul'shalom, b'yom Rosh Hochodesh hazeh.
Zochrenu, Adonai, Eloheinu, bo l'tovah, ufok'denu vo liv'rachah, v'hoshee-enu vo l'chayim, uvid'var y'shu-ah v'rachameem, chus v'chonenu, v'rachem aleinu v'hoshee-enu, kee eleicha eineinu, kee El melech chanun v'rachum atah.

מעריב לשבת

אַתָּה קִדַּשְׁתָּ אֶת יוֹם הַשְּׁבִיעִי לִשְׁמֶךָ. תַּכְלִית מַעֲשֵׂה שָׁמַיִם וָאָרֶץ. וּבֵרַכְתּוֹ מִכָּל הַיָּמִים, וְקִדַּשְׁתּוֹ מִכָּל הַזְּמַנִּים וְכֵן כָּתוּב בְּתוֹרָתֶךָ:

וַיְכֻלּוּ הַשָּׁמַיִם וְהָאָרֶץ וְכָל צְבָאָם: וַיְכַל אֱלֹהִים בַּיּוֹם הַשְּׁבִיעִי מְלַאכְתּוֹ אֲשֶׁר עָשָׂה, וַיִּשְׁבֹּת בַּיּוֹם הַשְּׁבִיעִי, מִכָּל מְלַאכְתּוֹ אֲשֶׁר עָשָׂה: וַיְבָרֶךְ אֱלֹהִים אֶת יוֹם הַשְּׁבִיעִי וַיְקַדֵּשׁ אֹתוֹ, כִּי בוֹ שָׁבַת מִכָּל מְלַאכְתּוֹ, אֲשֶׁר בָּרָא אֱלֹהִים לַעֲשׂוֹת:

אֱלֹהֵינוּ וֵאלֹהֵי אֲבוֹתֵינוּ, רְצֵה בִמְנוּחָתֵנוּ, קַדְּשֵׁנוּ בְּמִצְוֹתֶיךָ וְתֵן חֶלְקֵנוּ בְּתוֹרָתֶךָ, שַׂבְּעֵנוּ מִטּוּבֶךָ וְשַׂמְּחֵנוּ בִּישׁוּעָתֶךָ, וְטַהֵר לִבֵּנוּ לְעָבְדְּךָ בֶּאֱמֶת, וְהַנְחִילֵנוּ יְיָ אֱלֹהֵינוּ בְּאַהֲבָה וּבְרָצוֹן שַׁבַּת קָדְשֶׁךָ, וְיָנוּחוּ בָהּ יִשְׂרָאֵל מְקַדְּשֵׁי שְׁמֶךָ. בָּרוּךְ אַתָּה יְיָ, מְקַדֵּשׁ הַשַּׁבָּת:

רְצֵה, יְיָ אֱלֹהֵינוּ, בְּעַמְּךָ יִשְׂרָאֵל וּבִתְפִלָּתָם, וְהָשֵׁב אֶת הָעֲבוֹדָה לִדְבִיר בֵּיתֶךָ, וּתְפִלָּתָם בְּאַהֲבָה תְקַבֵּל בְּרָצוֹן, וּתְהִי לְרָצוֹן תָּמִיד עֲבוֹדַת יִשְׂרָאֵל עַמֶּךָ.

On ראש חדש, *add the following:*

אֱלֹהֵינוּ וֵאלֹהֵי אֲבוֹתֵינוּ, יַעֲלֶה וְיָבֹא וְיַגִּיעַ, וְיֵרָאֶה וְיֵרָצֶה וְיִשָּׁמַע, וְיִפָּקֵד וְיִזָּכֵר זִכְרוֹנֵנוּ וּפִקְדוֹנֵנוּ, וְזִכְרוֹן אֲבוֹתֵינוּ, וְזִכְרוֹן מָשִׁיחַ בֶּן דָּוִד עַבְדֶּךָ, וְזִכְרוֹן יְרוּשָׁלַיִם עִיר קָדְשֶׁךָ, וְזִכְרוֹן כָּל עַמְּךָ בֵּית יִשְׂרָאֵל לְפָנֶיךָ, לִפְלֵיטָה, לְטוֹבָה, לְחֵן וּלְחֶסֶד וּלְרַחֲמִים, לְחַיִּים וּלְשָׁלוֹם, בְּיוֹם רֹאשׁ הַחֹדֶשׁ הַזֶּה.
זָכְרֵנוּ, יְיָ אֱלֹהֵינוּ, בּוֹ לְטוֹבָה, וּפָקְדֵנוּ בוֹ לִבְרָכָה, וְהוֹשִׁיעֵנוּ בוֹ לְחַיִּים, וּבִדְבַר יְשׁוּעָה וְרַחֲמִים חוּס וְחָנֵּנוּ, וְרַחֵם עָלֵינוּ וְהוֹשִׁיעֵנוּ, כִּי אֵלֶיךָ עֵינֵינוּ, כִּי אֵל מֶלֶךְ חַנּוּן וְרַחוּם אָתָּה.

Shabbat Evening Prayers

Shabbat Evening Amidah

We take three steps back and three steps forward as we say:

Adonai, open my lips so I may speak Your praise.

Adonai s'fatai tif'tach ufi yagid t'hilatecha.

Praised are You, Adonai our God and God of our ancestors, God of Abraham, God of Isaac, and God of Jacob, God of Sarah, God of Rebecca, God of Rachel, and God of Leah, the great, strong and awe-inspiring God, God on high. You act with lovingkindness and create everything. God remembers the loving deeds of our ancestors, and will bring a redeemer to their children's children because that is God's loving nature.

Baruch atah Adonai Eloheinu vElohei avoteinu, Elohei Av'raham, Elohei Yitz'chak, vElohei Ya-akov, Elohei Sarah, Elohei Riv'ka, Elohei Rachel, vElohei Le-ah. Ha-El hagadol hagibur v'hanora, El el'yon, gomel chasideem toveem, v'koneh hakol, v'zocher chasdei avot, umevee go-el liv'nei v'neihem l'ma-an sh'mo b'ahavah.

You are a helping, guarding, saving and shielding Ruler. Praised are You, Adonai, Shield of Abraham and Guardian of Sarah.

Melech ozer ufoked umoshee-a umagen. Baruch atah Adonai, magen Av'raham ufoked Sarah.

You are mighty forever, Adonai. You give life to the dead with Your great saving power.

Atah gibor l'olam Adonai, m'chayeh meteem atah rav l'hoshee-a.

From Shemini Atzeret until Pesach:

You cause the wind to blow and the rain to fall.

Masheev haru-ach umoreed hagashem.

You support the living with kindness. You give life to the dead with great mercy. You support the fallen, heal the sick and set free those in prison. You keep faith with those who sleep in the dust. Who is like You, mighty Ruler, and who can compare to You, Ruler of life and death who causes salvation to bloom.

M'chal'kel chayim b'chesed, m'chayeh meteem b'rachameem rabeem, somech nofleem, v'rofeh choleem, umateer asureem, um'kayem emunato leeshenei afar, mee chamocha ba-al g'vurot umee domeh lach, melech memeet um'chayeh umatz'mee-ach y'shu-ah.

You are trustworthy in giving life to the dead. Praised are You Adonai, who gives life to the dead.

V'ne-eman atah l'hachayot meteem. Baruch atah Adonai, m'chayeh hameteem.

You are holy and Your name is holy and holy beings praise You every day. Praised are You Adonai, the holy God.

Atah kadosh v'shim'cha kadosh uk'dosheem b'chol yom y'hal'lucha, selah. Baruch atah Adonai, ha-El hakadosh.

מעריב לשבת

עֲמִידָה שֶׁל מַעֲרִיב לְשַׁבָּת

DID YOU KNOW THAT... On Shabbat, the *Amidah* has the same basic structure as the weekday version, with one big difference. Instead of all of the usual blessings in the middle, we replace them with a special blessing that praises the holiness of Shabbat.

We take three steps back and three steps forward as we say:

אֲדֹנָי שְׂפָתַי תִּפְתָּח וּפִי יַגִּיד תְּהִלָּתֶךָ:

בָּרוּךְ אַתָּה יְיָ אֱלֹהֵינוּ וֵאלֹהֵי אֲבוֹתֵינוּ, אֱלֹהֵי אַבְרָהָם, אֱלֹהֵי יִצְחָק, וֵאלֹהֵי יַעֲקֹב, אֱלֹהֵי שָׂרָה, אֱלֹהֵי רִבְקָה, אֱלֹהֵי רָחֵל וֵאלֹהֵי לֵאָה. הָאֵל הַגָּדוֹל הַגִּבּוֹר וְהַנּוֹרָא, אֵל עֶלְיוֹן, גּוֹמֵל חֲסָדִים טוֹבִים, וְקוֹנֵה הַכֹּל, וְזוֹכֵר חַסְדֵי אָבוֹת, וּמֵבִיא גוֹאֵל לִבְנֵי בְנֵיהֶם לְמַעַן שְׁמוֹ בְּאַהֲבָה.

מֶלֶךְ עוֹזֵר וּפוֹקֵד וּמוֹשִׁיעַ וּמָגֵן: בָּרוּךְ אַתָּה יְיָ, מָגֵן אַבְרָהָם וּפוֹקֵד שָׂרָה:

אַתָּה גִּבּוֹר לְעוֹלָם אֲדֹנָי, מְחַיֵּה מֵתִים אַתָּה, רַב לְהוֹשִׁיעַ:

From Shemini Atzeret until Pesach:
מַשִּׁיב הָרוּחַ וּמוֹרִיד הַגֶּשֶׁם:

מְכַלְכֵּל חַיִּים בְּחֶסֶד, מְחַיֵּה מֵתִים בְּרַחֲמִים רַבִּים, סוֹמֵךְ נוֹפְלִים, וְרוֹפֵא חוֹלִים, וּמַתִּיר אֲסוּרִים, וּמְקַיֵּם אֱמוּנָתוֹ לִישֵׁנֵי עָפָר, מִי כָמוֹךָ בַּעַל גְּבוּרוֹת וּמִי דּוֹמֶה לָּךְ, מֶלֶךְ מֵמִית וּמְחַיֶּה וּמַצְמִיחַ יְשׁוּעָה:

וְנֶאֱמָן אַתָּה לְהַחֲיוֹת מֵתִים. בָּרוּךְ אַתָּה יְיָ, מְחַיֵּה הַמֵּתִים:

אַתָּה קָדוֹשׁ וְשִׁמְךָ קָדוֹשׁ וּקְדוֹשִׁים בְּכָל יוֹם יְהַלְלוּךָ, סֶּלָה. בָּרוּךְ אַתָּה יְיָ, הָאֵל הַקָּדוֹשׁ:

Shabbat Evening Prayers

Hash'keevenu

Adonai our God, keep us safe when we lie down to sleep, and wake us up in the morning, our Ruler, to life. Spread Your *sukkah* of peace over us; guide us with Your good advice. Shield us and protect us from enemies, sickness, war, hunger, and sadness. Hide us in the shadow of Your wings, because You are our protecting and rescuing God, a gracious and merciful Ruler. Always guard our going and our return with life and peace. Spread over us the *sukkah* of Your peace. Praised are You, Adonai who spreads a *sukkah* of peace over us, over our people Israel, and over Jerusalem.

Hash'keevenu Adonai Eloheinu l'shalom, v'ha-ameedenu malkenu l'chayeem uf'ros aleinu sukat sh'lomecha, v'tak'nenu b'etzah tovah mil'faneicha, v'hoshee-enu l'ma-an sh'mecha, v'hagen ba-adenu, v'haser me-aleinu oyev, dever, v'cherev, v'ra-av v'yagon, v'haser shatan mil'faneinu ume-acharenu, uv'tzal k'nafeicha tas'teerenu. Kee El shom'renu umatzeelenu atah, kee El melech chanun v'rachum atah, ❖ ush'mor tzetenu uvo-enu, l'chayeem ul'shalom, me-atah v'ad olam. Uf'ros aleinu sukat sh'lomecha. Baruch atah Adonai, hapores sukat shalom aleinu v'al kol amo yisra-el v'al y'rushalayim.

V'shamru

We rise.

The people of Israel shall keep the Shabbat, to make Shabbat in every generation as a forever covenant. It is a sign between Me and the people of Israel forever, that in six days Adonai made the heavens and the earth, and on the seventh day God stopped working and rested.

V'sham'ru v'nei Yisra-el et haShabbat,
La-asot et haShabbat l'dorotam b'reet olam.
Beinee uvein b'nei Yisra-el ot hee l'olam,
Kee sheshet yameem asah Adonai et hashamayim v'et ha-aretz,
Uvayom hash'vee'ee shavat vayinafash.

Chatzi Kaddish

Leader:

May God's great name be made great and holy in the world which God created according to God's will. May God establish Divine rule soon, in our days, quickly and in the near future, and let us say, Amen.

Yit'gadal v'yit'kadash sh'meh rabah. B'al'mah dee v'rah chir'utei, v'yam'leech mal'chutei b'chayeichon uv'yomeichon uv'chayei d'chol beit Yisra-el. Ba-agalah uviz'man kareev v'im'ru amen.

Everyone:

May God's great name be praised for ever and ever.

Y'heh sh'meh rabah m'varach l'alam ul'al'mei al'mayah.

Leader:

Blessed, praised, glorified and raised high, honored and elevated be the name of the Blessed Holy One, far beyond all blessings and songs, praises and words of comfort which people can say, and let us say: Amen.

Yit'barach v'yishtabach v'yitpa-ar v'yit'romam v'yit'naseh v'yit'hadar v'yit'aleh v'yit'halal sh'meh d'kud'shah b'reech hu l'elah min kol bir'chatah v'sheeratah tush'b'chatah v'nechematah, da-ameeran b'al'mah, v'im'ru amen.

מעריב לשבת

הַשְׁכִּיבֵנוּ

הַשְׁכִּיבֵנוּ יְיָ אֱלֹהֵינוּ לְשָׁלוֹם, וְהַעֲמִידֵנוּ מַלְכֵּנוּ לְחַיִּים וּפְרוֹשׂ עָלֵינוּ סֻכַּת שְׁלוֹמֶךָ, וְתַקְּנֵנוּ בְּעֵצָה טוֹבָה מִלְּפָנֶיךָ, וְהוֹשִׁיעֵנוּ לְמַעַן שְׁמֶךָ, וְהָגֵן בַּעֲדֵנוּ, וְהָסֵר מֵעָלֵינוּ אוֹיֵב, דֶּבֶר, וְחֶרֶב, וְרָעָב וְיָגוֹן, וְהָסֵר שָׂטָן מִלְּפָנֵינוּ וּמֵאַחֲרֵינוּ, וּבְצֵל כְּנָפֶיךָ תַּסְתִּירֵנוּ. כִּי אֵל שׁוֹמְרֵנוּ וּמַצִּילֵנוּ אָתָּה, כִּי אֵל מֶלֶךְ חַנּוּן וְרַחוּם אָתָּה, ❖ וּשְׁמוֹר צֵאתֵנוּ וּבוֹאֵנוּ, לְחַיִּים וּלְשָׁלוֹם, מֵעַתָּה וְעַד עוֹלָם. וּפְרוֹשׂ עָלֵינוּ סֻכַּת שְׁלוֹמֶךָ. בָּרוּךְ אַתָּה יְיָ, הַפּוֹרֵשׂ סֻכַּת שָׁלוֹם עָלֵינוּ וְעַל כָּל עַמּוֹ יִשְׂרָאֵל וְעַל יְרוּשָׁלָיִם.

וְשָׁמְרוּ
We rise.

וְשָׁמְרוּ בְנֵי יִשְׂרָאֵל אֶת הַשַּׁבָּת,
לַעֲשׂוֹת אֶת הַשַּׁבָּת לְדֹרֹתָם בְּרִית עוֹלָם:
בֵּינִי וּבֵין בְּנֵי יִשְׂרָאֵל אוֹת הִיא לְעוֹלָם,
כִּי שֵׁשֶׁת יָמִים עָשָׂה יְיָ אֶת הַשָּׁמַיִם וְאֶת הָאָרֶץ,
וּבַיּוֹם הַשְּׁבִיעִי שָׁבַת וַיִּנָּפַשׁ.
EXODUS 31:16–17

חֲצִי קַדִּישׁ
Leader:

יִתְגַּדַּל וְיִתְקַדַּשׁ שְׁמֵהּ רַבָּא. בְּעָלְמָא דִּי בְרָא כִרְעוּתֵיהּ, וְיַמְלִיךְ מַלְכוּתֵהּ בְּחַיֵּיכוֹן וּבְיוֹמֵיכוֹן וּבְחַיֵּי דְכָל בֵּית יִשְׂרָאֵל. בַּעֲגָלָא וּבִזְמַן קָרִיב וְאִמְרוּ אָמֵן.

Everyone:

יְהֵא שְׁמֵהּ רַבָּא מְבָרַךְ לְעָלַם וּלְעָלְמֵי עָלְמַיָּא:

Leader:

יִתְבָּרַךְ וְיִשְׁתַּבַּח וְיִתְפָּאַר וְיִתְרוֹמַם וְיִתְנַשֵּׂא וְיִתְהַדָּר וְיִתְעַלֶּה וְיִתְהַלָּל שְׁמֵהּ דְּקֻדְשָׁא בְּרִיךְ הוּא לְעֵלָּא מִן כָּל בִּרְכָתָא וְשִׁירָתָא תֻּשְׁבְּחָתָא וְנֶחֱמָתָא, דַּאֲמִירָן בְּעָלְמָא, וְאִמְרוּ אָמֵן:

Shabbat Evening Prayers

Adonai said to Moses: Speak to the people Israel and tell them to make fringes for the corners of their clothes in all future generations. They shall put a blue thread in the fringe of each corner. When they look at them they will remember all of Adonai's mitzvot, and do them, and they won't be led astray by their hearts or their eyes. Do this so that you will remember and do all My mitzvot, and you will be holy for your God. I am Adonai your God, who took you out of the land of Egypt to be your God. I, Adonai, am your God.

Vayomer Adonai el-Mosheh lemor. Daber el-b'nei Yisra-el v'amar'ta alehem v'asu lahem tzeetzit al-can'fei vig'deihem l'dorotam v'nat'nu al-tzeetzit hakanaf p'til t'chelet. V'haya lachem l'tzeetzit ur'eetem oto uz'char'tem et-kol-mitzvot Adonai va-aseetem otam v'lo taturu acharei l'vav'chem v'acharei eineichem asher-atem zoneem achareihem. L'ma'an tiz'k'ru va-aseetem et-kol mitz'votai vih'yeetem k'dosheem leloheichem. Ani Adonai Eloheichem asher hotzetee et'chem me-eretz mitz'rayim lih'yot lachem lEloheem ani Adonai Eloheichem.

Adonai, your God, is truth.

❖ Adonai Eloheichem emet.

Mee Chamocha

When the people of Israel saw God's wonders at the sea, They gave thanks to God in these words:

❖ Umal'chuto b'ratzon keeb'lu aleiheim, Moshe uv'nei Yisra-el l'cha anu sheera b'sim'cha rabah, v'am'ru chulam:

Who is like You, Adonai, among the mighty?
Who is like You, special in holiness,
Inspiring praises, doing wonders?

Mee chamocha ba-elim Adonai,
Mee kamocha ne'dar bakodesh,
Nora t'hilot oseh fele.

As You divided the sea before Moses, Your children beheld Your sovereignty. They said:

❖ Mal'chut'cha ra-u vaneicha, boke-a lif'nei moshe, zeh elee anu v'am'ru:

Adonai will rule for ever and ever.

Adonai yimloch l'olam va-ed.

And it is written: Adonai has rescued Jacob; God redeemed him from those more powerful. Praised are You, Adonai, who rescues Israel.

❖ V'ne-emar: Kee fadah Adonai et Ya'akov, ug'alo miyad chazak mimenu. Baruch atah Adonai, ga-al Yisra-el.

מעריב לשבת

וַיֹּאמֶר יְהֹוָה אֶל־מֹשֶׁה לֵּאמֹר: דַּבֵּר אֶל־בְּנֵי יִשְׂרָאֵל וְאָמַרְתָּ אֲלֵהֶם וְעָשׂוּ לָהֶם צִיצִת עַל־כַּנְפֵי בִגְדֵיהֶם לְדֹרֹתָם וְנָתְנוּ עַל־צִיצִת הַכָּנָף פְּתִיל תְּכֵלֶת: וְהָיָה לָכֶם לְצִיצִת וּרְאִיתֶם אֹתוֹ וּזְכַרְתֶּם אֶת־כָּל־מִצְוֹת יְהֹוָה וַעֲשִׂיתֶם אֹתָם וְלֹא תָתוּרוּ אַחֲרֵי לְבַבְכֶם וְאַחֲרֵי עֵינֵיכֶם אֲשֶׁר־אַתֶּם זֹנִים אַחֲרֵיהֶם: לְמַעַן תִּזְכְּרוּ וַעֲשִׂיתֶם אֶת־כָּל־מִצְוֹתָי וִהְיִיתֶם קְדֹשִׁים לֵאלֹהֵיכֶם: אֲנִי יְהֹוָה אֱלֹהֵיכֶם אֲשֶׁר הוֹצֵאתִי אֶתְכֶם מֵאֶרֶץ מִצְרַיִם לִהְיוֹת לָכֶם לֵאלֹהִים אֲנִי יְהֹוָה אֱלֹהֵיכֶם:

NUMBERS 15:37–41

❖ יְיָ אֱלֹהֵיכֶם אֱמֶת.

מִי כָמֹכָה

❖ וּמַלְכוּתוֹ בְּרָצוֹן קִבְּלוּ עֲלֵיהֶם, מֹשֶׁה וּבְנֵי יִשְׂרָאֵל לְךָ עָנוּ שִׁירָה בְּשִׂמְחָה רַבָּה, וְאָמְרוּ כֻלָּם:

מִי כָמֹכָה בָּאֵלִים יְיָ,
מִי כָּמֹכָה נֶאְדָּר בַּקֹּדֶשׁ,
נוֹרָא תְהִלֹּת, עֹשֵׂה פֶלֶא:

EXODUS 15:11

❖ מַלְכוּתְךָ רָאוּ בָנֶיךָ, בּוֹקֵעַ יָם לִפְנֵי מֹשֶׁה, זֶה אֵלִי עָנוּ וְאָמְרוּ: יְיָ יִמְלֹךְ לְעוֹלָם וָעֶד.

EXODUS 15:18

❖ וְנֶאֱמַר: כִּי פָדָה יְיָ אֶת יַעֲקֹב, וּגְאָלוֹ מִיַּד חָזָק מִמֶּנּוּ. בָּרוּךְ אַתָּה יְיָ, גָּאַל יִשְׂרָאֵל:

Shabbat Evening Prayers

Shema

God is a faithful ruler.	*If there is no minyan, add:* El melech ne-eman.
Hear O Israel, Adonai is our God, Adonai is One.	Sh'ma Yisra-el, Adonai Eloheinu, Adonai echad.
	Silently:
Praised be God's glorious name forever.	Baruch shem k'vod mal'chuto l'olam va-ed.

You will love Adonai your God with all your mind, soul, and might. Take to heart these words which I command you today. Teach them carefully to your children. Repeat them at home and away, morning and night. Bind them as a sign on your hand, and let them be a symbol above your eyes. Write them on the doorposts of your homes and on your gates.

V'ahav'ta et Adonai Eloheicha b'chol-l'vav'cha uv'chol-naf'sh'cha uv'chol-m'odecha. V'hayu had'vareem ha-eleh ahser anochi m'tzav'cha hayom al-l'vavecha. V'shinan'tam l'vaneicha v'dibar'ta bam b'shiv't'cha b'veitecha uv'lech't'cha baderech uv'shoch'b'cha uv'kumecha. Uk'shar'tam l'ot al-yadecha v'hayu l'totafot bein eineicha. Uch'tav'tam al m'zuzot beitecha uvish'areicha.

If you will really listen to My commandments which I command you today, to love Adonai your God and to serve God with all your heart and soul, then I will give your land rain at the proper season—rain in autumn and rain in spring—and you will gather in your grain and wine and oil. I will give grass in the fields for your cattle, and you will eat your fill. Beware that you are not tempted to turn aside and worship other gods. For then God will be angry at you and will shut up the skies and there will be no rain, and the earth will not give you its produce, and you will quickly disappear from the good land which God is giving to you. So keep these words in mind and take them to heart, and bind them as a sign on your hand, and let them be a symbol between your eyes. Teach them to your children, speaking of them at home and away, when you lie down and when you get up. Write them upon the doorposts of your house and upon your gates, so that your days and the days of your children will last long on the land which Adonai promised to your ancestors, to give to them for as long as the heavens and earth last.

V'haya im-shamo-a tish'm'u el-mitzvotai asher anochi m'tzaveh et'chem hayom l'ahavah et-Adonai Eloheichem ul'av'do b'chol-l'vav'chem uv'chol-naf'sh'chem. V'natatee m'tar-ar'tz'chem b'ito yoreh umal'kosh v'asaf'ta d'gonecha v'teerosh'cha v'yitz'harecha. V'natatee esev b'sad'cha liv'hem'techa v'achal'ta v'sava'ta. Hisham'ru lachem pen-yif'teh l'vav'chem v'sar'tem v-avad'tem Eloheem achereem v'hish'tachaveetem lahem. V'chara af-Adonai bachem v'atzar et-hashamayim v'lo-yih'yeh matar v'ha-adamah lo titen et-y'vulah va-avad'tem m'herah me-al ha-aretz hatovah asher Adonai noten lachem. V'sam'tem et-d'varai eleh al-l'vav'chem v'al-naf'sh'chem uk'shar'tem otam l'ot al-yedchem v'hayu l'totafot bein eineichem. V'limad'tem otam et-b'neichem l'daber bam b'shiv't'cha b'veitecha uv'lech't'cha baderech uv'shoch'b'cha uv'kumecha. Uch'tav'tam al-m'zuzot beitecha uvish'areicha. L'ma-an yirbu y'meichem veemei v'neichem al ha-adamah asher nish'ba Adonai la-avoteichem latet lahem keemei hashamayim al-ha-aretz.

מעריב לשבת

קְרִיאַת שְׁמַע

If there is no miyan, add: אֵל מֶלֶךְ נֶאֱמָן

שְׁמַע יִשְׂרָאֵל, יְיָ אֱלֹהֵינוּ, יְיָ אֶחָד:

Silently:
בָּרוּךְ שֵׁם כְּבוֹד מַלְכוּתוֹ לְעוֹלָם וָעֶד.

וְאָהַבְתָּ אֵת יְהֹוָה אֱלֹהֶיךָ בְּכָל־לְבָבְךָ וּבְכָל־נַפְשְׁךָ וּבְכָל־מְאֹדֶךָ: וְהָיוּ הַדְּבָרִים הָאֵלֶּה אֲשֶׁר אָנֹכִי מְצַוְּךָ הַיּוֹם עַל־לְבָבֶךָ: וְשִׁנַּנְתָּם לְבָנֶיךָ וְדִבַּרְתָּ בָּם בְּשִׁבְתְּךָ בְּבֵיתֶךָ וּבְלֶכְתְּךָ בַדֶּרֶךְ וּבְשָׁכְבְּךָ וּבְקוּמֶךָ: וּקְשַׁרְתָּם לְאוֹת עַל־יָדֶךָ וְהָיוּ לְטֹטָפֹת בֵּין עֵינֶיךָ: וּכְתַבְתָּם עַל־מְזֻזוֹת בֵּיתֶךָ וּבִשְׁעָרֶיךָ:

DEUTERONOMY 6:4–9

וְהָיָה אִם־שָׁמֹעַ תִּשְׁמְעוּ אֶל־מִצְוֺתַי אֲשֶׁר אָנֹכִי מְצַוֶּה אֶתְכֶם הַיּוֹם לְאַהֲבָה אֶת־יְהֹוָה אֱלֹהֵיכֶם וּלְעָבְדוֹ בְּכָל־לְבַבְכֶם וּבְכָל־נַפְשְׁכֶם: וְנָתַתִּי מְטַר־אַרְצְכֶם בְּעִתּוֹ יוֹרֶה וּמַלְקוֹשׁ וְאָסַפְתָּ דְגָנֶךָ וְתִירֹשְׁךָ וְיִצְהָרֶךָ: וְנָתַתִּי עֵשֶׂב בְּשָׂדְךָ לִבְהֶמְתֶּךָ וְאָכַלְתָּ וְשָׂבָעְתָּ: הִשָּׁמְרוּ לָכֶם פֶּן־יִפְתֶּה לְבַבְכֶם וְסַרְתֶּם וַעֲבַדְתֶּם אֱלֹהִים אֲחֵרִים וְהִשְׁתַּחֲוִיתֶם לָהֶם: וְחָרָה אַף־יְהֹוָה בָּכֶם וְעָצַר אֶת־הַשָּׁמַיִם וְלֹא־יִהְיֶה מָטָר וְהָאֲדָמָה לֹא תִתֵּן אֶת־יְבוּלָהּ וַאֲבַדְתֶּם מְהֵרָה מֵעַל הָאָרֶץ הַטֹּבָה אֲשֶׁר יְהֹוָה נֹתֵן לָכֶם: וְשַׂמְתֶּם אֶת־דְּבָרַי אֵלֶּה עַל־לְבַבְכֶם וְעַל־נַפְשְׁכֶם וּקְשַׁרְתֶּם אֹתָם לְאוֹת עַל־יֶדְכֶם וְהָיוּ לְטוֹטָפֹת בֵּין עֵינֵיכֶם: וְלִמַּדְתֶּם אֹתָם אֶת־בְּנֵיכֶם לְדַבֵּר בָּם בְּשִׁבְתְּךָ בְּבֵיתֶךָ וּבְלֶכְתְּךָ בַדֶּרֶךְ וּבְשָׁכְבְּךָ וּבְקוּמֶךָ: וּכְתַבְתָּם עַל־מְזוּזוֹת בֵּיתֶךָ וּבִשְׁעָרֶיךָ: לְמַעַן יִרְבּוּ יְמֵיכֶם וִימֵי בְנֵיכֶם עַל הָאֲדָמָה אֲשֶׁר נִשְׁבַּע יְהֹוָה לַאֲבֹתֵיכֶם לָתֵת לָהֶם כִּימֵי הַשָּׁמַיִם עַל־הָאָרֶץ:

DEUTERONOMY 11:13–21

Shabbat Evening Prayers

Shabbat Evening Prayers

Barchu

We rise and the leader sings:
Praise Adonai, who is to be praised.
Bar'chu et Adonai ham'vorach.

Everyone replies, then the leader repeats:
Praised be Adonai who is to be praised for ever and ever.
Baruch Adonai ham'vorach l'olam va-ed.

Praised are You, Adonai our God, Ruler of the universe, whose word brings the evening. With wisdom God opens the gates of the heavens, changes the times of day with understanding, exchanges the seasons, and puts the stars in their proper place and order in the sky. Creator of day and night, rolling the light away before the darkness and the darkness before the light. God causes the day to pass and brings night, separating between day and night—*Adonai Tzeva'ot* is God's name. The God who lives forever will rule over us for ever and ever. Praised are You, Adonai, who brings the evening.

Baruch atah Adonai, Eloheinu melech ha-olam, asher bid'varo ma-ariv Araveem, b'chochmah pote-ach sh'areem, uvit'vunah m'shaneh iteem, umachaleef et haz'maneem, umsader et hakochaveem, b'meesh'm'roteihem barakee-a kir'tzono. Boreh yom valai'la, golel or mip'nei choshech, v'choshech mip'nei or. ❖ Uma-aveer yom umevee lai'lah, umav'deel bein yom uvein lai'lah, Adonai tzeva-ot sh'mo. El chai v'kayam, tameed yim'loch aleinu l'olam va-ed. Baruch atah Adonai, hama-areev araveem.

Ahavat Olam

You have always loved Your people Israel by teaching us Torah, mitzvot, laws and justice. Therefore, Adonai our God, when we lie down at night and when we get up in the morning we will talk about Your laws. We will always be happy with the words of Your Torah and Your commandments, because they are our life, and they give long life; we will think about them day and night. May You never take Your love away from us. Praised are You, Adonai, who loves the people Israel.

Ahavat olam beit Yisra-el am'cha ahav'ta, Torah umitz'vot, chukeem umish'pateem, otanu limad'ta al ken Adonai Eloheinu, b'shoch'venu uv'kumenu nasee-ach b'chukecha, v'nis'mach b'div'rei Toratecha uv'mitz'voteicha l'olam va-ed. Kee hem chayeinu v'orech yameimu, uvahem neh'geh yomam valai'lah, ❖ v'ahavat'cha al tasir mimenu l'olamim. Baruch atah Adonai, ohev amo Yisra-el.

מַעֲרִיב לְשַׁבָּת

> Now that we have welcomed the Shabbat Queen, we are ready to say our *Ma-ariv* prayers for Shabbat. Just like Weekday *Ma-ariv*, we say the *Sh'ma* and the *Amidah*. But, there are a few differences; we add a few special prayers to celebrate Shabbat.

בָּרְכוּ

We rise and the leader sings:

בָּרְכוּ אֶת יְיָ הַמְבֹרָךְ:

Everyone replies, then the leader repeats:

בָּרוּךְ יְיָ הַמְבֹרָךְ לְעוֹלָם וָעֶד:

בָּרוּךְ אַתָּה יְיָ, אֱלֹהֵינוּ מֶלֶךְ הָעוֹלָם, אֲשֶׁר בִּדְבָרוֹ מַעֲרִיב עֲרָבִים, בְּחָכְמָה פּוֹתֵחַ שְׁעָרִים, וּבִתְבוּנָה מְשַׁנֶּה עִתִּים, וּמַחֲלִיף אֶת הַזְּמַנִּים, וּמְסַדֵּר אֶת הַכּוֹכָבִים, בְּמִשְׁמְרוֹתֵיהֶם בָּרָקִיעַ כִּרְצוֹנוֹ. בּוֹרֵא יוֹם וָלָיְלָה, גּוֹלֵל אוֹר מִפְּנֵי חֹשֶׁךְ, וְחֹשֶׁךְ מִפְּנֵי אוֹר. ❖ וּמַעֲבִיר יוֹם וּמֵבִיא לָיְלָה, וּמַבְדִּיל בֵּין יוֹם וּבֵין לָיְלָה, יְיָ צְבָאוֹת שְׁמוֹ. אֵל חַי וְקַיָּם, תָּמִיד יִמְלֹךְ עָלֵינוּ לְעוֹלָם וָעֶד. בָּרוּךְ אַתָּה יְיָ, הַמַּעֲרִיב עֲרָבִים:

אַהֲבַת עוֹלָם

אַהֲבַת עוֹלָם בֵּית יִשְׂרָאֵל עַמְּךָ אָהָבְתָּ, תּוֹרָה וּמִצְוֹת, חֻקִּים וּמִשְׁפָּטִים, אוֹתָנוּ לִמַּדְתָּ עַל כֵּן יְיָ אֱלֹהֵינוּ, בְּשָׁכְבֵנוּ וּבְקוּמֵנוּ נָשִׂיחַ בְּחֻקֶּיךָ, וְנִשְׂמַח בְּדִבְרֵי תוֹרָתֶךָ וּבְמִצְוֹתֶיךָ לְעוֹלָם וָעֶד. כִּי הֵם חַיֵּינוּ וְאֹרֶךְ יָמֵינוּ, וּבָהֶם נֶהְגֶּה יוֹמָם וָלָיְלָה, ❖ וְאַהֲבָתְךָ אַל תָּסִיר מִמֶּנּוּ לְעוֹלָמִים. בָּרוּךְ אַתָּה יְיָ, אוֹהֵב עַמּוֹ יִשְׂרָאֵל:

Shabbat Evening Prayers

The good will bloom like a date-palm,	Tzadeek katamar yif'rach
They will grow strong like a cedar of Lebanon.	K'erez bal'vanon yis'geh.
Planted in Adonai's house,	Sh'tuleem b'veit Adonai
They blossom in our God's courts.	B'chatz'rot Eloheinu yaf'richu.
They still bear fruit even in old age, still healthy and fresh.	Od y'nuvun b'seivah D'sheneem v'ra-ananeem yih'yu.
Still telling all: Adonai is just,	L'hageed kee yashar Adonai
My Rock, who can do no wrong.	Tzuree v'lo av'latah bo.

"Grant me the privilege of the liberating joy of Shabbat, the privilege of truly tasting the delight of Shabbat. May I be undisturbed by sadness, by sorrow, or by sighing during the holy hours of Shabbat. Fill Your servant's heart with joy, for to You, Adonai, I offer my entire being. Let me hear joy and jubilation. Help me to expand the dimensions of all Shabbat delights. Help me to extend the joy of Shabbat to the other days of the week, until I attain the goal of deep joy always. Show me the path of life, the full joy of Your Presence, the bliss of being close to You forever."

—Rabbi Jules Harlow

צַדִּיק כַּתָּמָר יִפְרָח כְּאֶרֶז בַּלְּבָנוֹן יִשְׂגֶּה:
שְׁתוּלִים בְּבֵית יְיָ בְּחַצְרוֹת אֱלֹהֵינוּ יַפְרִיחוּ:
עוֹד יְנוּבוּן בְּשֵׂיבָה דְּשֵׁנִים וְרַעֲנַנִּים יִהְיוּ:
לְהַגִּיד כִּי יָשָׁר יְיָ צוּרִי וְלֹא עַוְלָתָה בּוֹ.

PSALM 92:13–16

In your redemption you will never be shamed,
Be not downcast, you will not be defamed.
Sheltered by you will my poor be reclaimed.
The city renewed from its ruins is raised.

Come, my beloved...

Then your destroyers will themselves be destroyed;
Ravagers, at great distance, will live in a void.
Your God then will celebrate you, overjoyed,
As a groom with his bride when her eyes meet his gaze.

Come, my beloved...

Break out of your confines, to the left and the right.
Revere Adonai in whom we delight.
The Messiah is coming to gladden our sight,
Bringing joy and rejoicing in fullness of days.

Come, my beloved...

We rise and face the entrance.

Come in peace, soul-mate, sweet Bride so adored,
Greeted with joy, in song and accord,
Amidst God's people, the faithful restored,
Come, Bride Shabbat; come, crown of the days.

Come, my beloved...

Lo tevoshee v'lo tikal'mee.
Mah tish'tochachee umah tehemee.
Bach yechesu aniyei amee,
V'niv'n'tah eer al tilah.

L'chah dodee lik'rat kalah.
Penei Shabbat n'kab'lah.

V'hayu lim'shisah Shosayich.
V'rachaku Kol m'val'ayich.
Yasis alayich Elohayich.
Kimsos chatan al kalah.

L'chah dodee lik'rat kalah.
Penei Shabbat n'kab'lah.

Yamin us'mol tif'rotzee.
V'et-Adonai Ta-aritzee.
Al yad eesh ben partzee.
V'nis'm'chah v'nageelah.

L'chah dodee lik'rat kalah.
Penei Shabbat n'kab'lah.

Bo-ee v'shalom ateret ba'lah.
Gam b'sim'cha uv'tzohalah.
Toch emunei am s'gulah.
Bo-ee chalah, bo-ee chalah.

L'chah dodee lik'rat kalah.
Penei Shabbat n'kab'lah.

We are seated.

לֹא תֵבוֹשִׁי וְלֹא תִכָּלְמִי.
מַה תִּשְׁתּוֹחֲחִי וּמַה תֶּהֱמִי.
בָּךְ יֶחֱסוּ עֲנִיֵּי עַמִּי,
וְנִבְנְתָה עִיר עַל תִּלָּהּ:

לְכָה דוֹדִי לִקְרַאת כַּלָּה. פְּנֵי שַׁבָּת נְקַבְּלָה:

וְהָיוּ לִמְשִׁסָּה שֹׁאסָיִךְ.
וְרָחֲקוּ כָּל מְבַלְּעָיִךְ.
יָשִׂישׂ עָלַיִךְ אֱלֹהָיִךְ.
כִּמְשׂוֹשׂ חָתָן עַל כַּלָּה:

לְכָה דוֹדִי לִקְרַאת כַּלָּה. פְּנֵי שַׁבָּת נְקַבְּלָה:

יָמִין וּשְׂמֹאל תִּפְרוֹצִי.
וְאֶת־יְיָ תַּעֲרִיצִי.
עַל יַד אִישׁ בֶּן פַּרְצִי.
וְנִשְׂמְחָה וְנָגִילָה:

לְכָה דוֹדִי לִקְרַאת כַּלָּה. פְּנֵי שַׁבָּת נְקַבְּלָה:

We rise and face the entrance.

בּוֹאִי בְשָׁלוֹם עֲטֶרֶת בַּעְלָהּ.
גַּם בְּשִׂמְחָה וּבְצָהֳלָה.
תּוֹךְ אֱמוּנֵי עַם סְגֻלָּה.
בּוֹאִי כַלָּה, בּוֹאִי כַלָּה:

לְכָה דוֹדִי לִקְרַאת כַּלָּה. פְּנֵי שַׁבָּת נְקַבְּלָה:

We are seated.

Welcoming Shabbat

L'cha Dodi

Come, my beloved, with chorus of praise;
Welcome Shabbat the Bride, Queen of our days.

Keep and remember, both uttered as one
By our Creator, beyond comparison.
Adonai is One and God's name is One,
Reflected in glory, in fame, and in praise.

Come, my beloved...

Come, let us greet Shabbat, Queen sublime,
Fountain of blessings in every clime.
Anointed and regal since earliest time,
In thought she preceded Creation's six days.

Come, my beloved...

Holy city, majestic, banish your fears.
Arise, emerge from your desolate years.
Too long have you dwelled in the valley of tears.
God will restore you with mercy and grace.

Come, my beloved...

Arise and shake off the dust of the earth.
Wear glorious garments reflecting your worth.
Messiah will lead us all soon to rebirth.
Let my soul now sense redemption's warm rays.

Come, my beloved...

Awake and arise to greet the new light
For in your radiance the world will be bright.
Sing out, for darkness is hidden from sight.
Through you Adonai's glory displays.

Come, my beloved...

L'chah dodee lik'rat kalah.
Penei Shabbat n'kab'lah.

Shamor v'zachor b'dibur echad,
Hish'meeanu El ham'yuchad.
Adonai echad ush'mo echad.
L'shem ul'tif'eret v'lit'hilah.

L'chah dodee lik'rat kalah.
Penei Shabbat n'kab'lah.

Lik'rat Shabbat l'chu v'nelcha.
Kee hee m'kor hab'rachah.
Merosh mikedem n'sucha.
Sof ma'aseh b'machashavah t'chilah.

L'chah dodee lik'rat kalah.
Penei Shabbat n'kab'lah.

Mikdash melech eer m'luchah.
Kumee tz'ee mitoch hahafechah.
Rav lach shevet b'emek habacha.
V'hu yachamol alayich chemlah.

L'chah dodee lik'rat kalah.
Penei Shabbat n'kab'lah.

Hit'na-ari me-afar kumee.
Liv'shee bigdei tif'ar'tech amee.
Al yad ben yishai beit halach'mee.
Kor'vah el naf'shee g'alah.

L'chah dodee lik'rat kalah.
Penei Shabbat n'kab'lah.

Hit'or'ree hit'or'ree.
Kee va orech kumee oree.
Uree uree sheer daberee.
K'vod Adonai alayich nig'la.

L'chah dodee lik'rat kalah.
Penei Shabbat n'kab'lah.

לְכָה דוֹדִי

לְכָה דוֹדִי לִקְרַאת כַּלָּה. פְּנֵי שַׁבָּת נְקַבְּלָה:

שָׁמוֹר וְזָכוֹר בְּדִבּוּר אֶחָד,
הִשְׁמִיעָנוּ אֵל הַמְיֻחָד.
יְיָ אֶחָד וּשְׁמוֹ אֶחָד.
לְשֵׁם וּלְתִפְאֶרֶת וְלִתְהִלָּה:

לְכָה דוֹדִי לִקְרַאת כַּלָּה. פְּנֵי שַׁבָּת נְקַבְּלָה:

לִקְרַאת שַׁבָּת לְכוּ וְנֵלְכָה.
כִּי הִיא מְקוֹר הַבְּרָכָה.
מֵרֹאשׁ מִקֶּדֶם נְסוּכָה.
סוֹף מַעֲשֶׂה בְּמַחֲשָׁבָה תְּחִלָּה:

לְכָה דוֹדִי לִקְרַאת כַּלָּה. פְּנֵי שַׁבָּת נְקַבְּלָה:

מִקְדַּשׁ מֶלֶךְ עִיר מְלוּכָה.
קוּמִי צְאִי מִתּוֹךְ הַהֲפֵכָה.
רַב לָךְ שֶׁבֶת בְּעֵמֶק הַבָּכָא.
וְהוּא יַחֲמוֹל עָלַיִךְ חֶמְלָה:

לְכָה דוֹדִי לִקְרַאת כַּלָּה. פְּנֵי שַׁבָּת נְקַבְּלָה:

הִתְנַעֲרִי מֵעָפָר קוּמִי.
לִבְשִׁי בִּגְדֵי תִפְאַרְתֵּךְ עַמִּי:
עַל יַד בֶּן יִשַׁי בֵּית הַלַּחְמִי.
קָרְבָה אֶל נַפְשִׁי גְאָלָהּ:

לְכָה דוֹדִי לִקְרַאת כַּלָּה. פְּנֵי שַׁבָּת נְקַבְּלָה:

הִתְעוֹרְרִי הִתְעוֹרְרִי.
כִּי בָא אוֹרֵךְ קוּמִי אוֹרִי.
עוּרִי עוּרִי שִׁיר דַּבֵּרִי.
כְּבוֹד יְיָ עָלַיִךְ נִגְלָה:

לְכָה דוֹדִי לִקְרַאת כַּלָּה. פְּנֵי שַׁבָּת נְקַבְּלָה:

Come let us sing to Adonai with joy,	L'chu n'ran'nah lAdonai
Shout with joy for our	Naree-ah l'tzur yish'enu.
Rock who saves us.	N'kad'mah fanav b'todah
Let us come before God with thanks,	Biz'mirot naree-a lo.
singing songs of praise!	Kee El gadol Adonai
Adonai is a great God, a great Ruler over	Umelech gadol al kol Eloheem.
all the heavenly beings.	Asher b'yado mech'k'rei aretz
God's hand holds the depths of the earth	v'to-afot hareem lo.
and the mountain tops.	

Let the heavens rejoice	Yis'm'chu hashamayeem v'tagel ha-aretz
and the earth be glad.	yir'am hayam um'lo-o.
Let the sea and all within it thunder.	

God is saving up a special light for those who are good,	Or zarua latzadeek ul'yishrei lev sim'cha.
And happiness for the honest.	

We rise.

A psalm of David.	Mizmor l'David.
Applaud Adonai, all the mighty.	Havu lAdonai b'nei eleem
Praise Adonai's glory and might.	Havu lAdonai kavod va-oz.
Praise Adonai's glorious name.	Havu lAdonai k'vod sh'mo
Bow down to Adonai's splendid holiness.	Hish'tachavu lAdonai b'had'rat kodesh.
Adonai's voice sounds over the waters,	Kol Adonai al hamayim
Thunders over many waters.	El hakavod hir'im
Adonai's voice is power.	Adonai al mayim rabeem.
Adonai's voice is majestic.	Kol Adonai bako-ach
Adonai's voice shatters the cedars of Lebanon.	Kol Adonai behadar.
	Kol Adonai shover arazeem
God makes them leap like a calf,	Vay'shaber Adonai et ar'zei hal'vanon,
The hills of Sirion like a young wild ox.	Vayar'keedem k'mo egel
Adonai's voice carves out flames of fire.	L'vanon v'sir'yon k'mo ven r'emeem,
Adonai's voice makes the wilderness shake.	Kol Adonai chotzev lahavot esh,
	Kol Adonai yacheel mid'bar,
Adonai's voice makes the trees dance,	Yachil Adonai midbar kadesh.
It strips the forest bare,	Kol Adonai y'cholel ayalot
While in God's Temple all say, "Glory!"	Vayechsof y'arot
Just as Adonai ruled at the time of the Flood,	uv'heichalo kulo omer kavod.
	Adonai lamabul yashav
So Adonai will rule forever.	Vayeshev Adonai melech l'olam.
Adonai will give strength to God's people.	Adonai oz l'amo yiten
Adonai will bless God's people with peace.	Adonai y'varech et amo vashalom.

We are seated.

קבלת שבת

לְכוּ נְרַנְּנָה לַיְיָ נָרִיעָה לְצוּר יִשְׁעֵנוּ:
נְקַדְּמָה פָנָיו בְּתוֹדָה בִּזְמִרוֹת נָרִיעַ לוֹ:
כִּי אֵל גָּדוֹל יְיָ וּמֶלֶךְ גָּדוֹל עַל כָּל אֱלֹהִים:
אֲשֶׁר בְּיָדוֹ מֶחְקְרֵי אָרֶץ וְתוֹעֲפוֹת הָרִים לוֹ:
PSALM 95:1–4

יִשְׂמְחוּ הַשָּׁמַיִם וְתָגֵל הָאָרֶץ יִרְעַם הַיָּם וּמְלֹאוֹ:
PSALM 96:11

אוֹר זָרֻעַ לַצַּדִּיק וּלְיִשְׁרֵי לֵב שִׂמְחָה:
PSALM 97:11

We rise.

מִזְמוֹר לְדָוִד
הָבוּ לַיְיָ בְּנֵי אֵלִים הָבוּ לַיְיָ כָּבוֹד וָעֹז:
הָבוּ לַיְיָ כְּבוֹד שְׁמוֹ הִשְׁתַּחֲווּ לַיְיָ בְּהַדְרַת קֹדֶשׁ:
קוֹל יְיָ עַל הַמָּיִם אֵל הַכָּבוֹד הִרְעִים
יְיָ עַל מַיִם רַבִּים:
קוֹל יְיָ בַּכֹּחַ קוֹל יְיָ בֶּהָדָר:
קוֹל יְיָ שֹׁבֵר אֲרָזִים וַיְשַׁבֵּר יְיָ אֶת אַרְזֵי הַלְּבָנוֹן,
וַיַּרְקִידֵם כְּמוֹ עֵגֶל לְבָנוֹן וְשִׂרְיֹן כְּמוֹ בֶן רְאֵמִים,
קוֹל יְיָ חֹצֵב לַהֲבוֹת אֵשׁ,
קוֹל יְיָ יָחִיל מִדְבָּר, יָחִיל יְיָ מִדְבַּר קָדֵשׁ:
קוֹל יְיָ יְחוֹלֵל אַיָּלוֹת
וַיֶּחֱשֹׂף יְעָרוֹת וּבְהֵיכָלוֹ כֻּלּוֹ אֹמֵר כָּבוֹד:
יְיָ לַמַּבּוּל יָשָׁב וַיֵּשֶׁב יְיָ מֶלֶךְ לְעוֹלָם:
יְיָ עֹז לְעַמּוֹ יִתֵּן יְיָ יְבָרֵךְ אֶת עַמּוֹ בַשָּׁלוֹם:
PSALM 29

We are seated.

Welcoming Shabbat

Y'deed Nefesh

Soul mate, loving God,
compassion's gentle source,
Take my disposition
and shape it to Your will.
Like a darting deer will I rush to You.
Before Your glorious Presence
humbly will I bow.
Let Your sweet love delight me
with its thrill,
Because no other dainty
will my hunger still.

How splendid is Your light,
illumining the world.
My soul is weary
yearning for Your love's delight.
Please, good God, do heal her;
reveal to her Your face,
The pleasure of Your Presence,
bathed in Your grace.
She will find strength
and healing in Your sight;
Forever will she serve You,
grateful, with all her might.

What mercy stirs in You
since days of old, my God.
Be kind to me, Your own child;
my love for You requite.
With deep and endless longing
I yearned for Your embrace,
To see my light in Your light,
basking in Your grace.
My heart's desire,
find me worthy in Your sight.
Do not delay Your mercy,
please hide not Your light.

Reveal Yourself,
Beloved, for all the world to see,
And shelter me in peace
beneath Your canopy.
Illumine all creation, lighting up the earth,
And we shall celebrate
You in choruses of mirth.
The time, my Love,
is now; rush, be quick, be bold.
Let Your favor grace me,
in the spirit of days of old.

Y'deed nefesh, av harachaman,
M'shoch av'dach el r'tzonach
Yarutz av'dach k'mo ayal,
Yish'tachaveh el mul hadarach
Ye-erav lo y'didutach
Minofet tzuf v'chol-ta-am.

Hadur, na-eh, zeev ha-olam,
Naf'shee cholat ahavatach
Ana, El na, r'fa na la
b'har'ot lah no-am zeevach
Az tit'chazek v'tit'rapeh,
V'hay'ta lach shif'chat olam.

Vateek, yehemu rachamecha,
V'chus na al ben ohavach
Kee zeh kamah nich'sof nich'saf
Lir'ot b'tif'eret uzach
Ana, Elee, mach'mad libee,
Chushah na, v'al tit'alam.

Higaleh na, uf'ros chaveev, alai
Et-sukat sh'lomach
Ta-eer eretz mik'vodach,
Nageelah v'nis'm'cha bach
Maher, Ahuv, kee va mo-ed,
V'chonenee keemei olam.

קבלת שבת

יְדִיד נֶפֶשׁ

יְדִיד נֶפֶשׁ, אָב הָרַחֲמָן, מְשׁוֹךְ עַבְדְּךָ אֶל רְצוֹנֶךְ
יָרוּץ עַבְדְּךָ כְּמוֹ אַיָּל, יִשְׁתַּחֲוֶה אֶל מוּל הֲדָרֶךְ
יֶעֱרַב לוֹ יְדִידוּתָךְ מִנֹּפֶת צוּף וְכָל־טָעַם.

הָדוּר, נָאֶה, זִיו הָעוֹלָם, נַפְשִׁי חוֹלַת אַהֲבָתָךְ
אָנָּא, אֵל נָא, רְפָא נָא לָהּ בְּהַרְאוֹת לָהּ נֹעַם זִיוֶךְ
אָז תִּתְחַזֵּק וְתִתְרַפֵּא, וְהָיְתָה לָךְ שִׁפְחַת עוֹלָם.

וָתִיק, יֶהֱמוּ רַחֲמֶךָ, וְחוּס נָא עַל בֵּן אוֹהֲבָךְ
כִּי זֶה כַּמָּה נִכְסוֹף נִכְסַף לִרְאוֹת בְּתִפְאֶרֶת עֻזֶּךְ
אָנָּא, אֵלִי, מַחְמַד לִבִּי, חוּשָׁה נָא, וְאַל תִּתְעַלָּם.

הִגָּלֶה נָא וּפְרֹשׂ, חָבִיב, עָלַי אֶת־סֻכַּת שְׁלוֹמֶךָ
תָּאִיר אֶרֶץ מִכְּבוֹדָךְ, נָגִילָה וְנִשְׂמְחָה בָּךְ
מַהֵר, אָהוּב, כִּי בָא מוֹעֵד, וְחָנֵּנִי כִּימֵי עוֹלָם.

Welcoming Shabbat

"In the beginning there was darkness and the spirit of God hovered over the darkness. Then God created light, and the work of creation was begun. As we kindle the Sabbath lights, we remember the majesty of creation and rejoice in our ability to attest to it. Light is a symbol of divinity and creative goodness. It is the outward sign of the inner spark God has shared with each of us. Light is the symbol of law and justice. It reminds us of our commitment to God's commandments. Light is a symbol of warmth and unity. It binds us together with Jews in all lands who are kindling the Sabbath lights."

—Congregation Beth El

Candle Lighting

Praised are You, Adonai our God, Ruler of the universe, who made us holy with mitzvot, and who gave us the mitzvah to light the Shabbat candles.

Baruch atah Adonai Eloheinu melech ha-olam, asher kid'shanu b'mitzvotav, v'tzivanu l'hadleek ner shel Shabbat.

קַבָּלַת שַׁבָּת

> Shabbat is a very special time at Camp Solomon Schechter. We clean up and make everything look nice, we put on nicer clothes, and we prepare good food. We make all these preparations to welcome Shabbat. After lighting the candles and singing The Sabbath Prayer, we sing selections from psalms that represent the six work days of the week. Then we sing *L'cha Dodi* to welcome the Shabbat Queen. Shabbat is so special that we welcome it into camp like royalty.

הַדְלָקַת נֵרוֹת

בָּרוּךְ אַתָּה יְיָ אֱלֹהֵינוּ מֶלֶךְ הָעוֹלָם, אֲשֶׁר קִדְּשָׁנוּ בְּמִצְוֹתָיו, וְצִוָּנוּ לְהַדְלִיק נֵר שֶׁל שַׁבָּת.

The Sabbath Prayer
May the Lord protect and defend you.
May God always shield you from shame.
May you come to be in Yisrael a shining name.
May you be like Ruth and like Esther.
May you be deserving of praise.
Strengthen us O Lord and keep us from the stranger's way.
W: May God bless you and grant you long life.
M: May the Lord fulfill our Sabbath Prayer for you.
W: May God keep you and shield you from strife.
M: May God in God's wisdom always care for you.
W: May the Lord protect and defend you.
M: (repeat)
W: May God always shield you from shame.
M: (repeat)
W: Favor us, O Lord.
M: (repeat)
W: With happiness and peace
M: With happiness, O...
O hear our Sabbath Prayer. Amen.
May the Lord protect and defend you. Amen.

Welcoming Shabbat

Hash'keevenu

Adonai our God, keep us safe when we lie down to sleep, and wake us up in the morning, our Ruler, to life. Spread Your *sukkah* of peace over us; guide us with Your good advice. Shield us and protect us from enemies, sickness, war, hunger, and sadness. Hide us in the shadow of Your wings, because You are our protecting and rescuing God, a gracious and merciful Ruler. Always guard our going and our return with life and peace. Praised are You Adonai, Guardian of Your people Israel.

Hash'keevenu Adonai Eloheinu l'shalom, v'ha-ameedenu malkenu l'chayeem uf'ros aleinu sukat sh'lomecha, v'tak'nenu b'etzah tovah mil'faneicha, v'hoshee-enu l'ma-an sh'mecha, v'hagen ba-adenu, v'haser me-aleinu oyev, dever, v'cherev, v'ra-av v'yagon, v'haser shatan mil'faneinu umeacharenu, uv'tzal k'nafeicha tas'teerenu. Kee El shom'renu umatzeelenu atah, kee El melech chanun v'rachum atah, ❖ ush'mor tzetenu uvo-enu, l'chayeem ul'shalom, meatah v'ad olam. Baruch atah Adonai, shomer amo Yisra-el la-ad.

Chatzi Kaddish

Leader:

May God's great name be made great and holy in the world which God created according to God's will. May God establish Divine rule soon, in our days, quickly and in the near future, and let us say, Amen.

Yit'gadal v'yit'kadash sh'meh rabah. B'al'mah dee v'rah chir'utei, v'yam'leech mal'chutei b'chayeichon uv'yomeichon uv'chayei d'chol beit Yisra-el. Ba-agalah uviz'man kareev v'im'ru amen.

Everyone:

May God's great name be praised for ever and ever.

Y'heh sh'meh rabah m'varach l'alam ul'al'mei al'mayah.

Leader:

Blessed, praised, glorified and raised high, honored and elevated be the name of the Blessed Holy One, far beyond all blessings and songs, praises and words of comfort which people can say, and let us say: Amen.

Yit'barach v'yishtabach v'yitpa-ar v'yit'romam v'yit'naseh v'yit'hadar v'yit'aleh v'yit'halal sh'meh d'kud'shah b'reech hu l'elah min kol bir'chatah v'sheeratah tush'b'chatah v'nechematah, da-ameeran b'al'mah, v'im'ru amen.

הַשְׁכִּיבֵנוּ

הַשְׁכִּיבֵנוּ יְיָ אֱלֹהֵינוּ לְשָׁלוֹם, וְהַעֲמִידֵנוּ מַלְכֵּנוּ לְחַיִּים וּפְרוֹשׂ עָלֵינוּ סֻכַּת שְׁלוֹמֶךָ, וְתַקְּנֵנוּ בְּעֵצָה טוֹבָה מִלְּפָנֶיךָ, וְהוֹשִׁיעֵנוּ לְמַעַן שְׁמֶךָ, וְהָגֵן בַּעֲדֵנוּ, וְהָסֵר מֵעָלֵינוּ אוֹיֵב, דֶּבֶר, וְחֶרֶב, וְרָעָב וְיָגוֹן, וְהָסֵר שָׂטָן מִלְּפָנֵינוּ וּמֵאַחֲרֵינוּ, וּבְצֵל כְּנָפֶיךָ תַּסְתִּירֵנוּ. כִּי אֵל שׁוֹמְרֵנוּ וּמַצִּילֵנוּ אָתָּה, כִּי אֵל מֶלֶךְ חַנּוּן וְרַחוּם אָתָּה, ❖ וּשְׁמוֹר צֵאתֵנוּ וּבוֹאֵנוּ, לְחַיִּים וּלְשָׁלוֹם, מֵעַתָּה וְעַד עוֹלָם. בָּרוּךְ אַתָּה יְיָ, שׁוֹמֵר עַמּוֹ יִשְׂרָאֵל לָעַד.

חֲצִי קַדִּישׁ

Leader:

יִתְגַּדַּל וְיִתְקַדַּשׁ שְׁמֵהּ רַבָּא. בְּעָלְמָא דִּי בְרָא כִרְעוּתֵיהּ, וְיַמְלִיךְ מַלְכוּתֵהּ בְּחַיֵּיכוֹן וּבְיוֹמֵיכוֹן וּבְחַיֵּי דְכָל בֵּית יִשְׂרָאֵל. בַּעֲגָלָא וּבִזְמַן קָרִיב וְאִמְרוּ אָמֵן:

Everyone:

יְהֵא שְׁמֵהּ רַבָּא מְבָרַךְ לְעָלַם וּלְעָלְמֵי עָלְמַיָּא:

Leader:

יִתְבָּרַךְ וְיִשְׁתַּבַּח וְיִתְפָּאַר וְיִתְרוֹמַם וְיִתְנַשֵּׂא וְיִתְהַדָּר וְיִתְעַלֶּה וְיִתְהַלָּל שְׁמֵהּ דְּקֻדְשָׁא בְּרִיךְ הוּא לְעֵלָּא מִן כָּל בִּרְכָתָא וְשִׁירָתָא תֻּשְׁבְּחָתָא וְנֶחֱמָתָא, דַּאֲמִירָן בְּעָלְמָא, וְאִמְרוּ אָמֵן:

Our prayers continue with:
    Weekday Amidah   p. 22
    Kaddish Shalem   p. 38
    Aleinu   p. 40
    Mourner's Kaddish   p. 42

Weekday Evening Prayers

Adonai said to Moses: Speak to the people Israel and tell them to make fringes for the corners of their clothes in all future generations. They shall put a blue thread in the fringe of each corner. When they look at them they will remember all of Adonai's mitzvot, and do them, and they won't be led astray by their hearts or their eyes. Do this so that you will remember and do all My mitzvot, and you will be holy for your God. I am Adonai your God, who took you out of the land of Egypt to be your God. I, Adonai, am your God.

Vayomer Adonai el-Mosheh lemor. Daber el-b'nei Yisra-el v'amar'ta alehem v'asu lahem tzeetzit al-can'fei vig'deihem l'dorotam v'nat'nu al-tzeetzit hakanaf p'til t'chelet. V'haya lachem l'tzeetzit ur'eetem oto uz'char'tem et-kol-mitzvot Adonai va-aseetem otam v'lo taturu acharei l'vav'chem v'acharei eineichem asher-atem zoneem achareihem. L'ma'an tiz'k'ru va-aseetem et-kol mitz'votai vih'yeetem k'dosheem leloheichem. Ani Adonai Eloheichem asher hotzetee et'chem me-eretz mitz'rayim lih'yot lachem lEloheem ani Adonai Eloheichem.

Adonai, your God, is truth.

❖ Adonai Eloheichem emet.

Mee Chamocha

When the people of Israel saw God's wonders at the sea, They gave thanks to God in these words:

❖ Umal'chuto b'ratzon keeb'lu aleiheim, Moshe uv'nei Yisra-el l'cha anu sheera b'sim'cha rabah, v'am'ru chulam:

Who is like You, Adonai, among the mighty?
Who is like You, special in holiness, Inspiring praises, doing wonders?

Mee chamocha ba-elim Adonai,
Mee kamocha ne'dar bakodesh,
Nora t'hilot oseh fele.

As You divided the sea before Moses, Your children beheld Your sovereignty. They said:

❖ Mal'chut'cha ra-u vaneicha, boke-a lif'nei moshe, zeh elee anu v'am'ru:

Adonai will rule for ever and ever.

Adonai yimloch l'olam va-ed.

And it is written: Adonai has rescued Jacob; God redeemed him from those more powerful. Praised are You, Adonai, who rescues Israel.

❖ V'ne-emar: Kee fadah Adonai et Ya'akov, ug'alo miyad chazak mimenu. Baruch atah Adonai, ga-al Yisra-el.

מעריב לחול

וַיֹּאמֶר יְהֹוָה אֶל־מֹשֶׁה לֵּאמֹר: דַּבֵּר אֶל־בְּנֵי יִשְׂרָאֵל וְאָמַרְתָּ אֲלֵהֶם וְעָשׂוּ לָהֶם צִיצִת עַל־כַּנְפֵי בִגְדֵיהֶם לְדֹרֹתָם וְנָתְנוּ עַל־צִיצִת הַכָּנָף פְּתִיל תְּכֵלֶת: וְהָיָה לָכֶם לְצִיצִת וּרְאִיתֶם אֹתוֹ וּזְכַרְתֶּם אֶת־כָּל־מִצְוֹת יְהֹוָה וַעֲשִׂיתֶם אֹתָם וְלֹא תָתוּרוּ אַחֲרֵי לְבַבְכֶם וְאַחֲרֵי עֵינֵיכֶם אֲשֶׁר־אַתֶּם זֹנִים אַחֲרֵיהֶם: לְמַעַן תִּזְכְּרוּ וַעֲשִׂיתֶם אֶת־כָּל־מִצְוֹתָי וִהְיִיתֶם קְדֹשִׁים לֵאלֹהֵיכֶם: אֲנִי יְהֹוָה אֱלֹהֵיכֶם אֲשֶׁר הוֹצֵאתִי אֶתְכֶם מֵאֶרֶץ מִצְרַיִם לִהְיוֹת לָכֶם לֵאלֹהִים אֲנִי יְהֹוָה אֱלֹהֵיכֶם:

NUMBERS 15:37–41

❖ יְיָ אֱלֹהֵיכֶם אֱמֶת.

מִי כָמֹכָה

❖ וּמַלְכוּתוֹ בְּרָצוֹן קִבְּלוּ עֲלֵיהֶם, מֹשֶׁה וּבְנֵי יִשְׂרָאֵל לְךָ עָנוּ שִׁירָה בְּשִׂמְחָה רַבָּה, וְאָמְרוּ כֻלָּם:

מִי כָמֹכָה בָּאֵלִים יְיָ,
מִי כָּמֹכָה נֶאְדָּר בַּקֹּדֶשׁ,
נוֹרָא תְהִלֹּת, עֹשֵׂה פֶלֶא:

EXODUS 15:11

❖ מַלְכוּתְךָ רָאוּ בָנֶיךָ, בּוֹקֵעַ יָם לִפְנֵי מֹשֶׁה, זֶה אֵלִי עָנוּ וְאָמְרוּ:

יְיָ יִמְלֹךְ לְעוֹלָם וָעֶד.

EXODUS 15:18

❖ וְנֶאֱמַר: כִּי פָדָה יְיָ אֶת יַעֲקֹב, וּגְאָלוֹ מִיַּד חָזָק מִמֶּנּוּ. בָּרוּךְ אַתָּה יְיָ, גָּאַל יִשְׂרָאֵל:

Shema

If there is no minyan, add:

God is a faithful ruler.   El melech ne-eman.

Hear O Israel, Adonai is our God, Adonai is One.

Sh'ma Yisra-el, Adonai Eloheinu, Adonai echad.

Silently:

Praised be God's glorious name forever.

Baruch shem k'vod mal'chuto l'olam va-ed.

You will love Adonai your God with all your mind, soul, and might. Take to heart these words which I command you today. Teach them carefully to your children. Repeat them at home and away, morning and night. Bind them as a sign on your hand, and let them be a symbol above your eyes. Write them on the doorposts of your homes and on your gates.

V'ahav'ta et Adonai Eloheicha b'chol-l'vav'cha uv'chol-naf'sh'cha uv'chol-m'odecha. V'hayu had'vareem ha-eleh ahser anochi m'tzav'cha hayom al-l'vavecha. V'shinan'tam l'vaneicha v'dibar'ta bam b'shiv't'cha b'veitecha uv'lech't'cha baderech uv'shoch'b'cha uv'kumecha. Uk'shar'tam l'ot al-yadecha v'hayu l'totafot bein eineicha. Uch'tav'tam al m'zuzot beitecha uvish'areicha.

If you will really listen to My commandments which I command you today, to love Adonai your God and to serve God with all your heart and soul, then I will give your land rain at the proper season—rain in autumn and rain in spring—and you will gather in your grain and wine and oil. I will give grass in the fields for your cattle, and you will eat your fill. Beware that you are not tempted to turn aside and worship other gods. For then God will be angry at you and will shut up the skies and there will be no rain, and the earth will not give you its produce, and you will quickly disappear from the good land which God is giving to you. So keep these words in mind and take them to heart, and bind them as a sign on your hand, and let them be a symbol between your eyes. Teach them to your children, speaking of them at home and away, when you lie down and when you get up. Write them upon the doorposts of your house and upon your gates, so that your days and the days of your children will last long on the land which Adonai promised to your ancestors, to give to them for as long as the heavens and earth last.

V'haya im-shamo-a tish'm'u el-mitzvotai asher anochi m'tazveh et'chem hayom l'ahavah et-Adonai Eloheichem ul'av'do b'chol-l'vav'chem uv'chol-naf'sh'chem. V'natatee m'tar-ar'tz'chem b'ito yoreh umal'kosh v'asaf'ta d'gonecha v'teerosh'cha v'yitz'harecha. V'natatee esev b'sad'cha liv'hem'techa v'achal'ta v'sava'ta. Hisham'ru lachem pen-yif'teh l'vav'chem v'sar'tem v-avad'tem Eloheem achereem v'hish'tachaveetem lahem. V'chara af-Adonai bachem v'atzar et-hashamayim v'lo-yih'yeh matar v'ha-adamah lo titen et-y'vulah va-avad'tem m'herah me-al ha-aretz hatovah asher Adonai noten lachem. V'sam'tem et-d'varai eleh al-l'vav'chem v'al-naf'sh'chem uk'shar'tem otam l'ot al-yedchem v'hayu l'totafot bein eineichem. V'limad'tem otam et-b'neichem l'daber bam b'shiv't'cha b'veitecha uv'lech't'cha baderech uv'shoch'b'cha uv'kumecha. Uch'tav'tam al-m'zuzot beitecha uvish'areicha. L'ma-an yi'bu y'meichem veemei v'neichem al ha-adamah asher nish'ba Adonai la-avoteichem latet lahem keemei hashamayim al-ha-aretz.

קְרִיאַת שְׁמַע

If there is no minyan, add: אֵל מֶלֶךְ נֶאֱמָן

שְׁמַע יִשְׂרָאֵל, יְיָ אֱלֹהֵינוּ, יְיָ אֶחָד:

Silently:
בָּרוּךְ שֵׁם כְּבוֹד מַלְכוּתוֹ לְעוֹלָם וָעֶד.

וְאָהַבְתָּ אֵת יְהֹוָה אֱלֹהֶיךָ בְּכָל־לְבָבְךָ וּבְכָל־נַפְשְׁךָ וּבְכָל־מְאֹדֶךָ: וְהָיוּ הַדְּבָרִים הָאֵלֶּה אֲשֶׁר אָנֹכִי מְצַוְּךָ הַיּוֹם עַל־לְבָבֶךָ: וְשִׁנַּנְתָּם לְבָנֶיךָ וְדִבַּרְתָּ בָּם בְּשִׁבְתְּךָ בְּבֵיתֶךָ וּבְלֶכְתְּךָ בַדֶּרֶךְ וּבְשָׁכְבְּךָ וּבְקוּמֶךָ: וּקְשַׁרְתָּם לְאוֹת עַל־יָדֶךָ וְהָיוּ לְטֹטָפֹת בֵּין עֵינֶיךָ: וּכְתַבְתָּם עַל־מְזֻזוֹת בֵּיתֶךָ וּבִשְׁעָרֶיךָ:
DEUTERONOMY 6:4–9

וְהָיָה אִם־שָׁמֹעַ תִּשְׁמְעוּ אֶל־מִצְוֹתַי אֲשֶׁר אָנֹכִי מְצַוֶּה אֶתְכֶם הַיּוֹם לְאַהֲבָה אֶת־יְהֹוָה אֱלֹהֵיכֶם וּלְעָבְדוֹ בְּכָל־לְבַבְכֶם וּבְכָל־נַפְשְׁכֶם: וְנָתַתִּי מְטַר־אַרְצְכֶם בְּעִתּוֹ יוֹרֶה וּמַלְקוֹשׁ וְאָסַפְתָּ דְגָנֶךָ וְתִירֹשְׁךָ וְיִצְהָרֶךָ: וְנָתַתִּי עֵשֶׂב בְּשָׂדְךָ לִבְהֶמְתֶּךָ וְאָכַלְתָּ וְשָׂבָעְתָּ: הִשָּׁמְרוּ לָכֶם פֶּן יִפְתֶּה לְבַבְכֶם וְסַרְתֶּם וַעֲבַדְתֶּם אֱלֹהִים אֲחֵרִים וְהִשְׁתַּחֲוִיתֶם לָהֶם: וְחָרָה אַף־יְהֹוָה בָּכֶם וְעָצַר אֶת־הַשָּׁמַיִם וְלֹא־יִהְיֶה מָטָר וְהָאֲדָמָה לֹא תִתֵּן אֶת־יְבוּלָהּ וַאֲבַדְתֶּם מְהֵרָה מֵעַל הָאָרֶץ הַטֹּבָה אֲשֶׁר יְהֹוָה נֹתֵן לָכֶם: וְשַׂמְתֶּם אֶת־דְּבָרַי אֵלֶּה עַל־לְבַבְכֶם וְעַל־נַפְשְׁכֶם וּקְשַׁרְתֶּם אֹתָם לְאוֹת עַל־יֶדְכֶם וְהָיוּ לְטוֹטָפֹת בֵּין עֵינֵיכֶם: וְלִמַּדְתֶּם אֹתָם אֶת־בְּנֵיכֶם לְדַבֵּר בָּם בְּשִׁבְתְּךָ בְּבֵיתֶךָ וּבְלֶכְתְּךָ בַדֶּרֶךְ וּבְשָׁכְבְּךָ וּבְקוּמֶךָ: וּכְתַבְתָּם עַל־מְזוּזוֹת בֵּיתֶךָ וּבִשְׁעָרֶיךָ: לְמַעַן יִרְבּוּ יְמֵיכֶם וִימֵי בְנֵיכֶם עַל הָאֲדָמָה אֲשֶׁר נִשְׁבַּע יְהֹוָה לַאֲבֹתֵיכֶם לָתֵת לָהֶם כִּימֵי הַשָּׁמַיִם עַל־הָאָרֶץ:
DEUTERONOMY 11:13–21

Weekday Evening Prayers

Weekday Evening Prayers

God, being merciful, grants atonement for sin and does not destroy. Time and again God restrains wrath, refuses to let rage be all-consuming. Save us, Adonai. Answer us, O sovereign, when we call.

V'hu rachum y'chaper avon v'lo yash'cheet, v'hir'bah l'hasheev apo, v'lo ya-eer kol chamato. Adonai hoshee-ah hamelech ya-anenu v'yom kor'enu.

Barchu

We rise and the leader sings:

Praise Adonai, who is to be praised.

Bar'chu et Adonai ham'vorach.

Everyone replies, then the leader repeats:

Praised be Adonai who is to be praised for ever and ever.

Baruch Adonai ham'vorach l'olam va-ed.

Praised are You, Adonai our God, Ruler of the universe, whose word brings the evening. With wisdom God opens the gates of the heavens, changes the times of day with understanding, exchanges the seasons, and puts the stars in their proper place and order in the sky. Creator of day and night, rolling the light away before the darkness and the darkness before the light. God causes the day to pass and brings night, separating between day and night—*Adonai Tzeva'ot* is God's name. The God who lives forever will rule over us for ever and ever. Praised are You, Adonai, who brings the evening.

Baruch atah Adonai, Eloheinu melech ha-olam, asher bid'varo ma-ariv Araveem, b'chochmah pote-ach sh'areem, uvit'vunah m'shaneh iteem, umachaleef et haz'maneem, umsader et hakochaveem, b'meesh'm'roteihem barakee-a kir'tzono. Boreh yom valai'la, golel or mip'nei choshech, v'choshech mip'nei or. ❖ Uma-aveer yom umevee lai'lah, umav'deel bein yom uvein lai'lah, Adonai tzeva-ot sh'mo. El chai v'kayam, tameed yim'loch aleinu l'olam va-ed. Baruch atah Adonai, hama-areev araveem.

Ahavat Olam

You have always loved Your people Israel by teaching us Torah, mitzvot, laws and justice. Therefore, Adonai our God, when we lie down at night and when we get up in the morning we will talk about Your laws. We will always be happy with the words of Your Torah and Your commandments, because they are our life, and they give long life; we will think about them day and night. May You never take Your love away from us. Praised are You, Adonai, who loves the people Israel.

Ahavat olam beit Yisra-el am'cha ahav'ta, Torah umitz'vot, chukeem umish'pateem, otanu limad'ta al ken Adonai Eloheinu, b'shoch'venu uv'kumenu nasee-ach b'chukecha, v'nis'mach b'div'rei Toratecha uv'mitz'voteicha l'olam va-ed. Kee hem chayeinu v'orech yameimu, uvahem neh'geh yomam valai'lah, ❖ v'ahavat'cha al tasir mimenu l'olamim. Baruch atah Adonai, ohev amo Yisra-el.

מַעֲרִיב לְחוֹל

> At the end of the day, we say the *Sh'ma* and the *Amidah* one more time in our *Ma-ariv* prayers. We also say a few things about the arrival of nightfall in the prayers before the *Sh'ma*.

וְהוּא רַחוּם יְכַפֵּר עָוֹן וְלֹא יַשְׁחִית, וְהִרְבָּה לְהָשִׁיב אַפּוֹ, וְלֹא יָעִיר כָּל חֲמָתוֹ. יְיָ הוֹשִׁיעָה הַמֶּלֶךְ יַעֲנֵנוּ בְיוֹם קָרְאֵנוּ:

בָּרְכוּ

We rise and the leader sings:

בָּרְכוּ אֶת יְיָ הַמְבֹרָךְ:

Everyone replies, then the leader repeats:

בָּרוּךְ יְיָ הַמְבֹרָךְ לְעוֹלָם וָעֶד:

בָּרוּךְ אַתָּה יְיָ, אֱלֹהֵינוּ מֶלֶךְ הָעוֹלָם, אֲשֶׁר בִּדְבָרוֹ מַעֲרִיב עֲרָבִים, בְּחָכְמָה פּוֹתֵחַ שְׁעָרִים, וּבִתְבוּנָה מְשַׁנֶּה עִתִּים, וּמַחֲלִיף אֶת הַזְּמַנִּים, וּמְסַדֵּר אֶת הַכּוֹכָבִים, בְּמִשְׁמְרוֹתֵיהֶם בָּרָקִיעַ כִּרְצוֹנוֹ. בּוֹרֵא יוֹם וָלָיְלָה, גּוֹלֵל אוֹר מִפְּנֵי חֹשֶׁךְ, וְחֹשֶׁךְ מִפְּנֵי אוֹר. ❖ וּמַעֲבִיר יוֹם וּמֵבִיא לָיְלָה, וּמַבְדִּיל בֵּין יוֹם וּבֵין לָיְלָה, יְיָ צְבָאוֹת שְׁמוֹ. אֵל חַי וְקַיָּם, תָּמִיד יִמְלוֹךְ עָלֵינוּ לְעוֹלָם וָעֶד. בָּרוּךְ אַתָּה יְיָ, הַמַּעֲרִיב עֲרָבִים:

אַהֲבַת עוֹלָם

אַהֲבַת עוֹלָם בֵּית יִשְׂרָאֵל עַמְּךָ אָהָבְתָּ, תּוֹרָה וּמִצְוֹת, חֻקִּים וּמִשְׁפָּטִים, אוֹתָנוּ לִמַּדְתָּ עַל כֵּן יְיָ אֱלֹהֵינוּ, בְּשָׁכְבֵנוּ וּבְקוּמֵנוּ נָשִׂיחַ בְּחֻקֶּיךָ, וְנִשְׂמַח בְּדִבְרֵי תוֹרָתֶךָ וּבְמִצְוֹתֶיךָ לְעוֹלָם וָעֶד. כִּי הֵם חַיֵּינוּ וְאֹרֶךְ יָמֵינוּ, וּבָהֶם נֶהְגֶּה יוֹמָם וָלָיְלָה, ❖ וְאַהֲבָתְךָ אַל תָּסִיר מִמֶּנּוּ לְעוֹלָמִים. בָּרוּךְ אַתָּה יְיָ, אוֹהֵב עַמּוֹ יִשְׂרָאֵל:

Weekday Evening Prayers

ס God holds up all who fall, and helps all who are bent over to stand straight.

ע The eyes of all look to You with hope, and You give them their food at the right time.

פ You open Your hand, and feed everything alive to its heart's content.

צ Adonai is righteous in every way, and kind in every deed.

ק Adonai is near to all who call, to all who call to God's sincerity.

ר God does the wishes of those who respect God, God hears their cry and saves them.

ש Adonai protects all who love God, but God will destroy the wicked.

ת My mouth shall speak praises of God, and all beings shall bless God's holy name forever and ever.

We shall praise God, now and forever. Halleluyah.

Somech Adonai l'chol hanof'leem, v'zokef l'chol hak'fufeem.

Einei chol eleicha y'saberu, v'atah noten lahem et ach'lam b'ito.

Pote-ach et yadecha, umas'bee-a l'chol chai ratzon.

Tzadeek Adonai b'chol d'rachav, v'chaseed b'chol ma-asav.

Karov Adonai l'chol korav l'chol asher yik'ra-uhu ve-emet.

R'tzon y're-av ya-aseh, v'et shav'atam yish'ma v'yoshee-em.

Shomer Adonai et kol ohavav, v'et kol har'sha-im yash'meed.

❖ T'hilat Adonai y'daber pee, Veevarech kol basar shem kod'sho, l'olam va-ed.

Va-anach'nu n'varech Yah, me-atah v'ad olam, hal'luyah.

Chatzi Kaddish

Leader:

May God's great name be made great and holy in the world which God created according to God's will. May God establish Divine rule soon, in our days, quickly and in the near future, and let us say, Amen.

Yit'gadal v'yit'kadash sh'meh rabah. B'al'mah dee v'rah chir'utei, v'yam'leech mal'chutei b'chayeichon uv'yomeichon uv'chayei d'chol beit Yisra-el. Ba-agalah uviz'man kareev v'im'ru amen.

Everyone:

May God's great name be praised for ever and ever.

Y'heh sh'meh rabah m'varach l'alam ul'al'mei al'mayah.

Leader:

Blessed, praised, glorified and raised high, honored and elevated be the name of the Blessed Holy One, far beyond all blessings and songs, praises and words of comfort which people can say, and let us say: Amen.

Yit'barach v'yishtabach v'yitpa-ar v'yit'romam v'yit'naseh v'yit'hadar v'yit'aleh v'yit'halal sh'meh d'kud'shah b'reech hu l'elah min kol bir'chatah v'sheeratah tush'b'chatah v'nechematah, da-ameeran b'al'mah, v'im'ru amen.

סוֹמֵךְ יְיָ לְכָל הַנֹּפְלִים, וְזוֹקֵף לְכָל הַכְּפוּפִים:

עֵינֵי כֹל אֵלֶיךָ יְשַׂבֵּרוּ, וְאַתָּה נוֹתֵן לָהֶם אֶת אָכְלָם בְּעִתּוֹ:
פּוֹתֵחַ אֶת יָדֶךָ, וּמַשְׂבִּיעַ לְכָל חַי רָצוֹן:

צַדִּיק יְיָ בְּכָל דְּרָכָיו, וְחָסִיד בְּכָל מַעֲשָׂיו:
קָרוֹב יְיָ לְכָל קֹרְאָיו, לְכֹל אֲשֶׁר יִקְרָאֻהוּ בֶאֱמֶת:

רְצוֹן יְרֵאָיו יַעֲשֶׂה, וְאֶת שַׁוְעָתָם יִשְׁמַע וְיוֹשִׁיעֵם:
שׁוֹמֵר יְיָ אֶת כָּל אֹהֲבָיו, וְאֵת כָּל הָרְשָׁעִים יַשְׁמִיד:

❖ תְּהִלַּת יְיָ יְדַבֶּר פִּי,
וִיבָרֵךְ כָּל בָּשָׂר שֵׁם קָדְשׁוֹ, לְעוֹלָם וָעֶד:
PSALM 145

וַאֲנַחְנוּ נְבָרֵךְ יָהּ, מֵעַתָּה וְעַד עוֹלָם, הַלְלוּיָהּ:
PSALM 115:18

חֲצִי קַדִּיש

Leader:

יִתְגַּדַּל וְיִתְקַדַּשׁ שְׁמֵהּ רַבָּא. בְּעָלְמָא דִּי בְרָא כִרְעוּתֵיהּ, וְיַמְלִיךְ מַלְכוּתֵהּ בְּחַיֵּיכוֹן וּבְיוֹמֵיכוֹן וּבְחַיֵּי דְכָל בֵּית יִשְׂרָאֵל. בַּעֲגָלָא וּבִזְמַן קָרִיב וְאִמְרוּ אָמֵן:

Everyone:

יְהֵא שְׁמֵהּ רַבָּא מְבָרַךְ לְעָלַם וּלְעָלְמֵי עָלְמַיָּא:

Leader:

יִתְבָּרַךְ וְיִשְׁתַּבַּח וְיִתְפָּאַר וְיִתְרוֹמַם וְיִתְנַשֵּׂא וְיִתְהַדָּר וְיִתְעַלֶּה וְיִתְהַלָּל שְׁמֵהּ דְּקֻדְשָׁא בְּרִיךְ הוּא לְעֵלָּא מִן כָּל בִּרְכָתָא וְשִׁירָתָא תֻּשְׁבְּחָתָא וְנֶחֱמָתָא, דַּאֲמִירָן בְּעָלְמָא, וְאִמְרוּ אָמֵן:

Our prayers continue with:
Weekday Amidah	p. 22
Kaddish Shalem	p. 38
Aleinu	p. 40
Mourner's Kaddish	p. 42

Weekday Afternoon Prayers

Ashrei

Happy are they who live in Your house;
They shall continue to praise You.

Happy are the people for whom this is so;
Happy are the people whose God is Adonai.

A Psalm of David.

א I will honor You, my God and Ruler, I will praise Your name forever and ever.

ב Every day I will praise You, and sing praises to Your name forever and ever.

ג Great is Adonai and greatly praised; there is no limit to God's greatness.

ד One generation shall praise Your deeds to another, and tell about Your mighty deeds.

ה I will speak about Your majesty, splendor and glory, and Your wonderful deeds.

ו They will talk about the power of Your mighty acts; and I will tell of Your greatness.

ז They recall Your great goodness, and sing of Your righteousness.

ח Adonai is gracious and caring, patient and very kind.

ט Adonai is good to all, and merciful to everything God made.

י All Your work shall praise You, Adonai, and Your faithful ones shall bless You.

כ They shall speak of the glory of Your rule, and talk of Your might.

ל To announce to humanity God's greatness, the splendor and glory of God's rule.

מ God, You rule eternally, Your kingdom is for all generations.

Ashrei yosh'vei veitecha,
od y'hal'lucha selah.

Ashrei ha-am shekacha lo,
ashrei ha-am she-Adonai elohav.

T'hilah l'David,

Aromim'cha elohai hamelech,
va-aver'chah shim'cha l'olam va-ed.

B'chol yom avar'checha,
va-ahal'lah shim'cha l'olam va-ed.

Gadol Adonai um'hulal m'od,
v'lig'dulato ein cheker.

Dor l'dor y'shabach ma-aseicha,
ug'vuroteicha yageedu.

Hadar k'vod hodecha,
v'div'rei nif'l'oteicha aseechah.

Ve-ezuz noroteicha yomeru,
ug'dulat'cha asap'renah.

Zecher rav tuv'cha yabee-u,
v'tzid'kat'cha y'ranenu.

Chanun v'rachum Adonai,
erech apayim ug'dal chased.

Tov Adonai lakol,
v'rachamav al kol ma-asav.

Yoducha Adonai kol ma-aseicha,
v'chaseedeicha y'varchucha.

K'vod mal'chut'cha yomeru,
ug'vurat'cha y'daberu.

L'hodee-ah liv'nei ha-adam g'vurotav,
uch'vod hadar mal'chuto.

Mal'chut'cha mal'chut kol olameem,
umem'shal't'cha b'chol dor vador.

מִנְחָה לְחוֹל

אַשְׁרֵי

אַשְׁרֵי יוֹשְׁבֵי בֵיתֶךָ, עוֹד יְהַלְלוּךָ סֶּלָה:
PSALM 84:5

אַשְׁרֵי הָעָם שֶׁכָּכָה לּוֹ, אַשְׁרֵי הָעָם שֶׁיְיָ אֱלֹהָיו:
PSALM 144:15

תְּהִלָּה לְדָוִד,
אֲרוֹמִמְךָ אֱלוֹהַי הַמֶּלֶךְ, וַאֲבָרְכָה שִׁמְךָ לְעוֹלָם וָעֶד:
בְּכָל יוֹם אֲבָרְכֶךָּ, וַאֲהַלְלָה שִׁמְךָ לְעוֹלָם וָעֶד:

גָּדוֹל יְיָ וּמְהֻלָּל מְאֹד, וְלִגְדֻלָּתוֹ אֵין חֵקֶר:
דּוֹר לְדוֹר יְשַׁבַּח מַעֲשֶׂיךָ, וּגְבוּרֹתֶיךָ יַגִּידוּ:

הֲדַר כְּבוֹד הוֹדֶךָ, וְדִבְרֵי נִפְלְאֹתֶיךָ אָשִׂיחָה:
וֶעֱזוּז נוֹרְאוֹתֶיךָ יֹאמֵרוּ, וּגְדֻלָּתְךָ אֲסַפְּרֶנָּה:

זֵכֶר רַב טוּבְךָ יַבִּיעוּ, וְצִדְקָתְךָ יְרַנֵּנוּ:
חַנּוּן וְרַחוּם יְיָ, אֶרֶךְ אַפַּיִם וּגְדָל חָסֶד:

טוֹב יְיָ לַכֹּל, וְרַחֲמָיו עַל כָּל מַעֲשָׂיו:
יוֹדוּךָ יְיָ כָּל מַעֲשֶׂיךָ, וַחֲסִידֶיךָ יְבָרְכוּכָה:

כְּבוֹד מַלְכוּתְךָ יֹאמֵרוּ, וּגְבוּרָתְךָ יְדַבֵּרוּ:
לְהוֹדִיעַ לִבְנֵי הָאָדָם גְּבוּרֹתָיו, וּכְבוֹד הֲדַר מַלְכוּתוֹ:

מַלְכוּתְךָ מַלְכוּת כָּל עוֹלָמִים, וּמֶמְשַׁלְתְּךָ בְּכָל דּוֹר וָדֹר:

Weekday Afternoon Prayers

We rise to return the Torah to the Ark. The leader chants:

Praise Adonai whose name alone is highly praised.

Y'hal'lu et shem Adonai, kee nis'gav sh'mo l'vado.

Everyone responds:

God's majesty is over the earth and the heavens. God will increase the pride and the praise of the people of Israel, the people close to God. Halleluyah.

Hodo al eretz v'shamayim. Vayarem keren l'amo, T'hilah l'chol chaseedav, liv'nei Yisra-el am k'rovo, hal'luyah.

The Torah is returned to the Ark, and we sing:

It is a tree of life for those who hold fast to it,
And all its supporters are happy.
Its paths are pleasant and all its ways are peaceful.
Return us to You, Adonai, and we shall return.

Etz chayeem hee lamachazeekeem bah, v'tomcheiha m'ushar.
D'racheiha dar'chei no-am, v'chol n'titvoteiha shalom.
Hasheevenu Adonai, eleicha v'nashuvah, chadesh yameinu k'kedem.

The Ark is closed.

It is a tree of life for those who hold fast to it, and all its supporters are happy!

We continue on page 39 with Kaddish Shalem.

סדר הוצאת התורה לחול

We rise to return the Torah to the Ark. The leader chants:

יְהַלְלוּ אֶת שֵׁם יְיָ, כִּי נִשְׂגָּב שְׁמוֹ לְבַדּוֹ.

Everyone responds:

הוֹדוֹ עַל אֶרֶץ וְשָׁמָיִם. וַיָּרֶם קֶרֶן לְעַמּוֹ, תְּהִלָּה לְכָל חֲסִידָיו, לִבְנֵי יִשְׂרָאֵל עַם קְרוֹבוֹ, הַלְלוּיָהּ.

The Torah is returned to the Ark, and we sing:

עֵץ חַיִּים הִיא לַמַּחֲזִיקִים בָּהּ, וְתֹמְכֶיהָ מְאֻשָּׁר.
דְּרָכֶיהָ דַרְכֵי נֹעַם, וְכָל נְתִיבוֹתֶיהָ שָׁלוֹם.
הֲשִׁיבֵנוּ יְיָ, אֵלֶיךָ וְנָשׁוּבָה, חַדֵּשׁ יָמֵינוּ כְּקֶדֶם.

The Ark is closed.

We continue on page 38 with קדיש שלם.

Torah Blessings

The leader sings:

Praise Adonai, who is to be praised. Bar'chu et Adonai ham'vorach.

Everyone replies, then the leader repeats:

Praised be Adonai who is to be praised for ever and ever. Baruch Adonai ham'vorach l'olam va-ed.

Praised are You, Adonai our God, Ruler of the universe, who chose us from among all peoples by giving us God's Torah. Praised are You, Adonai, who gives the Torah. Baruch atah Adonai, Eloheinu melech ha-olam, asher bachar banu mikol ha-ameem v'natan lanu et Torato. Baruch atah Adonai, noten haTorah.

After the Torah is read:

Praised are You, Adonai our God, Ruler of the universe, who gave us a Torah of truth and planted within us lasting life. Praised are You, Adonai, who gives the Torah. Baruch atah Adonai, Eloheinu melech ha-olam, asher natan lanu Torat emet, v'chayei olam nata b'tochenu. Baruch atah Adonai, noten haTorah.

We rise as the Hagbah lifts up the Torah and shows its written side to us and chant:

This is the Torah that Moses placed before the Israelites, by God's authority, through Moses. V'zot haTorah asher sam Moshe lif'nei b'nei Yisra-el al pee Adonai b'yad Moshe.

The Torah which Moses handed down to us is the heritage of the community of Jacob. Torah tzivah lanu Moshe, Morasha k'hilat Ya-akov.

בִּרְכוֹת הַתּוֹרָה

The leader sings:

בָּרְכוּ אֶת יְיָ הַמְבֹרָךְ:

Everyone replies, then the leader repeats:

בָּרוּךְ יְיָ הַמְבֹרָךְ לְעוֹלָם וָעֶד:

בָּרוּךְ אַתָּה יְיָ אֱלֹהֵינוּ מֶלֶךְ הָעוֹלָם, אֲשֶׁר בָּחַר בָּנוּ מִכָּל הָעַמִּים וְנָתַן לָנוּ אֶת תּוֹרָתוֹ: בָּרוּךְ אַתָּה יְיָ, נוֹתֵן הַתּוֹרָה:

After the Torah is read:

בָּרוּךְ אַתָּה יְיָ אֱלֹהֵינוּ מֶלֶךְ הָעוֹלָם, אֲשֶׁר נָתַן לָנוּ תּוֹרַת אֱמֶת, וְחַיֵּי עוֹלָם נָטַע בְּתוֹכֵנוּ: בָּרוּךְ אַתָּה יְיָ, נוֹתֵן הַתּוֹרָה:

We rise as the Hagbah lifts up the Torah and shows its written side to us and chant:

וְזֹאת הַתּוֹרָה אֲשֶׁר שָׂם מֹשֶׁה לִפְנֵי בְּנֵי יִשְׂרָאֵל, עַל פִּי יְיָ בְּיַד מֹשֶׁה:

תּוֹרָה צִוָּה לָנוּ מֹשֶׁה, מוֹרָשָׁה קְהִלַּת יַעֲקֹב:

The leader faces the Ark, bows, and chants:

Declare Adonai's greatness with me; let us praise God together.	Gad'lu lAdonai itee, un'rom'mah sh'mo yach'dav.

The Torah is carried around in procession as we sing:

Greatness, might, wonder, triumph, and majesty are Yours, Adonai—yes, all that is in heaven and on earth; to You, Adonai, belong kingship and rule over all.	L'cha Adonai hag'dulah v'hag'vurah v'hatif'eret v'hanetzach v'hahod, kee chol bashamayim uva-aretz. L'cha Adonai hamam'lacha v'hamit'naseh l'chol l'rosh:
Praise Adonai and bow down to God's presence; God is holy!	Rom'mu Adonai Eloheinu, v'hishtachavu lahadom rag'lav kadosh hu.
Praise Adonai, our God, bow to God's holy mountain. Adonai our God is holy.	Rom'mu Adonai Eloheinu, v'hishtachavu l'har kod'sho, kee kadosh Adonai Eloheinu.

Once the Torah is set down, we are seated.

The Gabbai calls up the first person to have an aliyah:

May God's sovereignty be revealed to us soon. May God favor the remnant of God's people Israel with grace and kindness, with compassion and love. And let us say: Amen. Let us all declare the greatness of God and give honor to the Torah.	V'tigaleh v'tera-eh mal'chuto aleinu biz'man karov, v'yachon p'letatenu uf'letat amo beit Yisra-el l'chein ul'chesed ul'rachameem ul'ratzon v'nomar amen. Hakol havu godel lEloheinu ut'nu chavod laTorah.
Let the first to be honored come forward.	Kohen, k'rav. Ya-amod _____ ben _____ hakohen.
	Bat kohen, kir'vee. Ta-amod _____ bat _____ hakohen.
	Ya-amod _____ ben _____ harishon.
	Ta-amod _____ bat _____ harishonah.
Praised is God who in holiness entrusted the Torah to God's people Israel.	Baruch shenatan Torah l'amo Yisra-el bik'dushto.

Everyone:

You who remain steadfast to Adonai your God have been sustained to this day.	V'atem had'vekeem bAdonai Eloheichem, chayeem kul'chem hayom.

סדר הוצאת התורה לחול

The leader faces the Ark, bows, and chants:

גַּדְּלוּ לַיְיָ אִתִּי, וּנְרוֹמְמָה שְׁמוֹ יַחְדָּו:

The Torah is carried around in procession as we sing:

לְךָ יְיָ הַגְּדֻלָּה וְהַגְּבוּרָה וְהַתִּפְאֶרֶת וְהַנֵּצַח וְהַהוֹד,
כִּי כֹל בַּשָּׁמַיִם וּבָאָרֶץ: לְךָ יְיָ הַמַּמְלָכָה וְהַמִּתְנַשֵּׂא לְכֹל לְרֹאשׁ:
רוֹמְמוּ יְיָ אֱלֹהֵינוּ, וְהִשְׁתַּחֲווּ לַהֲדֹם רַגְלָיו קָדוֹשׁ הוּא:
רוֹמְמוּ יְיָ אֱלֹהֵינוּ, וְהִשְׁתַּחֲווּ לְהַר קָדְשׁוֹ, כִּי קָדוֹשׁ יְיָ אֱלֹהֵינוּ:

Once the Torah is set down, we are seated.

The Gabbai calls up the first person to have an aliyah:

וְתִגָּלֶה וְתֵרָאֶה מַלְכוּתוֹ עָלֵינוּ בִּזְמַן קָרוֹב, וְיָחֹן פְּלֵטָתֵנוּ וּפְלֵטַת
עַמּוֹ בֵּית יִשְׂרָאֵל לְחֵן וּלְחֶסֶד וּלְרַחֲמִים וּלְרָצוֹן וְנֹאמַר אָמֵן.
הַכֹּל הָבוּ גֹדֶל לֵאלֹהֵינוּ וּתְנוּ כָבוֹד לַתּוֹרָה.
כֹּהֵן, קְרַב. יַעֲמֹד _____ בֶּן _____ הַכֹּהֵן.
בַּת כֹּהֵן, קִרְבִי. תַּעֲמֹד _____ בַּת _____ הַכֹּהֵן.
יַעֲמֹד _____ בֶּן _____ הָרִאשׁוֹן.
תַּעֲמֹד _____ בַּת _____ הָרִאשׁוֹנָה.
בָּרוּךְ שֶׁנָּתַן תּוֹרָה לְעַמּוֹ יִשְׂרָאֵל בִּקְדֻשָּׁתוֹ.

Everyone:

וְאַתֶּם הַדְּבֵקִים בַּיְיָ אֱלֹהֵיכֶם, חַיִּים כֻּלְּכֶם הַיּוֹם:

Weekday Torah Service   48

Weekday Torah Service

> "Pray with an attentive heart, and see all of heaven's doors open before you."
> —Rav Nachman, ABB 70

Chatzi Kaddish

Leader:

May God's great name be made great and holy in the world which God created according to God's will. May God establish Divine rule soon, in our days, quickly and in the near future, and let us say, Amen.

Yit'gadal v'yit'kadash sh'meh rabah. B'al'mah dee v'rah chir'utei, v'yam'leech mal'chutei b'chayeichon uv'yomeichon uv'chayei d'chol beit Yisra-el. Ba-agalah uviz'man kareev v'im'ru amen.

Everyone:

May God's great name be praised for ever and ever.

Y'heh sh'meh rabah m'varach l'alam ul'al'mei al'mayah.

Leader:

Blessed, praised, glorified and raised high, honored and elevated be the name of the Blessed Holy One, far beyond all blessings and songs, praises and words of comfort which people can say, and let us say: Amen.

Yit'barach v'yishtabach v'yitpa-ar v'yit'romam v'yit'naseh v'yit'hadar v'yit'aleh v'yit'halal sh'meh d'kud'shah b'reech hu l'elah min kol bir'chatah v'sheeratah tush'b'chatah v'nechematah, da-ameeran b'al'mah, v'im'ru amen.

We rise as the Ark is opened and sing:

Whenever the Ark would travel, Moses would say,
Arise, Adonai, and scatter Your enemies;
May those that hate You flee from You.
For Torah shall come from Zion,
The word of Adonai from Jerusalem.
Blessed is the One who in holiness gave the Torah to Israel.

Vay'hee bin'so-a ha-aron vayomer Moshe,
Kuma Adonai v'yafutzu oy'vecha,
V'yanusu m'san'eicha mipaneicha.
Kee mitzee-on tetzeh Torah,
ud'var Adonai mirushalayim.
Baruch shenatan Torah l'amo Yisra-el bik'dushato.

סדר הוצאת התורה לחול

סֵדֶר הוֹצָאַת הַתּוֹרָה לְחוֹל

> We read from the Torah on three days every week. Those days are Monday, Thursday, and Shabbat. When the children of Israel were wandering in the desert, they went three days without water and became very unhappy. All through history, rabbis have thought of water as a symbol for the Torah. Without water, we can't survive and the rabbis tell us that the Torah is just as important. For this reason, we never go three days without reading the Torah. Monday and Thursday were chosen to be Torah days because they used to be the market days, when everyone would go shopping. They used to read the Torah while everyone was at the market so they could all hear it!

חֲצִי קַדִישׁ

Leader:

יִתְגַּדַּל וְיִתְקַדַּשׁ שְׁמֵהּ רַבָּא. בְּעָלְמָא דִּי בְרָא כִרְעוּתֵיהּ, וְיַמְלִיךְ מַלְכוּתֵהּ בְּחַיֵּיכוֹן וּבְיוֹמֵיכוֹן וּבְחַיֵּי דְכָל בֵּית יִשְׂרָאֵל. בַּעֲגָלָא וּבִזְמַן קָרִיב וְאִמְרוּ אָמֵן:

Everyone:

יְהֵא שְׁמֵהּ רַבָּא מְבָרַךְ לְעָלַם וּלְעָלְמֵי עָלְמַיָּא:

Leader:

יִתְבָּרַךְ וְיִשְׁתַּבַּח וְיִתְפָּאַר וְיִתְרוֹמַם וְיִתְנַשֵּׂא וְיִתְהַדָּר וְיִתְעַלֶּה וְיִתְהַלָּל שְׁמֵהּ דְּקֻדְשָׁא בְּרִיךְ הוּא לְעֵלָּא מִן כָּל בִּרְכָתָא וְשִׁירָתָא תֻּשְׁבְּחָתָא וְנֶחֱמָתָא, דַּאֲמִירָן בְּעָלְמָא, וְאִמְרוּ אָמֵן:

We rise as the Ark is opened and sing:

וַיְהִי בִּנְסֹעַ הָאָרֹן וַיֹּאמֶר מֹשֶׁה:
קוּמָה יְיָ, וְיָפֻצוּ אֹיְבֶיךָ, וְיָנֻסוּ מְשַׂנְאֶיךָ מִפָּנֶיךָ.
כִּי מִצִּיּוֹן תֵּצֵא תוֹרָה, וּדְבַר יְיָ מִירוּשָׁלָיִם.
בָּרוּךְ שֶׁנָּתַן תּוֹרָה לְעַמּוֹ יִשְׂרָאֵל בִּקְדֻשָּׁתוֹ.

Weekday Torah Service

Adon Olam

Master of the universe	Adon olam asher malach,
Who ruled before anything was created,	b'terem kol y'tzeer niv'ra.
You are called Ruler	L'et na-asah b'chef'tzo kol,
Because You created everything.	Azai melech sh'mo nik'ra.
When everything ends at the end of time,	V'acharei kich'lot hakol,
God will still rule alone.	L'vado yim'loch nora.
God was, God is,	V'hu hayah, v'hu hoveh,
God always will be glorious.	V'hu yih'yeh, b'tif'arah.
God is one,	V'hu echad v'ein shenee,
There is no other being that compares.	l'ham'sheel lo l'hach'beerah.
God is without beginning, without end,	B'lee resheet b'lee tachleet,
Power and authority are God's.	V'lo ha-oz v'hamis'rah.
My God and living Rescuer,	V'hu elee v'chai go-alee,
My sheltering Rock in times of trouble,	V'tzur chev'lee b'et tzarah.
God is my banner and my shelter,	V'hu nisee umanos lee
Filling my cup on the day I call.	M'nat kosee b'yom ekra.
Into God's hand I place my spirit,	B'yado af'keed ruchee,
When I sleep and when I awake,	B'et eeshan v'a-eerah.
And with my spirit, my body too.	V'im ruchee g'vee-atee,
Adonai is with me, I shall not fear.	Adonai lee v'lo eera.

אֲדוֹן עוֹלָם

DID YOU KNOW THAT... The authors of our Jewish liturgy express their personal opinions of God and faith through their writings. What do you think the author of *Adon Olam* meant when he wrote "Adonai is with me, I shall not fear"?

אֲדוֹן עוֹלָם אֲשֶׁר מָלַךְ, בְּטֶרֶם כָּל יְצִיר נִבְרָא.
לְעֵת נַעֲשָׂה בְחֶפְצוֹ כֹּל, אֲזַי מֶלֶךְ שְׁמוֹ נִקְרָא.

וְאַחֲרֵי כִּכְלוֹת הַכֹּל, לְבַדּוֹ יִמְלוֹךְ נוֹרָא.
וְהוּא הָיָה, וְהוּא הֹוֶה, וְהוּא יִהְיֶה, בְּתִפְאָרָה.

וְהוּא אֶחָד וְאֵין שֵׁנִי, לְהַמְשִׁיל לוֹ לְהַחְבִּירָה.
בְּלִי רֵאשִׁית בְּלִי תַכְלִית, וְלוֹ הָעֹז וְהַמִּשְׂרָה.

וְהוּא אֵלִי וְחַי גֹּאֲלִי, וְצוּר חֶבְלִי בְּעֵת צָרָה.
וְהוּא נִסִּי וּמָנוֹס לִי, מְנָת כּוֹסִי בְּיוֹם אֶקְרָא.

בְּיָדוֹ אַפְקִיד רוּחִי, בְּעֵת אִישַׁן וְאָעִירָה.
וְעִם רוּחִי גְוִיָּתִי, יְיָ לִי וְלֹא אִירָא.

Mourner's Kaddish

Mourners:

May God's great name be made great and holy in the world which God created according to God's will. May God establish Divine rule soon, in our days, quickly and in the near future, and let us say: Amen.

Yit'gadal v'yit'kadash sh'meh rabah. B'al'mah dee v'rah chir'utei, v'yam'leech mal'chutei b'chayeichon uv'yomeichon uv'chayei d'chol beit Yisra-el. Ba-agalah uviz'man kareev v'im'ru amen.

Everyone:

May God's great name be praised for ever and ever.

Y'heh sh'meh rabah m'varach l'alam ul'al'mei al'mayah.

Mourners:

Blessed, praised, glorified and raised high, honored and elevated be the name of the Holy Blessed One, far beyond all blessings and songs, praises and words of comfort which people can say, and let us say: Amen.

Yit'barach v'yishtabach v'yitpa-ar v'yit'romam v'yit'naseh v'yit'hadar v'yit'aleh v'yit'halal sh'meh d'kud'shah b'reech hu l'elah min kol bir'chatah v'sheeratah tush'b'chatah v'nechematah, da-ameeran b'al'mah, v'im'ru amen.

May there be abundant peace from heaven and life for us and for all Israel, and let us say: Amen.

Y'hei sh'lamah rabah min sh'mayah v'chayeem aleinu v'al kol Yisra-el, v'im'ru amen.

May the One who makes peace in the high heavens make peace for us and for all Israel, and let us say: Amen.

Oseh shalom bim'romav, hu ya-aseh shalom aleinu, v'al kol Yisra-el v'im'ru amen.

קַדִּישׁ יָתוֹם

DID YOU KNOW THAT... The Mourner's Kaddish is a prayer for us to recite in honor of those loved ones who are no longer with us physically in this world. Out of respect for the memories of our loved ones and the millions of Jews that died in the Holocaust we say the Mourner's Kaddish.

Mourners:

יִתְגַּדַּל וְיִתְקַדַּשׁ שְׁמֵהּ רַבָּא. בְּעָלְמָא דִּי בְרָא כִרְעוּתֵיהּ, וְיַמְלִיךְ מַלְכוּתֵהּ בְּחַיֵּיכוֹן וּבְיוֹמֵיכוֹן וּבְחַיֵּי דְכָל בֵּית יִשְׂרָאֵל. בַּעֲגָלָא וּבִזְמַן קָרִיב וְאִמְרוּ אָמֵן:

Everyone:

יְהֵא שְׁמֵהּ רַבָּא מְבָרַךְ לְעָלַם וּלְעָלְמֵי עָלְמַיָּא:

Mourners:

יִתְבָּרַךְ וְיִשְׁתַּבַּח וְיִתְפָּאַר וְיִתְרוֹמַם וְיִתְנַשֵּׂא וְיִתְהַדָּר וְיִתְעַלֶּה וְיִתְהַלָּל שְׁמֵהּ דְּקֻדְשָׁא בְּרִיךְ הוּא לְעֵלָּא מִן כָּל בִּרְכָתָא וְשִׁירָתָא תֻּשְׁבְּחָתָא וְנֶחֱמָתָא, דַּאֲמִירָן בְּעָלְמָא, וְאִמְרוּ אָמֵן:

יְהֵא שְׁלָמָא רַבָּא מִן שְׁמַיָּא וְחַיִּים עָלֵינוּ וְעַל כָּל יִשְׂרָאֵל, וְאִמְרוּ אָמֵן:

עֹשֶׂה שָׁלוֹם בִּמְרוֹמָיו הוּא יַעֲשֶׂה שָׁלוֹם עָלֵינוּ וְעַל כָּל יִשְׂרָאֵל, וְאִמְרוּ אָמֵן:

Weekday Prayers

Aleinu

We rise.

We should praise God for not making us like the other peoples and families of the earth. We bend the knee and bow and give thanks to the Ruler of all earthly rulers, the Blessed Holy One. God spread out the heavens and built the earth's foundations. God's mighty presence is in the highest heights. God is our God—no one else. Our Ruler is true. There is nothing besides God, as it is written in God's Torah: "You shall know therefore this day and keep in mind that Adonai alone is God in heaven above and on earth below; there is no other."

And so we hope in You, Adonai our God, soon to see Your power used in a wonderful way: removing false gods from the earth, fixing the brokenness of the world so that it will be a world truly ruled by God. All humanity will call Your name, and all the wicked of the earth will turn toward You. All who live in the world will know and understand that everyone should accept You as their God. They will bow to You, Adonai our God, honoring the glory of Your name. For You will rule the world, and You will always rule over it in glory, as it is written in the Torah: "Adonai will rule for ever and ever." And as the prophet Zechariah said: "Then God will be Ruler over all the earth. On that day Adonai will be One and God's name will be One."

Aleinu l'shabe-ach la-adon hakol, latet g'dulah l'yotzer b'resheet, shelo asanu k'goyei ha-aratzot, v'lo samanu k'mish'p'chot ha-adamah, shelo sam chel'kenu kahem, v'goralenu k'chol hamonam. Va-anachnu kor'eem umish'tachaveem umodeem, lifnei melech, malchei ham'lacheem, hakadosh baruch hu. Shehu noteh shamayeem v'yosed aretz, umoshav y'karo bashamayim mima-al, ush'cheenat uzo b'gav'hei m'romeem, hu Eloheinu ein od. Emet malkenu efes zulato, kakatuv b'Torato: V'yada'ta hayom vahashevota El l'vavecha, kee Adonai hu haEloheem bashamayim mima-al, v'al ha-aretz mitachat, ein od.

Al ken n'kaveh l'cha Adonai Eloheinu, lir'ot m'hera b'tif'eret uzecha, l'ha-aveer giluleem min ha-aretz v'ha-eleeleem karot yikaretun. L'taken olam b'mal'chut shadai, v'chol b'nei vasar yik'r'u vish'mecha. L'haf'not eleicha kol rish'ei aretz. Yakeeru v'yed'u kol yosh'vei tevel, kee l'cha tich'ra kol berech, tishava kol lashon. L'faneicha Adonai Eloheinu yich'r'u v'yipolu. V'lich'vod shim'cha y'kar yitenu. Veekab'lu chulam et ol mal'chutecha. V'tim'loch aleihem m'herah l'olam va-ed.
❖ Kakatuv b'toratecha, Adonai yim'loch l'olam va-ed. V'ne-emar, v'haya Adonai l'melech al kol ha-aretz, bayom hahu yih'yeh Adonai echad, ush'mo echad.

We are seated.

תפילות לחול

עָלֵינוּ

DID YOU KNOW THAT... The first paragraph of *Aleinu* praises God for our uniqueness as Jews, while the second looks to the future, hoping for the day when the world will belong to God and be a place of harmony and peace. How can we create a world that is a place of peace and harmony?

We rise.

עָלֵינוּ לְשַׁבֵּחַ לַאֲדוֹן הַכֹּל, לָתֵת גְּדֻלָּה לְיוֹצֵר בְּרֵאשִׁית, שֶׁלֹּא עָשָׂנוּ כְּגוֹיֵי הָאֲרָצוֹת, וְלֹא שָׂמָנוּ כְּמִשְׁפְּחוֹת הָאֲדָמָה, שֶׁלֹּא שָׂם חֶלְקֵנוּ כָּהֶם, וְגוֹרָלֵנוּ כְּכָל הֲמוֹנָם:

וַאֲנַחְנוּ כּוֹרְעִים וּמִשְׁתַּחֲוִים וּמוֹדִים,

לִפְנֵי מֶלֶךְ, מַלְכֵי הַמְּלָכִים, הַקָּדוֹשׁ בָּרוּךְ הוּא.

שֶׁהוּא נוֹטֶה שָׁמַיִם וְיוֹסֵד אָרֶץ, וּמוֹשַׁב יְקָרוֹ בַּשָּׁמַיִם מִמַּעַל, וּשְׁכִינַת עֻזּוֹ בְּגָבְהֵי מְרוֹמִים, הוּא אֱלֹהֵינוּ אֵין עוֹד. אֱמֶת מַלְכֵּנוּ אֶפֶס זוּלָתוֹ, כַּכָּתוּב בְּתוֹרָתוֹ: וְיָדַעְתָּ הַיּוֹם וַהֲשֵׁבֹתָ אֶל לְבָבֶךָ, כִּי יְיָ הוּא הָאֱלֹהִים בַּשָּׁמַיִם מִמַּעַל, וְעַל הָאָרֶץ מִתָּחַת, אֵין עוֹד:

עַל כֵּן נְקַוֶּה לְךָ יְיָ אֱלֹהֵינוּ, לִרְאוֹת מְהֵרָה בְּתִפְאֶרֶת עֻזֶּךָ, לְהַעֲבִיר גִּלּוּלִים מִן הָאָרֶץ וְהָאֱלִילִים כָּרוֹת יִכָּרֵתוּן. לְתַקֵּן עוֹלָם בְּמַלְכוּת שַׁדַּי, וְכָל בְּנֵי בָשָׂר יִקְרְאוּ בִשְׁמֶךָ. לְהַפְנוֹת אֵלֶיךָ כָּל רִשְׁעֵי אָרֶץ. יַכִּירוּ וְיֵדְעוּ כָּל יוֹשְׁבֵי תֵבֵל, כִּי לְךָ תִּכְרַע כָּל בֶּרֶךְ, תִּשָּׁבַע כָּל לָשׁוֹן: לְפָנֶיךָ יְיָ אֱלֹהֵינוּ יִכְרְעוּ וְיִפֹּלוּ. וְלִכְבוֹד שִׁמְךָ יְקָר יִתֵּנוּ. וִיקַבְּלוּ כֻלָּם אֶת עוֹל מַלְכוּתֶךָ. וְתִמְלֹךְ עֲלֵיהֶם מְהֵרָה לְעוֹלָם וָעֶד. כִּי הַמַּלְכוּת שֶׁלְּךָ הִיא, וּלְעוֹלְמֵי עַד תִּמְלוֹךְ בְּכָבוֹד:

❖ כַּכָּתוּב בְּתוֹרָתֶךָ, יְיָ יִמְלֹךְ לְעוֹלָם וָעֶד: וְנֶאֱמַר, וְהָיָה יְיָ לְמֶלֶךְ עַל כָּל הָאָרֶץ, בַּיּוֹם הַהוּא יִהְיֶה יְיָ אֶחָד, וּשְׁמוֹ אֶחָד:

We are seated.

Kaddish Shalem

Leader:

May God's great name be made great and holy in the world which God created according to God's will. May God establish Divine rule soon, in our days, quickly and in the near future, and let us say: Amen.

Yit'gadal v'yit'kadash sh'meh rabah. B'al'mah dee v'rah chir'utei, v'yam'leech mal'chutei b'chayeichon uv'yomeichon uv'chayei d'chol beit Yisra-el. Ba-agalah uviz'man kareev v'im'ru amen.

Everyone:

May God's great name be praised for ever and ever.

Y'heh sh'meh rabah m'varach l'alam ul'al'mei al'mayah.

Leader:

Blessed, praised, glorified and raised high, honored and elevated be the name of the Holy Blessed One, far beyond all blessings and songs, praises and words of comfort which people can say, and let us say: Amen.

Yit'barach v'yishtabach v'yitpa-ar v'yit'romam v'yit'naseh v'yit'hadar v'yit'aleh v'yit'halal sh'meh d'kud'shah b'reech hu l'elah min kol bir'chatah v'sheeratah tush'b'chatah v'nechematah, da-ameeran b'al'mah, v'im'ru amen.

May the prayers and pleas of the entire House of Israel be accepted before their Parent in heaven. And let us say: Amen.

Tit'kabal tz'lot'hon uva-ut'hon d'chol Yisra-el kadam avuhon dee vish'mayah v'im'ru amen.

May there be abundant peace from heaven and life for us and for all Israel, and let us say: Amen.

Y'hei sh'lamah rabah min sh'mayah v'chayeem aleinu v'al kol Yisra-el, v'im'ru amen.

May the One who makes peace in the high heavens make peace for us and for all Israel, and let us say: Amen.

Oseh shalom bim'romav, hu ya-aseh shalom aleinu, v'al kol Yisra-el v'im'ru amen.

קַדִּישׁ שָׁלֵם

DID YOU KNOW THAT... The *Kaddish* is sometimes used to mark the end of a section of our *T'fillot*. This *Kaddish Shalem* tells us that we are at the end of our prayers and are ready to wrap things up.

Leader:

יִתְגַּדַּל וְיִתְקַדַּשׁ שְׁמֵהּ רַבָּא. בְּעָלְמָא דִּי בְרָא כִרְעוּתֵיהּ, וְיַמְלִיךְ מַלְכוּתֵהּ בְּחַיֵּיכוֹן וּבְיוֹמֵיכוֹן וּבְחַיֵּי דְכָל בֵּית יִשְׂרָאֵל. בַּעֲגָלָא וּבִזְמַן קָרִיב וְאִמְרוּ אָמֵן:

Everyone:

יְהֵא שְׁמֵהּ רַבָּא מְבָרַךְ לְעָלַם וּלְעָלְמֵי עָלְמַיָּא:

Leader:

יִתְבָּרַךְ וְיִשְׁתַּבַּח וְיִתְפָּאַר וְיִתְרוֹמַם וְיִתְנַשֵּׂא וְיִתְהַדָּר וְיִתְעַלֶּה וְיִתְהַלָּל שְׁמֵהּ דְּקֻדְשָׁא בְּרִיךְ הוּא לְעֵלָּא מִן כָּל בִּרְכָתָא וְשִׁירָתָא תֻּשְׁבְּחָתָא וְנֶחֱמָתָא, דַּאֲמִירָן בְּעָלְמָא, וְאִמְרוּ אָמֵן:

תִּתְקַבֵּל צְלוֹתְהוֹן וּבָעוּתְהוֹן דְּכָל יִשְׂרָאֵל קֳדָם אֲבוּהוֹן דִּי בִשְׁמַיָּא וְאִמְרוּ אָמֵן:

יְהֵא שְׁלָמָא רַבָּא מִן שְׁמַיָּא וְחַיִּים עָלֵינוּ וְעַל כָּל יִשְׂרָאֵל, וְאִמְרוּ אָמֵן:

עֹשֶׂה שָׁלוֹם בִּמְרוֹמָיו הוּא יַעֲשֶׂה שָׁלוֹם עָלֵינוּ וְעַל כָּל יִשְׂרָאֵל, וְאִמְרוּ אָמֵן:

Weekday Prayers

My God, help me not to say bad things or to tell lies. Help me to ignore people who say bad things about me. Open my heart to Your Torah, so that I can do Your mitzvot. Quickly stop the ideas and spoil the plans of anyone who wants to hurt me. Do this because of Your love, Your holiness, and Your Torah: so that those You love will be free. May the words of my mouth and the thoughts of my heart find favor with You, my Rock and my Protector. May the One who makes peace up above give peace to us and to all the people of Israel. Amen.

Elohai, n'tzor l'shonee mera. Us'fatai midaber mir'mah. V'lim'kal'lai naf'shee tidom, v'naf'shee ke-afar lakol tih'yeh. P'tach libee b'Torahtecha, uv'mitzvoteicha tir'dof naf'shee. V'chol hachosh'veem alai ra-ah, m'herah hafer atzatam v'kal'kel macahshav'tam. Aseh l'ma-an Toratecha. Lama-an yechal'tzun y'deedeicha, hoshee-ah y'meen'cha va-anenee. Yih'yu l'ratzon im'rei fee v'heg'yon libee l'faneicha, Adonai tzuree v'go-alee. Oseh shalom bim'romav, hu ya-aseh shalom aleinu, v'al kol Yisra-el v'im'ru amen.

We are seated.

"You have blessed me with many gifts, God, but I know it is my task to realize them. May I never underestimate my potential, may I never lose hope. May I find the strength to strive for better, the courage to be different, the energy to give all that I have to offer."
—Rabbi Naomi Levy 189

On Monday and Thursday mornings, we continue with the Torah Service on page 47.

On Rosh Chodesh mornings, we continue with Hallel on page 193 and then the Torah Service on page 47.

On Fast Day mornings, we continue with Aveenu Malkenu on page 199 and then the Torah Service on page 47.

At all other times, we continue with Kaddish Shalem on the next page.

תפילות לחול

אֱלֹהַי, נְצוֹר לְשׁוֹנִי מֵרָע. וּשְׂפָתַי מִדַּבֵּר מִרְמָה: וְלִמְקַלְלַי נַפְשִׁי תִדֹּם, וְנַפְשִׁי כֶּעָפָר לַכֹּל תִּהְיֶה. פְּתַח לִבִּי בְּתוֹרָתֶךָ, וּבְמִצְוֹתֶיךָ תִּרְדּוֹף נַפְשִׁי. וְכָל הַחוֹשְׁבִים עָלַי רָעָה, מְהֵרָה הָפֵר עֲצָתָם וְקַלְקֵל מַחֲשַׁבְתָּם. עֲשֵׂה לְמַעַן שְׁמֶךָ, עֲשֵׂה לְמַעַן יְמִינֶךָ, עֲשֵׂה לְמַעַן קְדֻשָּׁתֶךָ. עֲשֵׂה לְמַעַן תּוֹרָתֶךָ. לְמַעַן יֵחָלְצוּן יְדִידֶיךָ, הוֹשִׁיעָה יְמִינְךָ וַעֲנֵנִי. יִהְיוּ לְרָצוֹן אִמְרֵי פִי וְהֶגְיוֹן לִבִּי לְפָנֶיךָ, יְיָ צוּרִי וְגוֹאֲלִי. עֹשֶׂה שָׁלוֹם בִּמְרוֹמָיו, הוּא יַעֲשֶׂה שָׁלוֹם עָלֵינוּ, וְעַל כָּל יִשְׂרָאֵל וְאִמְרוּ: אָמֵן.

We are seated.

On Monday and Thursday mornings,
we continue with the Torah Service on page 46.

On ראש חדש *mornings,*
we continue with הלל *on page 192*
and then the Torah Service on page 46.

On Fast Day mornings,
we continue with אבינו מלכנו *on page 198*
and then the Torah Service on page 46.

At all other times,
we continue with קדיש שלם *on the next page.*

Weekday Prayers

We thank You for being our God and God of our ancestors for ever and ever. You are the Rock of our lives and our saving Shield. In every generation we will thank and praise You for our lives which are in Your power, for our souls which are in Your keeping, for Your miracles which are with us every day, and for Your wonders and good things that are with us at all times, evening, morning, and noon. O Good One, Your mercies have never stopped. O Merciful One, Your kindness has never stopped. We have always placed our hope in You.

Modeem anach'nu lach, sha-atah hu, Adonai Eloheinu vElohei avoteinu, l'olam va-ed, tzur chayeinu, magen yish'enu, atah hu l'dor vador nodeh l'cha un'saper t'hilatecha. Al chayeinu ham'sureem b'yadecha, v'al nish'moteinu hap'kudot lach, v'al niseicha sheb'chol yom imanu, v'al nif'l'oteicha v'tovoteicha sheb'chol et, erev vavoker v'tzohorayim, hatov kee lo chalu rachameicha, v'ham'rachem kee lo tamu chasadeicha me-olam kiveenu lach.

For all these things, our Ruler, may Your name be blessed and honored forever.

V'al kulam yitbarach v'yit'romam shim'cha, mal'kenu, tameed l'olam va-ed.

May every living thing thank You and praise You sincerely, O God, our rescue and help. Praised are You, Your name is "the Good One," and it is good to thank You.

V'chol hachayeem yoducha selah, veehal'lu et shim'cha be-emet, ha-El y'shu-atenu v'ez'ratenu selah. Baruch atah Adonai, hatov shim'cha ul'cha na-eh l'hodot.

Shacharit (and Mincha on Fast Days):

Make peace in the world, with goodness, blessing, grace, lovingkindness and mercy for us and for all Your people Israel. Bless us, our Parent, all of us together, with Your light, by which You taught us Your Torah of life, love and kindness, justice and mercy, life and peace. May it be good in Your sight to bless Your people Israel at all times with peace.

Sim shalom tovah uv'racha, chen vachesed v'rachameem, aleinu v'al kol Yisra-el amecha. Bar'chenu, aveenu, kulanu k'echad b'or paneicha, kee v'or paneicha natata lanu, Adonai Eloheinu, Torat chayeem v'ahavat chesed, utz'dakah uv'racha v'rachameem v'chayeem v'shalom, v'tov b'eineicha l'varech et am'cha Yisra-el b'chol et uv'chol sha-ah bish'lomecha.

Mincha (except on Fast Days) and Ma-ariv:

Give peace to Your people Israel and to the whole world forever, for You are the Ruler of peace. May it please You always to bless Your people Israel with Your peace.

Shalom rav al Yisra-el am'cha taseem l'olam, kee atah hu melech adon l'chol hashalom. V'tov b'eineicha l'varech et am'cha Yisra-el b'chol et uv'chol sha-ah bish'lomecha.

Praised are You, Adonai, who blesses Your people Israel with peace.

Baruch atah Adonai, ham'varech et amo Yisra-el bashalom.

מוֹדִים אֲנַחְנוּ לָךְ, שָׁאַתָּה הוּא, יְיָ אֱלֹהֵינוּ וֵאלֹהֵי אֲבוֹתֵינוּ, לְעוֹלָם וָעֶד, צוּר חַיֵּינוּ, מָגֵן יִשְׁעֵנוּ, אַתָּה הוּא לְדוֹר וָדוֹר נוֹדֶה לְּךָ וּנְסַפֵּר תְּהִלָּתֶךָ. עַל חַיֵּינוּ הַמְּסוּרִים בְּיָדֶךָ, וְעַל נִשְׁמוֹתֵינוּ הַפְּקוּדוֹת לָךְ, וְעַל נִסֶּיךָ שֶׁבְּכָל יוֹם עִמָּנוּ, וְעַל נִפְלְאוֹתֶיךָ וְטוֹבוֹתֶיךָ שֶׁבְּכָל עֵת, עֶרֶב וָבֹקֶר וְצָהֳרָיִם, הַטּוֹב כִּי לֹא כָלוּ רַחֲמֶיךָ, וְהַמְרַחֵם כִּי לֹא תַמּוּ חֲסָדֶיךָ מֵעוֹלָם קִוִּינוּ לָךְ.

וְעַל כֻּלָּם יִתְבָּרַךְ וְיִתְרוֹמַם שִׁמְךָ, מַלְכֵּנוּ, תָּמִיד לְעוֹלָם וָעֶד.

וְכֹל הַחַיִּים יוֹדוּךָ סֶּלָה, וִיהַלְלוּ אֶת שִׁמְךָ בֶּאֱמֶת, הָאֵל יְשׁוּעָתֵנוּ וְעֶזְרָתֵנוּ סֶלָה. בָּרוּךְ אַתָּה יְיָ, הַטּוֹב שִׁמְךָ וּלְךָ נָאֶה לְהוֹדוֹת.

Shacharit (and Mincha on Fast Days):

שִׂים שָׁלוֹם טוֹבָה וּבְרָכָה, חֵן וָחֶסֶד וְרַחֲמִים, עָלֵינוּ וְעַל כָּל יִשְׂרָאֵל עַמֶּךָ. בָּרְכֵנוּ, אָבִינוּ, כֻּלָּנוּ כְּאֶחָד בְּאוֹר פָּנֶיךָ, כִּי בְאוֹר פָּנֶיךָ נָתַתָּ לָּנוּ, יְיָ אֱלֹהֵינוּ, תּוֹרַת חַיִּים וְאַהֲבַת חֶסֶד, וּצְדָקָה וּבְרָכָה וְרַחֲמִים וְחַיִּים וְשָׁלוֹם, וְטוֹב בְּעֵינֶיךָ לְבָרֵךְ אֶת עַמְּךָ יִשְׂרָאֵל בְּכָל עֵת וּבְכָל שָׁעָה בִּשְׁלוֹמֶךָ.

Mincha (except on Fast Days) and Ma-ariv:

שָׁלוֹם רָב עַל יִשְׂרָאֵל עַמְּךָ תָּשִׂים לְעוֹלָם, כִּי אַתָּה הוּא מֶלֶךְ אָדוֹן לְכָל הַשָּׁלוֹם. וְטוֹב בְּעֵינֶיךָ לְבָרֵךְ אֶת עַמְּךָ יִשְׂרָאֵל בְּכָל עֵת וּבְכָל שָׁעָה בִּשְׁלוֹמֶךָ.

בָּרוּךְ אַתָּה יְיָ, הַמְבָרֵךְ אֶת עַמּוֹ יִשְׂרָאֵל בַּשָּׁלוֹם.

Answer us, Adonai, answer us on our Fast Day, for grievous trouble has overtaken us. Consider not our guilt, turn not away from us. Be mindful of our plea and heed our supplication. Your love is our comfort; answer before we call. This is the promise uttered by Your prophet: "I shall answer before they have spoken, I shall heed their call before it is uttered." You, Adonai answer us in time of trouble; You rescue and redeem in time of distress. You mercifully heed Your people's supplication. Praised are You Adonai, who hears prayer.

Anenu, Adonai, Anenu, b'yom tzum ta-aneetenu, kee b'tzarah g'dolah anach'nu. al tefen el rish'enu, v'al tas'ter paneicha mimenu, v'al tit'alam mit'chintenu. Heyeh na karov l'shav'atenu, y'hee na chas'd'cha l'nachmenu, terem nik'ra anenu, kadavar shene-emar. V'haya terem yik'ra-u va-anee e-eneh, od hem m'dab'reem va-anee esh'ma. kee atah, Adonai, ha-oneh b'et tzarah, podeh umatzeel b'chol et tzarah v'tzukah. Kee atah shome-a t'filat am'cha Yisra-el b'rachameem. Baruch atah Adonai shome-a t'filah.

Adonai, be pleased with Your people Israel and with their prayer. Restore worship to Your Temple. May the prayer of Your people Israel always be accepted with love and favor.

R'tzeh, Adonai Eloheinu, b'am'cha Yisra-el uvit'filatam, v'hashev et ha-avodah lid'veer beitecha, ut'filatam b'ahavah t'kabel b'ratzon, ut'hee l'ratzon tameed avodat Yisra-el amecha.

On Rosh Chodesh, add the following:

Our God and God of our ancestors, show us Your care and concern. Remember our ancestors; recall Your anointed, descended from David Your servant. Protect Jerusalem, Your holy city, and exalt all Your people, Israel, with life and well-being, contentment and peace on this Rosh Hodesh.

Eloheinu vElohei avoteinu, ya-aleh v'yavo, v'yagee-a, v'yera-eh, v'yeratzeh, v'yishama, v'yipaked, v'yizacher zich'ronenu ufikdonenu, v'zich'ron avoteinu mashiach ben David av'decha, v'zich'ron Y'rushalayim eer kod'shecha, v'zich'ron kol am'cha beit Yisra-el l'faneicha, lif'leitah, l'tovah, l'chen ul'chesed ul'rachameem, l'chayim ul'shalom, b'yom Rosh Hachodesh hazeh.

Grant us life and blessing, and remember us for good. Recall Your promise of mercy and redemption. Be merciful to us and save us, for we place our hope in You, loving and merciful God.

Zochrenu, Adonai, Eloheinu, bo l'tovah, ufok'denu vo liv'rachah, v'hoshee-enu vo l'chayim, uvid'var y'shu-ah v'rachameem, chus v'chonenu, v'rachem aleinu v'hoshee-enu, kee eleicha eineinu, kee El melech chanun v'rachum atah.

May we see Your merciful return to Zion. Praised are You, Adonai, who restores Your presence to Zion.

V'techezeinah eineinu b'shuv'cha l'tzee-on b'rachameem. Baruch atah Adonai, hamachazeer sh'cheenato l'tzee-on.

עֲנֵנוּ, יְיָ, עֲנֵנוּ, בְּיוֹם צוֹם תַּעֲנִיתֵנוּ, כִּי בְצָרָה גְדוֹלָה אֲנָחְנוּ. אַל תֵּפֶן אֶל רִשְׁעֵנוּ, וְאַל תַּסְתֵּר פָּנֶיךָ מִמֶּנּוּ, וְאַל תִּתְעַלַּם מִתְּחִנָּתֵנוּ. הֱיֵה נָא קָרוֹב לְשַׁוְעָתֵנוּ, יְהִי נָא חַסְדְּךָ לְנַחֲמֵנוּ, טֶרֶם נִקְרָא אֵלֶיךָ עֲנֵנוּ, כַּדָּבָר שֶׁנֶּאֱמַר, וְהָיָה טֶרֶם יִקְרָאוּ וַאֲנִי אֶעֱנֶה, עוֹד הֵם מְדַבְּרִים וַאֲנִי אֶשְׁמָע. כִּי אַתָּה, יְיָ, הָעוֹנֶה בְּעֵת צָרָה, פּוֹדֶה וּמַצִּיל בְּכָל עֵת צָרָה וְצוּקָה, כִּי אַתָּה שׁוֹמֵעַ תְּפִלַּת עַמְּךָ יִשְׂרָאֵל בְּרַחֲמִים. בָּרוּךְ אַתָּה יְיָ, שׁוֹמֵעַ תְּפִלָּה.

רְצֵה, יְיָ אֱלֹהֵינוּ, בְּעַמְּךָ יִשְׂרָאֵל וּבִתְפִלָּתָם, וְהָשֵׁב אֶת הָעֲבוֹדָה לִדְבִיר בֵּיתֶךָ, וּתְפִלָּתָם בְּאַהֲבָה תְקַבֵּל בְּרָצוֹן, וּתְהִי לְרָצוֹן תָּמִיד עֲבוֹדַת יִשְׂרָאֵל עַמֶּךָ.

On ראש חדש, *add the following:*

אֱלֹהֵינוּ וֵאלֹהֵי אֲבוֹתֵינוּ, יַעֲלֶה וְיָבֹא, וְיַגִּיעַ וְיֵרָאֶה, וְיֵרָצֶה וְיִשָּׁמַע, וְיִפָּקֵד, וְיִזָּכֵר זִכְרוֹנֵנוּ וּפִקְדוֹנֵנוּ, וְזִכְרוֹן אֲבוֹתֵינוּ, וְזִכְרוֹן מָשִׁיחַ בֶּן דָּוִד עַבְדֶּךָ, וְזִכְרוֹן יְרוּשָׁלַיִם עִיר קָדְשֶׁךָ, וְזִכְרוֹן כָּל עַמְּךָ בֵּית יִשְׂרָאֵל לְפָנֶיךָ, לִפְלֵיטָה, לְטוֹבָה, לְחֵן וּלְחֶסֶד וּלְרַחֲמִים, לְחַיִּים וּלְשָׁלוֹם, בְּיוֹם רֹאשׁ הַחֹדֶשׁ הַזֶּה.

זָכְרֵנוּ, יְיָ אֱלֹהֵינוּ, בּוֹ לְטוֹבָה, וּפָקְדֵנוּ בוֹ לִבְרָכָה, וְהוֹשִׁיעֵנוּ בוֹ לְחַיִּים וּבִדְבַר יְשׁוּעָה וְרַחֲמִים, חוּס וְחָנֵּנוּ, וְרַחֵם עָלֵינוּ וְהוֹשִׁיעֵנוּ, כִּי אֵלֶיךָ עֵינֵינוּ, כִּי אֵל מֶלֶךְ חַנּוּן וְרַחוּם אָתָּה.

וְתֶחֱזֶינָה עֵינֵינוּ בְּשׁוּבְךָ לְצִיּוֹן בְּרַחֲמִים. בָּרוּךְ אַתָּה יְיָ, הַמַּחֲזִיר שְׁכִינָתוֹ לְצִיּוֹן.

Weekday Prayers

Have mercy and return to Jerusalem, Your city. May Your presence dwell there as You have promised. Build it now, in our days and for all time. Reestablish there the majesty of David, Your servant.

V'leerushalayim eer'cha b'rachameem tashuv, v'tish'kon b'tochah ka-asher dibar'ta, uv'neh otah b'karov b'yameinu bin'yan olam, v'chiseh David m'herah l'tochah tacheen.

Mincha—On Tisha B'Av, replace the following with "Comfort..."

Praised are You Adonai, who builds Jerusalem.

Baruch atah Adonai, boneh Y'rushalayim.

Comfort, Adonai our God, the mourners of Zion and those who grieve for Jerusalem, the city which once was so desolate in mourning, like a woman bereft of her children. For Your people Israel, smitten by the sword, and for her children who gave their lives for her, Zion cries with bitter tears, Jerusalem voices her anguish: "My heart, my heart goes out for the slain; my entire being mourns for the slain." Have mercy, Adonai our God, in Your great compassion for us and for Your city, Jerusalem, rebuilt from destruction and restored from desolation. Adonai who causes Zion to rejoice at her children's return, may all who love Jerusalem exult in her, may all who mourn Jerusalem of old rejoice with her now. May they hear in the cities of Judah and in the streets of Jerusalem sounds of joy and gladness, voices of bride and groom. Grant peace to the city which You have redeemed, and protect her, as proclaimed by Your prophet: "I will surround her," says Adonai, "as a wall of fire, and I will be the glory in her midst." Praised are You, Adonai who comforts Zion and rebuilds Jerusalem.

Nachem Adonai Eloheinu et avelei tzee-on, v'et avelei Y'rushalayim, v'et ha-eer shecharevah hai'tah, va-avelah mib'lee vaneicha. Al am'cha Yisra-el shehutal lecharev v'al baneiha asher mas'ru naf'sham aleiha, tzee-on b'mar tiv'keh, virushalayim titen kolah. Libee libee al chal'leihem, me-ai me-ai al chal'leihem. Rachem Adonai Eloheinu, b'rachameicha harabeem, aleinu v'al Y'rushalayim eer'cha haniv'neit mechur'banah, v'ham'yushevet mishom'mutah. Y'hee ratzon mil'faneicha, m'same'ach tzee-on b'vaneiha, sheish'm'chu et Y'rushalayim kol ohaveiha v'yaseesu itah kol hamit'ab'leem aleiha, v'yish'm'u b'arei y'huday uv'chutzot Y'rushalayim kol sason v'kol sim'cha, kol chatan v'kol kalah. Ten shalom l'eer'cha asher pareeta v'hagen aleiha, ca-amur: Va-anee eh'yeh lah, n'um Adonai, chomat esh saveev ul'chavod eh'yeh v'tochah. Baruch atah Adonai, m'nachem tzee-on uvoneh y'rushalayim.

Cause the offspring of Your servant David to flourish, and hasten the coming of Messianic deliverance. We hope continually for Your redemption. Praised are You Adonai, who assures our redemption.

Et tzemach David av'd'cha m'hera tatz'mee-ach, v'kar'no tarum beeshu-atecha, kee leeshu-atecha kiveenu kol hayom. Baruch atah Adonai, matz'mee-ach keren y'shu-ah.

Hear our voice, Adonai our God. Have compassion upon us, pity us. Accept our prayer with loving favor. You listen to entreaty and prayer. Do not turn us away unanswered, our Sovereign.

Sh'ma kolenu, Adonai Eloheinu, chus v'rachem aleinu, v'kabel b'rachameem uv'ratzon et t'filatenu, kee el shome-a t'filot v'tachanuneem atah, umil'faneicha, mal'kenu, reikam al t'sheevenu.

Mincha—On Fast Days, replace the following with "Answer us..."

You mercifully heed Your people's supplication. Praised are You Adonai, who hears prayer.

Kee atah shome-a t'filat am'cha Yisra-el b'rachameem. Baruch atah Adonai shome-a t'filah.

וְלִירוּשָׁלַיִם עִירְךָ בְּרַחֲמִים תָּשׁוּב, וְתִשְׁכּוֹן בְּתוֹכָהּ כַּאֲשֶׁר דִּבַּרְתָּ, וּבְנֵה אוֹתָהּ בְּקָרוֹב בְּיָמֵינוּ בִּנְיַן עוֹלָם, וְכִסֵּא דָוִד מְהֵרָה לְתוֹכָהּ תָּכִין.

Mincha—On תשעה באב, replace the following with נחם

בָּרוּךְ אַתָּה יְיָ, בּוֹנֵה יְרוּשָׁלָיִם.

נַחֵם יְיָ אֱלֹהֵינוּ, אֶת אֲבֵלֵי צִיּוֹן וְאֶת אֲבֵלֵי יְרוּשָׁלָיִם, וְאֶת הָעִיר שֶׁחָרְבָה הָיְתָה, וַאֲבֵלָה מִבְּלִי בָנֶיהָ. עַל עַמְּךָ יִשְׂרָאֵל שֶׁחוֹטַל לַחֶרֶב וְעַל בָּנֶיהָ אֲשֶׁר מָסְרוּ נַפְשָׁם עָלֶיהָ, צִיּוֹן בְּמַר תִּבְכֶּה, וִירוּשָׁלַיִם תִּתֵּן קוֹלָהּ. לִבִּי לִבִּי עַל חַלְלֵיהֶם, מֵעַי מֵעַי עַל חַלְלֵיהֶם, רַחֵם יְיָ אֱלֹהֵינוּ, בְּרַחֲמֶיךָ הָרַבִּים, עָלֵינוּ וְעַל יְרוּשָׁלַיִם עִירְךָ הַנִּבְנֵית מֵחָרְבָּנָהּ וְהַמְיֻשֶּׁבֶת מִשּׁוֹמְמוּתָהּ. יְהִי רָצוֹן מִלְּפָנֶיךָ, מְשַׂמֵּחַ צִיּוֹן בְּבָנֶיהָ, שֶׁיִּשְׂמְחוּ אֶת יְרוּשָׁלַיִם כָּל אוֹהֲבֶיהָ וְיָשִׂישׂוּ אִתָּהּ כָּל הַמִּתְאַבְּלִים עָלֶיהָ, וְיִשָּׁמְעוּ בְּעָרֵי יְהוּדָה וּבְחוּצוֹת יְרוּשָׁלַיִם קוֹל שָׂשׂוֹן וְקוֹל שִׂמְחָה, קוֹל חָתָן וְקוֹל כַּלָּה. תֵּן שָׁלוֹם לְעִירְךָ אֲשֶׁר פָּדִיתָ וְהָגֵן עָלֶיהָ, כָּאָמוּר: וַאֲנִי אֶהְיֶה לָּהּ, נְאֻם יְיָ, חוֹמַת אֵשׁ סָבִיב וּלְכָבוֹד אֶהְיֶה בְתוֹכָהּ. בָּרוּךְ אַתָּה יְיָ, מְנַחֵם צִיּוֹן וּבוֹנֵה יְרוּשָׁלָיִם.

אֶת צֶמַח דָּוִד עַבְדְּךָ מְהֵרָה תַצְמִיחַ, וְקַרְנוֹ תָּרוּם בִּישׁוּעָתֶךָ, כִּי לִישׁוּעָתְךָ קִוִּינוּ כָּל הַיּוֹם. בָּרוּךְ אַתָּה יְיָ, מַצְמִיחַ קֶרֶן יְשׁוּעָה.

שְׁמַע קוֹלֵנוּ, יְיָ אֱלֹהֵינוּ, חוּס וְרַחֵם עָלֵינוּ, וְקַבֵּל בְּרַחֲמִים וּבְרָצוֹן אֶת תְּפִלָּתֵנוּ, כִּי אֵל שׁוֹמֵעַ תְּפִלּוֹת וְתַחֲנוּנִים אָתָּה, וּמִלְּפָנֶיךָ, מַלְכֵּנוּ, רֵיקָם אַל תְּשִׁיבֵנוּ.

Mincha—On Fast Days, replace the following with ענני

כִּי אַתָּה שׁוֹמֵעַ תְּפִלַּת עַמְּךָ יִשְׂרָאֵל בְּרַחֲמִים. בָּרוּךְ אַתָּה יְיָ, שׁוֹמֵעַ תְּפִלָּה.

Weekday Prayers

Adonai our God, make this a blessed year. May its varied produce bring us happiness.

Summer: Grant blessing
Winter: Grant dew and rain

upon the earth, satisfy us with its abundance, and bless our year as the best of years. Praised are You Adonai, who blesses the years.

Sound the great shofar to herald our freedom, raise high the banner to gather all exiles. Gather the dispersed from the ends of the earth. Praised are You Adonai, who gathers the dispersed of the people Israel.

Restore our judges as in days of old, restore our counselors as in former times. Remove from us sorrow and anguish. Reign over us, alone, with lovingkindness; with justice and mercy sustain our cause. Praised are You Adonai, Ruler who loves justice with compassion.

Frustrate the hopes of all those who malign us; let all evil very soon disappear. Let all Your enemies soon be destroyed. May You quickly uproot and crush the arrogant; may You subdue and humble them in our time. Praised are You Adonai, who humbles the arrogant.

Let Your tender mercies be stirred for the righteous, the pious, and the leaders of the House of Israel, devoted scholars and faithful proselytes. Be merciful to us of the House of Israel. Reward all who trust in You, cast our lot with those who are faithful to You. May we never come to despair, for our trust is in You. Praised are You Adonai, who sustains the righteous.

Barech aleinu, Adonai Eloheinu, et hashana hazot v'et kol meenei t'vu-atah l'tovah

Summer: v'ten b'racha
Winter: v'ten tal umatar liv'rachah

al p'nei ha-adamah, v'sab'enu mituvecha, uvarech sh'natenu kashaneem hatovot. Baruch atah Adonai, m'varech hashaneem.

T'ka b'shofar gadol l'cherutenu, v'sa nes l'kabetz galuyoteinu, v'kab'tzenu yachad me-ar'ba kan'fot ha-aretz. Baruch atah Adonai, m'kabetz nidchei amo Yisra-el.

Hasheevah shof'teinu k'varishonah v'yo-atzeinu k'vat'chilah, v'haser mimenu yagon va-anacha, um'loch aleinu atah Adonai, l'vad'cha b'chesed uv'rachameem, v'tzad'kenu bamish'pat. Baruch atah Adonai, melech ohev tz'dakah umish'pat.

V'lamal'sheeneem al t'hee tikvah, v'chol harish'ah k'rega toved, v'chol oy'veicha m'herah yikaretu, v'hazedeem m'herah t'aker ut'shaber ut'mager v'tach'nee-a bim'herah v'yameinu. Baruch atah Adonai, shover oy'veem umach'nee-a zedeem.

Al hatzadeekeem v'al hachaseedeem v'al ziknei am'cha beit Yisra-el, v'al p'leitat sof'reihem, v'al gerei hatzedek v'aleinu, yehemu na rachameicha, Adonai Eloheinu, v'ten sachar tov l'chol habot'cheem b'shim'cha be-emet, v'seem chel'kenu imahem l'olam, v'lo nevosh kee v'cha batach'nu. Baruch atah Adonai, mish'an umiv'tach latzadeekeem.

בָּרֵךְ עָלֵינוּ, יְיָ אֱלֹהֵינוּ, אֶת הַשָּׁנָה הַזֹּאת וְאֶת כָּל מִינֵי תְבוּאָתָהּ לְטוֹבָה

וְתֵן בְּרָכָה *Between Pesach and December fourth:*
וְתֵן טַל וּמָטָר לִבְרָכָה *Between December fifth and Pesach:*

עַל פְּנֵי הָאֲדָמָה, וְשַׂבְּעֵנוּ מִטּוּבֶךָ, וּבָרֵךְ שְׁנָתֵנוּ כַּשָּׁנִים הַטּוֹבוֹת. בָּרוּךְ אַתָּה יְיָ, מְבָרֵךְ הַשָּׁנִים.

תְּקַע בְּשׁוֹפָר גָּדוֹל לְחֵרוּתֵנוּ, וְשָׂא נֵס לְקַבֵּץ גָּלֻיּוֹתֵינוּ, וְקַבְּצֵנוּ יַחַד מֵאַרְבַּע כַּנְפוֹת הָאָרֶץ. בָּרוּךְ אַתָּה יְיָ, מְקַבֵּץ נִדְחֵי עַמּוֹ יִשְׂרָאֵל.

הָשִׁיבָה שׁוֹפְטֵינוּ כְּבָרִאשׁוֹנָה וְיוֹעֲצֵינוּ כְּבַתְּחִלָּה, וְהָסֵר מִמֶּנּוּ יָגוֹן וַאֲנָחָה, וּמְלוֹךְ עָלֵינוּ אַתָּה, יְיָ, לְבַדְּךָ בְּחֶסֶד וּבְרַחֲמִים, וְצַדְּקֵנוּ בַּמִּשְׁפָּט. בָּרוּךְ אַתָּה יְיָ, מֶלֶךְ אוֹהֵב צְדָקָה וּמִשְׁפָּט.

וְלַמַּלְשִׁינִים אַל תְּהִי תִקְוָה, וְכָל הָרִשְׁעָה כְּרֶגַע תֹּאבֵד, וְכָל אוֹיְבֶיךָ מְהֵרָה יִכָּרֵתוּ, וְהַזֵּדִים מְהֵרָה תְעַקֵּר וּתְשַׁבֵּר וּתְמַגֵּר וְתַכְנִיעַ בִּמְהֵרָה בְיָמֵינוּ. בָּרוּךְ אַתָּה יְיָ, שׁוֹבֵר אֹיְבִים וּמַכְנִיעַ זֵדִים.

עַל הַצַּדִּיקִים וְעַל הַחֲסִידִים וְעַל זִקְנֵי עַמְּךָ בֵּית יִשְׂרָאֵל, וְעַל פְּלֵיטַת סוֹפְרֵיהֶם, וְעַל גֵּרֵי הַצֶּדֶק וְעָלֵינוּ, יֶהֱמוּ נָא רַחֲמֶיךָ, יְיָ אֱלֹהֵינוּ, וְתֵן שָׂכָר טוֹב לְכָל הַבּוֹטְחִים בְּשִׁמְךָ בֶּאֱמֶת, וְשִׂים חֶלְקֵנוּ עִמָּהֶם לְעוֹלָם, וְלֹא נֵבוֹשׁ כִּי בְךָ בָּטָחְנוּ. בָּרוּךְ אַתָּה יְיָ, מִשְׁעָן וּמִבְטָח לַצַּדִּיקִים.

Weekday Prayers

> *Ma-ariv—At the end of Shabbat recite this blessing in place of the one which follows it.*
>
> You graciously endow mortals with intelligence, teaching us wisdom and understanding. You graciously granted us knowledge of Your Torah, teaching us to fulfill the laws You have willed. You set apart the sacred from the profane, even as You separated light from darkness, singled out the people Israel from among the nations, and distinguished Shabbat from all other days. Our Parent, our Ruler, may the coming days bring us peace. May they be free of sin and cleansed of wrongdoing; may they find us more closely attached to You. Grant us knowledge, discernment, and wisdom. Praised are You Adonai, who graciously grants us intelligence.
>
> Atah chonen l'adam da-at, um'lamed le-enosh beenah. Atah chonan'tanu l'mada Toratecha, vat'lam'denu la-asot chukei r'tzonecha, vatav'del Adonai Eloheinu bein kodesh l'chol, bein or l'choshech, bein Yisra-el la-ameem bein yom hash'vee-ee l'sheshet y'mei hama-aseh. Avinu malkenu, hachel aleinu hayameem haba-eem lik-ratenu l'shalom, chasucheem mikol chet, um'nukeem mikol avon, um'dubakeem b'yir'atecha. V'chonenu me-it'cha de-ah, beenah v'has'kel. Baruch atah Adonai, chonen hada-at.

You graciously endow mortals with intelligence, teaching us wisdom and understanding. Grant us knowledge, discernment, and wisdom. Praised are You Adonai, who graciously grants us intelligence.

Atah chonen l'adam da-at, um'lamed le-enosh beenah. Chonenu me-it'cha de-ah, beenah v'has'kel. Baruch atah Adonai, chonen hada-at.

Bring us back, our Parent, to Your Torah. Draw us near, our Ruler, to Your service. Lead us back to You, truly repentant. Praised are You Adonai, who welcomes repentance.

Hasheevenu aveenu l'Toratecha, v'kor'venu mal'kenu la-avodatecha, v'chachazeerenu bit'shuvah sh'lemah l'faneicha. Baruch atah Adonai, harotzeh bit'shuvah.

Forgive us, our Parent, for we have sinned. Pardon us, our Ruler, for we have transgressed; for You forgive and pardon. Praised are You Adonai, gracious and forgiving.

S'lach lanu, aveenu, kee chatanu, m'chal lanu, mal'keinu kee fasha'nu, kee mochel v'sole-ach atah. Baruch atah Adonai, chanun hamar'beh lis'lo-ach.

Behold our adversity and deliver us. Redeem us soon because of Your mercy, for You are the mighty Redeemer. Praised are You Adonai, Redeemer of the people Israel.

R'eh v'on'yenu, v'reevah reevenu, ug'alenu m'herah l'ma-an sh'mecha, kee go-el chazak atah. Baruch atah Adonai, go-el Yisra-el.

Heal us, Adonai, and we shall be healed. Help us and save us, for You are our glory. Grant complete healing for all our afflictions, for You are the faithful and merciful God of healing. Praised are You Adonai, Healer of the people Israel.

R'fa-enu Adonai v'nerafeh, hoshee-enu v'nivashe-ah, kee t'hilatenu atah, v'ha-ahleh r'fu-ah sh'lemah l'chol makoteinu. Kee el melech rofeh ne-eman v'rachaman atah. Baruch atah Adonai, rofeh cholei amo Yisra-el.

> **Ma-ariv**—At the end of שבת
> recite this blessing in place of the one which follows it.
>
> אַתָּה חוֹנֵן לְאָדָם דַּעַת, וּמְלַמֵּד לֶאֱנוֹשׁ בִּינָה. אַתָּה חוֹנַנְתָּנוּ לְמַדַּע תּוֹרָתֶךָ, וַתְּלַמְּדֵנוּ לַעֲשׂוֹת חֻקֵּי רְצוֹנֶךָ, וַתַּבְדֵּל יְיָ אֱלֹהֵינוּ בֵּין קֹדֶשׁ לְחוֹל, בֵּין אוֹר לְחוֹשֶׁךְ, בֵּין יִשְׂרָאֵל לָעַמִּים בֵּין יוֹם הַשְּׁבִיעִי לְשֵׁשֶׁת יְמֵי הַמַּעֲשֶׂה. אָבִינוּ מַלְכֵּנוּ, הָחֵל עָלֵינוּ הַיָּמִים הַבָּאִים לִקְרָאתֵנוּ לְשָׁלוֹם, חֲשׂוּכִים מִכָּל חֵטְא, וּמְנֻקִּים מִכָּל עָוֹן, וּמְדֻבָּקִים בְּיִרְאָתֶךָ. וְחָנֵּנוּ מֵאִתְּךָ דֵּעָה, בִּינָה וְהַשְׂכֵּל. בָּרוּךְ אַתָּה יְיָ, חוֹנֵן הַדָּעַת.

אַתָּה חוֹנֵן לְאָדָם דַּעַת, וּמְלַמֵּד לֶאֱנוֹשׁ בִּינָה. חָנֵּנוּ מֵאִתְּךָ דֵּעָה, בִּינָה וְהַשְׂכֵּל. בָּרוּךְ אַתָּה יְיָ, חוֹנֵן הַדָּעַת.

הֲשִׁיבֵנוּ אָבִינוּ לְתוֹרָתֶךָ, וְקָרְבֵנוּ מַלְכֵּנוּ לַעֲבוֹדָתֶךָ, וְהַחֲזִירֵנוּ בִּתְשׁוּבָה שְׁלֵמָה לְפָנֶיךָ. בָּרוּךְ אַתָּה יְיָ, הָרוֹצֶה בִּתְשׁוּבָה.

סְלַח לָנוּ, אָבִינוּ, כִּי חָטָאנוּ, מְחַל לָנוּ, מַלְכֵּנוּ כִּי פָשָׁעְנוּ, כִּי מוֹחֵל וְסוֹלֵחַ אָתָּה. בָּרוּךְ אַתָּה יְיָ, חַנּוּן הַמַּרְבֶּה לִסְלֹחַ.

רְאֵה בְעָנְיֵנוּ, וְרִיבָה רִיבֵנוּ, וּגְאָלֵנוּ מְהֵרָה לְמַעַן שְׁמֶךָ, כִּי גּוֹאֵל חָזָק אָתָּה. בָּרוּךְ אַתָּה יְיָ, גּוֹאֵל יִשְׂרָאֵל.

רְפָאֵנוּ יְיָ וְנֵרָפֵא, הוֹשִׁיעֵנוּ וְנִוָּשֵׁעָה, כִּי תְהִלָּתֵנוּ אָתָּה, וְהַעֲלֵה רְפוּאָה שְׁלֵמָה לְכָל מַכּוֹתֵינוּ. כִּי אֵל מֶלֶךְ רוֹפֵא נֶאֱמָן וְרַחֲמָן אָתָּה. בָּרוּךְ אַתָּה יְיָ, רוֹפֵא חוֹלֵי עַמּוֹ יִשְׂרָאֵל.

Weekday Prayers

K'dushah

*When the Amidah is chanted out loud,
the K'dushah is substituted for "You are holy..." at the bottom of the page.*

We shall tell of Your holiness on earth just as it is told in the heavens above. As Your prophet wrote, the angels called to one another, saying:

> Holy, holy, holy is *Adonai Tzeva'ot*, the whole world is filled with God's glory.

Then the Serafim responded in a mighty chorus:

> Praised is God's glory from God's place.

With Your holy words it is written:

> Adonai will rule forever, your God, O Zion, for all generations. Halleluyah.

For all generations we will tell Your greatness, and forever and ever we will add our holiness to Yours. We will never stop praising You, for You are a great and holy God. Praised are You Adonai, the holy God.

N'kadesh et shim'cha ba-olam, k'shem shemakdisheem oto bish'mei marom, kakatuv al yad n'vee-echa, v'kara zeh el zeh v'amar:

> Kadosh, kadosh, kadosh Adonai Tzeva-ot, m'lo chol ha-aretz k'vodo.

L'umatam baruch yomeru:

> Baruch k'vod Adonai mim'komo.

Uv'div'rei kod'sh'cha katuv lemor:

> Yimloch Adonai l'olam, Elohayich Tzion l'dor vador, hal'luyah.

L'dor vador nageed god'lecha, ul'netzach n'tzacheem k'dushat'cha nakdeesh, v'shiv'chacha, Eloheinu, mipeenu lo yamush l'olam va-ed, kee El melech gadol v'kadosh atah. Baruch atah Adonai, ha-El hakadosh.

When the Amidah is recited silently:

You are holy and Your name is holy and holy beings praise You every day. Praised are You Adonai, the holy God.

Atah kadosh v'shim'cha kadosh uk'dosheem b'chol yom y'hal'lucha, selah. Baruch atah Adonai, ha-El hakadosh.

קְדוּשָׁה

When the עמידה *is chanted out loud,
the* קדושה *is substituted for* אתה קדוש *at the bottom of the page.*

נְקַדֵּשׁ אֶת שִׁמְךָ בָּעוֹלָם, כְּשֵׁם שֶׁמַּקְדִּישִׁים אוֹתוֹ בִּשְׁמֵי מָרוֹם, כַּכָּתוּב עַל יַד נְבִיאֶךָ: וְקָרָא זֶה אֶל זֶה וְאָמַר:

קָדוֹשׁ, קָדוֹשׁ, קָדוֹשׁ יְיָ צְבָאוֹת, מְלֹא כָל הָאָרֶץ כְּבוֹדוֹ.

לְעֻמָּתָם בָּרוּךְ יֹאמֵרוּ:

בָּרוּךְ כְּבוֹד יְיָ מִמְּקוֹמוֹ.

וּבְדִבְרֵי קָדְשְׁךָ כָּתוּב לֵאמֹר:

יִמְלֹךְ יְיָ לְעוֹלָם, אֱלֹהַיִךְ צִיּוֹן לְדֹר וָדֹר, הַלְלוּיָהּ.

לְדוֹר וָדוֹר נַגִּיד גָּדְלֶךָ, וּלְנֵצַח נְצָחִים קְדֻשָּׁתְךָ נַקְדִּישׁ, וְשִׁבְחֲךָ, אֱלֹהֵינוּ, מִפִּינוּ לֹא יָמוּשׁ לְעוֹלָם וָעֶד, כִּי אֵל מֶלֶךְ גָּדוֹל וְקָדוֹשׁ אָתָּה. בָּרוּךְ אַתָּה יְיָ, הָאֵל הַקָּדוֹשׁ.

When the עמידה *is recited silently:*

אַתָּה קָדוֹשׁ וְשִׁמְךָ קָדוֹשׁ וּקְדוֹשִׁים בְּכָל יוֹם יְהַלְלוּךָ, סֶּלָה. בָּרוּךְ אַתָּה יְיָ, הָאֵל הַקָּדוֹשׁ.

Weekday Prayers

Weekday Amidah

> "Speech has a great power to awaken a person spiritually. Address God in your own words. Compose your own prayers. Doing this will draw forth your soul."
> —Rav Nachman, LM 2:98

We rise and take three steps back and three steps forward as we say:

Adonai, open my lips so I may speak Your praise.

Adonai s'fatai tif'tach ufi yagid t'hilatecha.

Praised are You, Adonai our God and God of our ancestors, God of Abraham, God of Isaac, and God of Jacob, God of Sarah, God of Rebecca, God of Rachel, and God of Leah, the great, strong and awe-inspiring God, God on high. You act with lovingkindness and create everything. God remembers the loving deeds of our ancestors, and will bring a redeemer to their children's children because that is God's loving nature.

Baruch atah Adonai Eloheinu vElohei avoteinu, Elohei Av'raham, Elohei Yitz'chak, vElohei Ya-akov, Elohei Sarah, Elohei Riv'ka, Elohei Rachel, vElohei Le-ah. Ha-El hagadol hagibur v'hanora, El el'yon, gomel chasideem toveem, v'koneh hakol, v'zocher chasdei avot, umevee go-el liv'nei v'neihem l'ma-an sh'mo b'ahavah.

You are a helping, guarding, saving and shielding Ruler. Praised are You, Adonai, Shield of Abraham and Guardian of Sarah.

Melech ozer ufoked umoshee-a umagen. Baruch atah Adonai, magen Av'raham ufoked Sarah.

You are mighty forever, Adonai. You give life to the dead with Your great saving power.

Atah gibor l'olam Adonai, m'chayeh meteem atah rav l'hoshee-a.

From Shemini Atzeret until Pesach:

You cause the wind to blow and the rain to fall.

Masheev haru-ach umoreed hagashem.

You support the living with kindness. You give life to the dead with great mercy. You support the fallen, heal the sick and set free those in prison. You keep faith with those who sleep in the dust. Who is like You, mighty Ruler, and who can compare to You, Ruler of life and death who causes salvation to bloom.

M'chal'kel chayim b'chesed, m'chayeh meteem b'rachameem rabeem, somech nofleem, v'rofeh choleem, umateer asureem, um'kayem emunato leeshenei afar, mee chamocha ba-al g'vurot umee domeh lach, melech memeet um'chayeh umatz'mee-ach y'shu-ah.

You are trustworthy in giving life to the dead. Praised are You Adonai, who gives life to the dead.

V'ne-eman atah l'hachayot meteem. Baruch atah Adonai, m'chayeh hameteem.

עֲמִידָה לְחוֹל

> At the core of our prayers is the *Amidah*. This prayer has had a few names over the years. It is called *Amidah* because we say it while standing (the root of the word is *omed*—to stand). It is also called The *Shmona Esrei* (Eighteen) because there were originally 18 blessings in the Amidah, now there are 19 (can you find them all?). The third name is *HaT'filah* (The Prayer). The rabbis gave it this name because it is the heart and soul of every one of our prayer services, so they felt that if anything could be called "The Prayer," this was the one.
>
> The first blessing of the Amidah praises God as the God of our ancestors. Here at camp we feel that it is just as important to remember the role that our female ancestors played in our history along with our male ancestors. For that reason, we include them in our *Amidah*.

We rise and take three steps back and three steps forward as we say:

אֲדֹנָי שְׂפָתַי תִּפְתָּח וּפִי יַגִּיד תְּהִלָּתֶךָ:

בָּרוּךְ אַתָּה יְיָ אֱלֹהֵינוּ וֵאלֹהֵי אֲבוֹתֵינוּ, אֱלֹהֵי אַבְרָהָם, אֱלֹהֵי יִצְחָק, וֵאלֹהֵי יַעֲקֹב, אֱלֹהֵי שָׂרָה, אֱלֹהֵי רִבְקָה, אֱלֹהֵי רָחֵל וֵאלֹהֵי לֵאָה. הָאֵל הַגָּדוֹל הַגִּבּוֹר וְהַנּוֹרָא, אֵל עֶלְיוֹן, גּוֹמֵל חֲסָדִים טוֹבִים, וְקוֹנֵה הַכֹּל, וְזוֹכֵר חַסְדֵי אָבוֹת, וּמֵבִיא גוֹאֵל לִבְנֵי בְנֵיהֶם לְמַעַן שְׁמוֹ בְּאַהֲבָה.

מֶלֶךְ עוֹזֵר וּפוֹקֵד וּמוֹשִׁיעַ וּמָגֵן: בָּרוּךְ אַתָּה יְיָ, מָגֵן אַבְרָהָם וּפוֹקֵד שָׂרָה:

אַתָּה גִּבּוֹר לְעוֹלָם אֲדֹנָי, מְחַיֵּה מֵתִים אַתָּה, רַב לְהוֹשִׁיעַ:

> *From Shemini Atzeret until Pesach:*
> מַשִּׁיב הָרוּחַ וּמוֹרִיד הַגֶּשֶׁם:

מְכַלְכֵּל חַיִּים בְּחֶסֶד, מְחַיֵּה מֵתִים בְּרַחֲמִים רַבִּים, סוֹמֵךְ נוֹפְלִים, וְרוֹפֵא חוֹלִים, וּמַתִּיר אֲסוּרִים, וּמְקַיֵּם אֱמוּנָתוֹ לִישֵׁנֵי עָפָר, מִי כָמוֹךָ בַּעַל גְּבוּרוֹת וּמִי דוֹמֶה לָּךְ, מֶלֶךְ מֵמִית וּמְחַיֶּה וּמַצְמִיחַ יְשׁוּעָה:

וְנֶאֱמָן אַתָּה לְהַחֲיוֹת מֵתִים. בָּרוּךְ אַתָּה יְיָ, מְחַיֵּה הַמֵּתִים:

Weekday Prayers

Adonai said to Moses: Speak to the people Israel and tell them to make fringes for the corners of their clothes in all future generations. They shall put a blue thread in the fringe of each corner. When they look at them they will remember all of Adonai's mitzvot, and do them, and they won't be led astray by their hearts or their eyes. Do this so that you will remember and do all My mitzvot, and you will be holy for your God. I am Adonai your God, who took you out of the land of Egypt to be your God. I, Adonai, am your God.

Adonai, your God, is truth.

Vayomer Adonai el-Mosheh lemor. Daber el-b'nei Yisra-el v'amar'ta alehem v'asu lahem tzeetzit al-can'fei vig'deihem l'dorotam v'nat'nu al-tzeetzit hakanaf p'til t'chelet. V'haya lachem l'tzeetzit ur'eetem oto uz'char'tem et-kol-mitzvot Adonai va-aseetem otam v'lo taturu acharei l'vav'chem v'acharei eineichem asher-atem zoneem achareihem. L'ma'an tiz'k'ru va-aseetem et-kol mitz'votai vih'yeetem k'dosheem leloheichem. Ani Adonai Eloheichem asher hotzetee et'chem me-eretz mitz'rayim lih'yot lachem lEloheem ani Adonai Eloheichem.

❖ Adonai Eloheichem emet.

Mee Chamocha

Praises to God supreme, who is ever praised. Moses and the Israelites sang a song to You with great joy, as they all said:

Who is like You, Adonai, among the mighty?
Who is like You, glorious in holiness, Awesome in praises, doing wonders.

Those who were rescued sang a new song at the shore of the sea. Together they thanked You and announced Your power:

Adonai will rule for ever and ever.

❖ T'hilot l'el el'yon, baruch hu um'vorach. Moshe uv'nei Yisra-el l'cha anu sheera b'sim'chah rabah v'am'ru chulam:

Mee chamocha ba-elim Adonai,
Mee kamocha ne'dar bakodesh,
Nora t'hilot oseh fele.

❖ Sheerah chadashah Shib'chu g'uleem l'shim'cha al s'fat hayam, yachad kulam hodu v'him'leechu v'am'ru:

Adonai yimloch l'olam va-ed.

Tzur Yisrael

We rise.

Rock of Israel, rise up to help Israel, and rescue Judah and Israel as You promised. Your are our Savior, *Adonai Tz'vaot* is Your name.
Praised are you, Adonai, who rescues Israel.

Tzur Yisra-el, kuma b'ezrat Yisra-el, uf'deh chin'umecha Y'hudah v'Yisra-el. Go-alenu Adonai tz'va-ot sh'mo, K'dosh Yisra-el.
Baruch atah Adonai ga-al Yisra-el.

וַיֹּאמֶר יְהֹוָה אֶל־מֹשֶׁה לֵּאמֹר: דַּבֵּר אֶל־בְּנֵי יִשְׂרָאֵל וְאָמַרְתָּ אֲלֵהֶם וְעָשׂוּ לָהֶם צִיצִת עַל־כַּנְפֵי בִגְדֵיהֶם לְדֹרֹתָם וְנָתְנוּ עַל־צִיצִת הַכָּנָף פְּתִיל תְּכֵלֶת: וְהָיָה לָכֶם לְצִיצִת וּרְאִיתֶם אֹתוֹ וּזְכַרְתֶּם אֶת־כָּל־מִצְוֹת יְהֹוָה וַעֲשִׂיתֶם אֹתָם וְלֹא תָתוּרוּ אַחֲרֵי לְבַבְכֶם וְאַחֲרֵי עֵינֵיכֶם אֲשֶׁר־אַתֶּם זֹנִים אַחֲרֵיהֶם: לְמַעַן תִּזְכְּרוּ וַעֲשִׂיתֶם אֶת־כָּל־מִצְוֹתָי וִהְיִיתֶם קְדֹשִׁים לֵאלֹהֵיכֶם: אֲנִי יְהֹוָה אֱלֹהֵיכֶם אֲשֶׁר הוֹצֵאתִי אֶתְכֶם מֵאֶרֶץ מִצְרַיִם לִהְיוֹת לָכֶם לֵאלֹהִים אֲנִי יְהֹוָה אֱלֹהֵיכֶם:

NUMBERS 15:37–41

❖ יְיָ אֱלֹהֵיכֶם אֱמֶת.

מִי כָמֹכָה

❖ תְּהִלּוֹת לְאֵל עֶלְיוֹן, בָּרוּךְ הוּא וּמְבוֹרָךְ. מֹשֶׁה וּבְנֵי יִשְׂרָאֵל לְךָ עָנוּ שִׁירָה בְּשִׂמְחָה רַבָּה וְאָמְרוּ כֻלָּם:

מִי כָמֹכָה בָּאֵלִם יְיָ,
מִי כָּמֹכָה נֶאְדָּר בַּקֹּדֶשׁ,
נוֹרָא תְהִלֹּת עֹשֵׂה פֶלֶא.

EXODUS 15:11

❖ שִׁירָה חֲדָשָׁה שִׁבְּחוּ גְאוּלִים לְשִׁמְךָ עַל שְׂפַת הַיָּם, יַחַד כֻּלָּם הוֹדוּ וְהִמְלִיכוּ וְאָמְרוּ:

יְיָ יִמְלֹךְ לְעֹלָם וָעֶד:

EXODUS 15:18

צוּר יִשְׂרָאֵל

We rise.

צוּר יִשְׂרָאֵל, קוּמָה בְּעֶזְרַת יִשְׂרָאֵל, וּפְדֵה כִנְאֻמֶךָ יְהוּדָה וְיִשְׂרָאֵל. גֹּאֲלֵנוּ יְיָ צְבָאוֹת שְׁמוֹ, קְדוֹשׁ יִשְׂרָאֵל. בָּרוּךְ אַתָּה יְיָ גָּאַל יִשְׂרָאֵל:

Shema

If there is no minyan, add:

God is a faithful ruler.   El melech ne-eman.

Hear O Israel, Adonai is our God, Adonai is One.	Sh'ma Yisra-el, Adonai Eloheinu, Adonai echad.

Silently:

Praised be God's glorious name forever.	Baruch shem k'vod mal'chuto l'olam va-ed.

You will love Adonai your God with all your mind, soul, and might. Take to heart these words which I command you today. Teach them carefully to your children. Repeat them at home and away, morning and night. Bind them as a sign on your hand, and let them be a symbol above your eyes. Write them on the doorposts of your homes and on your gates.

V'ahav'ta et Adonai Eloheicha b'chol-l'vav'cha uv'chol-naf'sh'cha uv'chol-m'odecha. V'hayu had'vareem ha-eleh asher anochi m'tzav'cha hayom al-l'vavecha. V'shinan'tam l'vaneicha v'dibar'ta bam b'shiv't'cha b'veitecha uv'lech't'cha baderech uv'shoch'b'cha uv'kumecha. Uk'shar'tam l'ot al-yadecha v'hayu l'totafot bein eineicha. Uch'tav'tam al m'zuzot beitecha uvish'areicha.

If you will really listen to My commandments which I command you today, to love Adonai your God and to serve God with all your heart and soul, then I will give your land rain at the proper season—rain in autumn and rain in spring—and you will gather in your grain and wine and oil. I will give grass in the fields for your cattle, and you will eat your fill. Beware that you are not tempted to turn aside and worship other gods. For then God will be angry at you and will shut up the skies and there will be no rain, and the earth will not give you its produce, and you will quickly disappear from the good land which God is giving to you. So keep these words in mind and take them to heart, and bind them as a sign on your hand, and let them be a symbol between your eyes. Teach them to your children, speaking of them at home and away, when you lie down and when you get up. Write them upon the doorposts of your house and upon your gates, so that your days and the days of your children will last long on the land which Adonai promised to your ancestors, to give to them for as long as the heavens and earth last.

V'haya im-shamo-a tish'm'u el-mitzvotai asher anochi m'tzaveh et'chem hayom l'ahavah et-Adonai Eloheichem ul'av'do b'chol-l'vav'chem uv'chol-naf'sh'chem. V'natatee m'tar-ar'tz'chem b'ito yoreh umal'kosh v'asaf'ta d'gonecha v'teerosh'cha v'yitz'harecha. V'natatee esev b'sad'cha liv'hem'techa v'achal'ta v'sava'ta. Hisham'ru lachem pen-yif'teh l'vav'chem v'sar'tem v-avad'tem Eloheem achereem v'hish'tachaveetem lahem. V'chara af-Adonai bachem v'atzar et-hashamayim v'lo-yih'yeh matar v'ha-adamah lo titen et-y'vulah va-avad'tem m'herah me-al ha-aretz hatovah asher Adonai noten lachem. V'sam'tem et-d'varai eleh al-l'vav'chem v'al-naf'sh'chem uk'shar'tem otam l'ot al-yedchem v'hayu l'totafot bein eineichem. V'limad'tem otam et-b'neichem l'daber bam b'shiv't'cha b'veitecha uv'lech't'cha baderech uv'shoch'b'cha uv'kumecha. Uch'tav'tam al-m'zuzot beitecha uvish'areicha. L'ma-an yirbu y'meichem veemei v'neichem al ha-adamah asher nish'ba Adonai la-avoteichem latet lahem keemei hashamayim al-ha-aretz.

קְרִיאַת שְׁמַע

DID YOU KNOW THAT... We are commanded to say the *Sh'ma* twice a day. One reason is hidden in the *Sh'ma* itself. The ayin of the word *sh'ma* and the daled of the word *echad* make the Hebrew word *ed* which means witness. Why do you think the three paragraphs of the *Sh'ma* helps us to be witnesses of God's mitzvot and wonders every day?

If there is no minyan, add: אֵל מֶלֶךְ נֶאֱמָן

שְׁמַע יִשְׂרָאֵל, יְיָ אֱלֹהֵינוּ, יְיָ אֶחָד:

Silently:
בָּרוּךְ שֵׁם כְּבוֹד מַלְכוּתוֹ לְעוֹלָם וָעֶד.

וְאָהַבְתָּ אֵת יְהֹוָה אֱלֹהֶיךָ בְּכָל־לְבָבְךָ וּבְכָל־נַפְשְׁךָ וּבְכָל־מְאֹדֶךָ: וְהָיוּ הַדְּבָרִים הָאֵלֶּה אֲשֶׁר אָנֹכִי מְצַוְּךָ הַיּוֹם עַל־לְבָבֶךָ: וְשִׁנַּנְתָּם לְבָנֶיךָ וְדִבַּרְתָּ בָּם בְּשִׁבְתְּךָ בְּבֵיתֶךָ וּבְלֶכְתְּךָ בַדֶּרֶךְ וּבְשָׁכְבְּךָ וּבְקוּמֶךָ: וּקְשַׁרְתָּם לְאוֹת עַל־יָדֶךָ וְהָיוּ לְטֹטָפֹת בֵּין עֵינֶיךָ: וּכְתַבְתָּם עַל־מְזֻזוֹת בֵּיתֶךָ וּבִשְׁעָרֶיךָ:

DEUTERONOMY 6:4–9

וְהָיָה אִם־שָׁמֹעַ תִּשְׁמְעוּ אֶל־מִצְוֹתַי אֲשֶׁר אָנֹכִי מְצַוֶּה אֶתְכֶם הַיּוֹם לְאַהֲבָה אֶת־יְהֹוָה אֱלֹהֵיכֶם וּלְעָבְדוֹ בְּכָל־לְבַבְכֶם וּבְכָל־נַפְשְׁכֶם: וְנָתַתִּי מְטַר־אַרְצְכֶם בְּעִתּוֹ יוֹרֶה וּמַלְקוֹשׁ וְאָסַפְתָּ דְגָנֶךָ וְתִירֹשְׁךָ וְיִצְהָרֶךָ: וְנָתַתִּי עֵשֶׂב בְּשָׂדְךָ לִבְהֶמְתֶּךָ וְאָכַלְתָּ וְשָׂבָעְתָּ: הִשָּׁמְרוּ לָכֶם פֶּן־יִפְתֶּה לְבַבְכֶם וְסַרְתֶּם וַעֲבַדְתֶּם אֱלֹהִים אֲחֵרִים וְהִשְׁתַּחֲוִיתֶם לָהֶם: וְחָרָה אַף־יְהֹוָה בָּכֶם וְעָצַר אֶת־הַשָּׁמַיִם וְלֹא־יִהְיֶה מָטָר וְהָאֲדָמָה לֹא תִתֵּן אֶת־יְבוּלָהּ וַאֲבַדְתֶּם מְהֵרָה מֵעַל הָאָרֶץ הַטֹּבָה אֲשֶׁר יְהֹוָה נֹתֵן לָכֶם: וְשַׂמְתֶּם אֶת־דְּבָרַי אֵלֶּה עַל־לְבַבְכֶם וְעַל־נַפְשְׁכֶם וּקְשַׁרְתֶּם אֹתָם לְאוֹת עַל־יֶדְכֶם וְהָיוּ לְטוֹטָפֹת בֵּין עֵינֵיכֶם: וְלִמַּדְתֶּם אֹתָם אֶת־בְּנֵיכֶם לְדַבֵּר בָּם בְּשִׁבְתְּךָ בְּבֵיתֶךָ וּבְלֶכְתְּךָ בַדֶּרֶךְ וּבְשָׁכְבְּךָ וּבְקוּמֶךָ: וּכְתַבְתָּם עַל־מְזוּזוֹת בֵּיתֶךָ וּבִשְׁעָרֶיךָ: לְמַעַן יִרְבּוּ יְמֵיכֶם וִימֵי בְנֵיכֶם עַל הָאֲדָמָה אֲשֶׁר נִשְׁבַּע יְהֹוָה לַאֲבֹתֵיכֶם לָתֵת לָהֶם כִּימֵי הַשָּׁמַיִם עַל־הָאָרֶץ:

DEUTERONOMY 11:13–21

Weekday Morning Prayers

Barchu

We rise and the leader sings:

Praise Adonai, who is to be praised.

Bar'chu et Adonai ham'vorach.

Everyone replies, then the leader repeats:

Praised be Adonai who is to be praised for ever and ever.

Baruch Adonai ham'vorach l'olam va-ed.

Praised are You, Adonai our God, Ruler of the universe, who forms light and creates darkness, who makes peace and creates everything.

Baruch atah Adonai, Eloheinu melech ha-olam, yotzeir or, uvoreh choshech, oseh shalom uvoreh et hakol.

We are seated.

Or Chadash

Cause a new light to shine upon Zion, and may we all soon be able to enjoy its light, Praised are You, Adonai, Creator of the heavenly lights.

Or chadash al tzee-on ta-eer v'niz'keh chulanu m'herah l'oro. Baruch atah Adonai yotzer ham'orot.

Ahavah Rabah

With great love have You loved us, Adonai our God; with great and extra tenderness You have cared for us. Our Parent, our Ruler, for the sake of our ancestors who trusted in You, and whom You taught for life-giving laws, be kind to us, too, and teach us. Our merciful Parent, treat us with mercy, and help our minds to understand Your Torah, teaching us to listen, to learn and to teach, to observe, to do, and to fulfill all its words with love. Light up our eyes with Your Torah and cause our hearts to hold tight to Your commandments. Unify our hearts to love and respect Your name so that we will never be ashamed. For we trust in Your holy, great, and awe-inspiring name—may we rejoice in Your saving power. Gather us in peace from the four corners of the earth, and lead us to our land with our heads held high, for You are a God who is able to rescue. You have chosen us from among all peoples and brought us near to You, to thank You sincerely, and to announce with love that You are One. Praised are You, Adonai, who lovingly chooses the people of Israel.

Ahavah rabah ahav'tanu, Adonai Eloheinu, chem'lah g'dolah veeterah chamal'ta aleinu. Aveenu mal'keinu, ba-avur avoteinu shebat'chu v'cha, vat'lam'dem chukei chayim, ken t'chonenu ut'lam'denu. Aveenu, ha-av harachaman, ham'rachem, rachem aleinu, v'ten b'libenu l'haveen ul'haskeel, lish'mo-ah, lil'mod ul'lamed, lish'mor v'la-asot ul'kayem et kol divrei tal'mud toratecha b'ahavah. V'ha-er eineinu b'Toratecha, v'dabek libenu b'mitz'voteicha, v'yached l'vavenu l'ahavah ul'yir'ah et sh'mecha, v'lo nevosh l'olam va-ed. Kee v'shem kod'sh'cha hagadol v'hanora batach'nu, nageelah v'nis'm'cha beeshu-atecha. Vahavee-enu l'shalom me-ar'ba can'fot ha-aretz, v'tolichenu kom'mee-ut l'ar'tzenu, kee El po-el y'shu-ot atah, uvanu vachar'ta mikol am v'lashon. ❖ V'kerav'tanu l'shim'cha hagadol selah be-emet l'hodot l'cha ul'yached'cha b'ahava. Baruch atah Adonai, habocher b'amo Yisra-el b'ahavah.

בָּרְכוּ

DID YOU KNOW THAT... Every Hebrew word comes from a three letter root word. The three letters that make the root of the word *Barchu* are bet, reish, and kaf. These letters also spell the word *Berech*, which means knee. It is important to remember that when we praise God we do it with our whole self, not just our words. This is why we bend our knees and bow when we say *Barchu*.

We rise and the leader sings:

בָּרְכוּ אֶת יְיָ הַמְבֹרָךְ:

Everyone replies, then the leader repeats:

בָּרוּךְ יְיָ הַמְבֹרָךְ לְעוֹלָם וָעֶד:

בָּרוּךְ אַתָּה יְיָ, אֱלֹהֵינוּ מֶלֶךְ הָעוֹלָם, יוֹצֵר אוֹר, וּבוֹרֵא חֹשֶׁךְ, עֹשֶׂה שָׁלוֹם וּבוֹרֵא אֶת הַכֹּל:

We are seated.

אוֹר חָדָשׁ

אוֹר חָדָשׁ עַל צִיּוֹן תָּאִיר וְנִזְכֶּה כֻלָּנוּ מְהֵרָה לְאוֹרוֹ: בָּרוּךְ אַתָּה יְיָ יוֹצֵר הַמְּאוֹרוֹת:

אַהֲבָה רַבָּה

אַהֲבָה רַבָּה אֲהַבְתָּנוּ, יְיָ אֱלֹהֵינוּ, חֶמְלָה גְדוֹלָה וִיתֵרָה חָמַלְתָּ עָלֵינוּ. אָבִינוּ מַלְכֵּנוּ, בַּעֲבוּר אֲבוֹתֵינוּ שֶׁבָּטְחוּ בְךָ, וַתְּלַמְּדֵם חֻקֵּי חַיִּים, כֵּן תְּחָנֵּנוּ וּתְלַמְּדֵנוּ. אָבִינוּ, הָאָב הָרַחֲמָן, הַמְרַחֵם, רַחֵם עָלֵינוּ, וְתֵן בְּלִבֵּנוּ לְהָבִין וּלְהַשְׂכִּיל, לִשְׁמֹעַ, לִלְמֹד וּלְלַמֵּד, לִשְׁמֹר וְלַעֲשׂוֹת וּלְקַיֵּם אֶת כָּל דִּבְרֵי תַלְמוּד תּוֹרָתֶךָ בְּאַהֲבָה. וְהָאֵר עֵינֵינוּ בְּתוֹרָתֶךָ, וְדַבֵּק לִבֵּנוּ בְּמִצְוֹתֶיךָ, וְיַחֵד לְבָבֵנוּ לְאַהֲבָה וּלְיִרְאָה אֶת שְׁמֶךָ, וְלֹא נֵבוֹשׁ לְעוֹלָם וָעֶד: כִּי בְשֵׁם קָדְשְׁךָ הַגָּדוֹל וְהַנּוֹרָא בָּטָחְנוּ, נָגִילָה וְנִשְׂמְחָה בִּישׁוּעָתֶךָ. וַהֲבִיאֵנוּ לְשָׁלוֹם מֵאַרְבַּע כַּנְפוֹת הָאָרֶץ, וְתוֹלִיכֵנוּ קוֹמְמִיּוּת לְאַרְצֵנוּ, כִּי אֵל פּוֹעֵל יְשׁוּעוֹת אָתָּה, וּבָנוּ בָחַרְתָּ מִכָּל עַם וְלָשׁוֹן. ❖ וְקֵרַבְתָּנוּ לְשִׁמְךָ הַגָּדוֹל סֶלָה בֶּאֱמֶת לְהוֹדוֹת לְךָ וּלְיַחֶדְךָ בְּאַהֲבָה. בָּרוּךְ אַתָּה יְיָ, הַבּוֹחֵר בְּעַמּוֹ יִשְׂרָאֵל בְּאַהֲבָה.

Weekday Morning Prayers

Yishtabach

We rise.

May Your name be praised forever, our Ruler, great and holy God, in heaven and on earth. Adonai our God and God of our ancestors, it is proper to sing songs of glory to You, songs of praise, of strength and rule, victory and greatness, power, praise and splendor, holiness and mastery; singing praises and thanks now and forever. Praised are You, Adonai, God and Ruler, great in praises, Master of wonders, who chooses songs of praise, Ruler, God, Life-giver of the universe.

Yishtabach shim'cha la-ad mal'kenu, ha-el hamelech hagadol v'hakadosh bashamayim uva-aretz. Kee l'cha na-eh, Adonai Eloheinu vElohei avoteinu: Sheer ush'vacha, halel v'zim'rah, oz umem'shala, netzach, g'dulah ug'vurah, t'hilah v'tif'eret, k'dushah umal'chut. ❖ B'rachot v'hoda-ot me-atah v'ad olam. Baruch atah Adonai, El melech gadol batish'bachot, El hahoda-ot, adon hanif'la-ot, habocher b'sheerei zim'rah, melech, El, chei ha-olameem.

Chatzi Kaddish

Leader:

May God's great name be made great and holy in the world which God created according to God's will. May God establish Divine rule soon, in our days, quickly and in the near future, and let us say, Amen.

Yit'gadal v'yit'kadash sh'meh rabah. B'al'mah dee v'rah chir'utei, v'yam'leech mal'chutei b'chayeichon uv'yomeichon uv'chayei d'chol beit Yisra-el. Ba-agalah uviz'man kareev v'im'ru amen.

Everyone:

May God's great name be praised for ever and ever.

Y'heh sh'meh rabah m'varach l'alam ul'al'mei al'mayah.

Leader:

Blessed, praised, glorified and raised high, honored and elevated be the name of the Blessed Holy One, far beyond all blessings and songs, praises and words of comfort which people can say, and let us say: Amen.

Yit'barach v'yishtabach v'yitpa-ar v'yit'romam v'yit'naseh v'yit'hadar v'yit'aleh v'yit'halal sh'meh d'kud'shah b'reech hu l'elah min kol bir'chatah v'sheeratah tush'b'chatah v'nechematah, da-ameeran b'al'mah, v'im'ru amen.

יִשְׁתַּבַּח

We rise.

יִשְׁתַּבַּח שִׁמְךָ לָעַד מַלְכֵּנוּ, הָאֵל הַמֶּלֶךְ הַגָּדוֹל וְהַקָּדוֹשׁ בַּשָּׁמַיִם וּבָאָרֶץ. כִּי לְךָ נָאֶה, יְיָ אֱלֹהֵינוּ וֵאלֹהֵי אֲבוֹתֵינוּ: שִׁיר וּשְׁבָחָה, הַלֵּל וְזִמְרָה, עֹז וּמֶמְשָׁלָה, נֶצַח, גְּדֻלָּה וּגְבוּרָה, תְּהִלָּה וְתִפְאֶרֶת, קְדֻשָּׁה וּמַלְכוּת. ❖ בְּרָכוֹת וְהוֹדָאוֹת מֵעַתָּה וְעַד עוֹלָם. בָּרוּךְ אַתָּה יְיָ, אֵל מֶלֶךְ גָּדוֹל בַּתִּשְׁבָּחוֹת, אֵל הַהוֹדָאוֹת, אֲדוֹן הַנִּפְלָאוֹת, הַבּוֹחֵר בְּשִׁירֵי זִמְרָה, מֶלֶךְ, אֵל, חֵי הָעוֹלָמִים.

חֲצִי קַדִּישׁ

The *Kaddish* is used to mark the end of a section in our *T'fillot*. This *Chatzi Kaddish* tells us that we are at the end of P'sukei D'zimra and are ready to start the next section.

Leader:

יִתְגַּדַּל וְיִתְקַדַּשׁ שְׁמֵהּ רַבָּא. בְּעָלְמָא דִּי בְרָא כִרְעוּתֵיהּ, וְיַמְלִיךְ מַלְכוּתֵהּ בְּחַיֵּיכוֹן וּבְיוֹמֵיכוֹן וּבְחַיֵּי דְכָל בֵּית יִשְׂרָאֵל. בַּעֲגָלָא וּבִזְמַן קָרִיב וְאִמְרוּ אָמֵן:

Everyone:

יְהֵא שְׁמֵהּ רַבָּא מְבָרַךְ לְעָלַם וּלְעָלְמֵי עָלְמַיָּא:

Leader:

יִתְבָּרַךְ וְיִשְׁתַּבַּח וְיִתְפָּאַר וְיִתְרוֹמַם וְיִתְנַשֵּׂא וְיִתְהַדָּר וְיִתְעַלֶּה וְיִתְהַלָּל שְׁמֵהּ דְּקֻדְשָׁא בְּרִיךְ הוּא לְעֵלָּא מִן כָּל בִּרְכָתָא וְשִׁירָתָא תֻּשְׁבְּחָתָא וְנֶחֱמָתָא, דַּאֲמִירָן בְּעָלְמָא, וְאִמְרוּ אָמֵן:

Now that we are all warmed up, we can start our formal *Shacharit* prayers. First, the *Shali-ach Tzeebur* (leader) invites us to pray with *Barchu*. Then we say the *Sh'ma* and the *Amidah*.

Weekday Morning Prayers

צ Adonai is righteous in every way, and kind in every deed.

ק Adonai is near to all who call, to all who call to God's sincerity.

ר God does the wishes of those who respect God, God hears their cry and saves them.

ש Adonai protects all who love God, but God will destroy the wicked.

ת My mouth shall speak praises of God, and all beings shall bless God's holy name forever and ever.

We shall praise God, now and forever. Halleluyah.

Tzadeek Adonai b'chol d'rachav,
v'chaseed b'chol ma-asav.

Karov Adonai l'chol kor'av,
l'chol asher yik'ra-uhu ve-emet.

R'tzon y're-av ya-aseh,
v'et shav'atam yish'ma v'yoshee-em.

Shomer Adonai et kol ohavav,
v'et kol har'sha-im yash'meed.

❖ T'hilat Adonai y'daber pee,
Veevarech kol basar shem kod'sho, l'olam va-ed.

Va-anach'nu n'varech Yah, me-atah v'ad olam, hal'luyah.

Halleluyah

Halleluyah! Praise God in God's holy place.
Praise God in the heavens.
Praise God for mighty deeds,
Praise God for endless greatness.
Praise God with the sound of the Shofar.
Praise God with harp and lyre.
Praise God with drum and dance,
Praise God with lute and pipe.
Praise God with loud cymbals,
Praise God with clashing cymbals.
Let everything the breathes praise God. Halleluyah!
Let everything the breathes praise God. Halleluyah!

Hal'luyah,
Hal'lu El b'kod'sho,
Hal'luhu bir'kee-a uzo.
Hal'luhu big'vurotav,
Hal'luhu k'rov gud'lo.
Hal'luhu b'teka shofar,
Hal'luhu b'nevel v'chinor.
Hal'luhu b'tof umachol,
Hal'luhu b'mineem v'ugav.
Hal'luhu v'tzil'tz'lei shama,
Hal'luhu b'tzil'tz'lei t'ruah.
❖ Kol han'shamah t'halel Yah hal'luyah.
Kol han'shamah t'halel Yah hal'luyah.

> "Always remember: you are never given an obstacle you cannot overcome."
> —Rav Nachman, LM II 4:6

צַדִּיק יְיָ בְּכָל דְּרָכָיו, וְחָסִיד בְּכָל מַעֲשָׂיו:
קָרוֹב יְיָ לְכָל קֹרְאָיו, לְכֹל אֲשֶׁר יִקְרָאֻהוּ בֶאֱמֶת:
רְצוֹן יְרֵאָיו יַעֲשֶׂה, וְאֶת שַׁוְעָתָם יִשְׁמַע וְיוֹשִׁיעֵם:
שׁוֹמֵר יְיָ אֶת כָּל אֹהֲבָיו, וְאֵת כָּל הָרְשָׁעִים יַשְׁמִיד:

❖ תְּהִלַּת יְיָ יְדַבֶּר פִּי,
וִיבָרֵךְ כָּל בָּשָׂר שֵׁם קָדְשׁוֹ, לְעוֹלָם וָעֶד:

PSALM 145

וַאֲנַחְנוּ נְבָרֵךְ יָהּ, מֵעַתָּה וְעַד עוֹלָם, הַלְלוּיָהּ:

PSALM 115:18

הַלְלוּיָהּ

הַלְלוּיָהּ,
הַלְלוּ אֵל בְּקָדְשׁוֹ,   הַלְלוּהוּ בִּרְקִיעַ עֻזּוֹ:
הַלְלוּהוּ בִגְבוּרֹתָיו,   הַלְלוּהוּ כְּרֹב גֻּדְלוֹ:
הַלְלוּהוּ בְּתֵקַע שׁוֹפָר,   הַלְלוּהוּ בְּנֵבֶל וְכִנּוֹר:
הַלְלוּהוּ בְּתֹף וּמָחוֹל,   הַלְלוּהוּ בְּמִנִּים וְעֻגָב:
הַלְלוּהוּ בְצִלְצְלֵי שָׁמַע,   הַלְלוּהוּ בְּצִלְצְלֵי תְרוּעָה:
❖ כֹּל הַנְּשָׁמָה תְּהַלֵּל יָהּ הַלְלוּיָהּ.
כֹּל הַנְּשָׁמָה תְּהַלֵּל יָהּ הַלְלוּיָהּ:

PSALM 150

Ashrei

Happy are they who live in Your house;
They shall continue to praise You.

Happy are the people for whom this is so;
Happy are the people whose God is Adonai.

A Psalm of David.

א I will honor You, my God and Ruler, I will praise Your name forever and ever.

ב Every day I will praise You, and sing praises to Your name forever and ever.

ג Great is Adonai and greatly praised; there is no limit to God's greatness.

ד One generation shall praise Your deeds to another, and tell about Your mighty deeds.

ה I will speak about Your majesty, splendor and glory, and Your wonderful deeds.

ו They will talk about the power of Your mighty acts; and I will tell of Your greatness.

ז They recall Your great goodness, and sing of Your righteousness.

ח Adonai is gracious and caring, patient and very kind.

ט Adonai is good to all, and merciful to everything God made.

י All Your work shall praise You, Adonai, and Your faithful ones shall bless You.

כ They shall speak of the glory of Your rule, and talk of Your might.

ל To announce to humanity God's greatness, the splendor and glory of God's rule.

מ God, You rule eternally, Your kingdom is for all generations.

ס God holds up all who fall, and helps all who are bent over to stand straight.

ע The eyes of all look to You with hope, and You give them their food at the right time.

פ You open Your hand, and feed everything alive to its heart's content.

Ashrei yosh'vei veitecha,
od y'hal'lucha selah.

Ashrei ha-am shekacha lo,
ashrei ha-am she-Adonai elohav.

T'hilah l'David,

Aromim'cha elohai hamelech,
va-aver'chah shim'cha l'olam va-ed.

B'chol yom avar'checha,
va-ahal'lah shim'cha l'olam va-ed.

Gadol Adonai um'hulal m'od,
v'lig'dulato ein cheker.

Dor l'dor y'shabach ma-aseicha,
ug'vuroteicha yageedu.

Hadar k'vod hodecha,
v'div'rei nif'l'oteicha aseechah.

Ve-ezuz noroteicha yomeru,
ug'dulat'cha asap'renah.

Zecher rav tuv'cha yabee-u,
v'tzid'kat'cha y'ranenu.

Chanun v'rachum Adonai,
erech apayim ug'dal chased.

Tov Adonai lakol,
v'rachamav al kol ma-asav.

Yoducha Adonai kol ma-aseicha,
v'chaseedeicha y'varchucha.

K'vod mal'chut'cha yomeru,
ug'vurat'cha y'daberu.

L'hodee-ah liv'nei ha-adam g'vurotav,
uch'vod hadar mal'chuto.

Mal'chut'cha mal'chut kol olameem,
umem'shal't'cha b'chol dor vador.

Somech Adonai l'chol hanof'leem,
v'zokef l'chol hak'fufeem.

Einei chol eleicha y'saberu,
v'atah noten lahem et ach'lam b'ito.

Pote-ach et yadecha,
umas'bee-a l'chol chai ratzon.

שחרית לחול

אַשְׁרֵי

DID YOU KNOW THAT... Ashrei has one line for every letter of the Hebrew alphabet except one. Can you find the missing one?

אַשְׁרֵי יוֹשְׁבֵי בֵיתֶךָ, עוֹד יְהַלְלוּךָ סֶּלָה:
PSALM 84:5

אַשְׁרֵי הָעָם שֶׁכָּכָה לּוֹ, אַשְׁרֵי הָעָם שֶׁיְיָ אֱלֹהָיו:
PSALM 144:15

תְּהִלָּה לְדָוִד,
אֲרוֹמִמְךָ אֱלוֹהַי הַמֶּלֶךְ, וַאֲבָרְכָה שִׁמְךָ לְעוֹלָם וָעֶד:
בְּכָל יוֹם אֲבָרְכֶךָּ, וַאֲהַלְלָה שִׁמְךָ לְעוֹלָם וָעֶד:

גָּדוֹל יְיָ וּמְהֻלָּל מְאֹד, וְלִגְדֻלָּתוֹ אֵין חֵקֶר:
דּוֹר לְדוֹר יְשַׁבַּח מַעֲשֶׂיךָ, וּגְבוּרֹתֶיךָ יַגִּידוּ:

הֲדַר כְּבוֹד הוֹדֶךָ, וְדִבְרֵי נִפְלְאֹתֶיךָ אָשִׂיחָה:
וֶעֱזוּז נוֹרְאוֹתֶיךָ יֹאמֵרוּ, וּגְדֻלָּתְךָ אֲסַפְּרֶנָּה:

זֵכֶר רַב טוּבְךָ יַבִּיעוּ, וְצִדְקָתְךָ יְרַנֵּנוּ:
חַנּוּן וְרַחוּם יְיָ, אֶרֶךְ אַפַּיִם וּגְדָל חָסֶד:

טוֹב יְיָ לַכֹּל, וְרַחֲמָיו עַל כָּל מַעֲשָׂיו:
יוֹדוּךָ יְיָ כָּל מַעֲשֶׂיךָ, וַחֲסִידֶיךָ יְבָרְכוּכָה:

כְּבוֹד מַלְכוּתְךָ יֹאמֵרוּ, וּגְבוּרָתְךָ יְדַבֵּרוּ:
לְהוֹדִיעַ לִבְנֵי הָאָדָם גְּבוּרֹתָיו, וּכְבוֹד הֲדַר מַלְכוּתוֹ:

מַלְכוּתְךָ מַלְכוּת כָּל עוֹלָמִים, וּמֶמְשַׁלְתְּךָ בְּכָל דּוֹר וָדֹר:
סוֹמֵךְ יְיָ לְכָל הַנֹּפְלִים, וְזוֹקֵף לְכָל הַכְּפוּפִים:

עֵינֵי כֹל אֵלֶיךָ יְשַׂבֵּרוּ, וְאַתָּה נוֹתֵן לָהֶם אֶת אָכְלָם בְּעִתּוֹ:
פּוֹתֵחַ אֶת יָדֶךָ, וּמַשְׂבִּיעַ לְכָל חַי רָצוֹן:

Baruch She-amar

Praised is the One who spoke—
and the world was!
Praised is God.

Praised is the One who...
...made Creation.
...speaks and it is done.

...decides and it happens.
...has mercy on the world.

...has mercy on all creatures.
...rewards those who respect God.

...lives for ever and exists eternally.
...redeems and rescues.
Praised be God's name.

We rise.

Baruch she-amar v'hayah ha-olam,
Baruch hu,

Baruch oseh v'resheet,
Baruch omer v'oseh,

Baruch gozer um'kayem,
Baruch m'rachem al ha-aretz,

Baruch m'rachem al hab'ree-ot,
Baruch m'shalem sachar tov leere-av,

Baruch chai la-ad v'kayam lanetzach,
Baruch podeh umatzeel,
Baruch sh'mo.

Praised are You, Adonai our God, Ruler of the universe, God, merciful Parent, Your people sing Your praises. Your loyal servants glorify You. We will sing to You, Adonai our God, with the songs written by Your servant David. We will tell how great You are with praises and Psalms. Unique One, Who lives forever, You are the Ruler whom we praise, whose great name is wonderful forever. Praised are You, Adonai, Ruler whom we praise with songs.

Baruch atah Adonai Eloheinu melech ha-olam, ha-el ha-av harachaman, ham'hulal b'fee amo, m'shubach um'fo-ar bil'shon chasidav va-avadav, uv'shirei david av'decha. N'halel'cha Adonai Eloheinu bish'vachot uviz'meerot, n'gadel'cha un'shabechacha un'fa-er'cha v'naz'keer shim'cha, v'nam'leech'cha, mal'keinu Eloheinu, ❖ yachid, chei ha-olameem, melech m'shubach um'fo-ar adei ad sh'mo hagadol. Baruch atah Adonai, melech m'hulal batish'bachot.

We are seated.

"Talk to God as you would talk to your
very best friend. Tell God everything."
—Rav Nachman, LM 11:99

> Before we can jump into our *T'fillot*, we need to get ourselves in the mood. These next few pages are called *P'sukei D'zimra* and they are some songs that we sing to help us get ready. We start with *Baruch She-amar*...

בָּרוּךְ שֶׁאָמַר

We rise.

בָּרוּךְ שֶׁאָמַר וְהָיָה הָעוֹלָם,
בָּרוּךְ הוּא,

בָּרוּךְ עֹשֶׂה בְרֵאשִׁית,
בָּרוּךְ אוֹמֵר וְעוֹשֶׂה,

בָּרוּךְ גּוֹזֵר וּמְקַיֵּם,
בָּרוּךְ מְרַחֵם עַל הָאָרֶץ,

בָּרוּךְ מְרַחֵם עַל הַבְּרִיּוֹת,
בָּרוּךְ מְשַׁלֵּם שָׂכָר טוֹב לִירֵאָיו,

בָּרוּךְ חַי לָעַד וְקַיָּם לָנֶצַח,
בָּרוּךְ פּוֹדֶה וּמַצִּיל,
בָּרוּךְ שְׁמוֹ.

בָּרוּךְ אַתָּה יְיָ אֱלֹהֵינוּ מֶלֶךְ הָעוֹלָם, הָאֵל הָאָב הָרַחֲמָן, הַמְהֻלָּל בְּפִי עַמּוֹ, מְשֻׁבָּח וּמְפֹאָר בִּלְשׁוֹן חֲסִידָיו וַעֲבָדָיו, וּבְשִׁירֵי דָוִד עַבְדֶּךָ. נְהַלֶּלְךָ יְיָ אֱלֹהֵינוּ בִּשְׁבָחוֹת וּבִזְמִירוֹת, נְגַדֶּלְךָ וּנְשַׁבֵּחֲךָ וּנְפָאֶרְךָ וְנַזְכִּיר שִׁמְךָ, וְנַמְלִיכְךָ, מַלְכֵּנוּ אֱלֹהֵינוּ, ❖ יָחִיד, חֵי הָעוֹלָמִים, מֶלֶךְ מְשֻׁבָּח וּמְפֹאָר עֲדֵי עַד שְׁמוֹ הַגָּדוֹל: בָּרוּךְ אַתָּה יְיָ, מֶלֶךְ מְהֻלָּל בַּתִּשְׁבָּחוֹת:

We are seated.

Modeh Ani

I am greateful to You, living, enduring Ruler, for restoring my soul to me in compassion. You are faithful beyond measure.

Modeh/Modah ani l'fanecha, melech chai v'kayam, shehechezarta bee nishmatee b'chem'lah rabah emunatecha.

Mah Tovu

How beautiful are your tents, O Jacob, your houses, O Israel. Your great love inspires me to enter Your house, to worship in Your holy sanctuary, filled with awe for You.

Mah tovu ohalecha ya-akov, Mish'k'notecha yisra-el. Va-ani b'rov chas'd'cha avo veitecha, Esh'tachaveh el heichal kod'sh'cha b'yir'atecha.

Birchot Hashachar

Praised are you Adonai our God, Ruler of the universe...
...who gave us the ability to tell day from night.
...who made me in God's image.
...who made me a Jew.
...who made me free.
...who opens the eyes of the blind.
...who clothes the unclothed.
...who frees the bound.
...who helps those who are bent over by trouble stand straight.
...who spreads out the earth over the waters.
...who made for me everything I need.
...who prepares the way for our footsteps.
...who gives the people of Israel strength.
...who crowns the people Israel with glory.
...who gives strength to the weary.
...who removes sleep from my eyes and slumber from my eyelids.

Baruch atah Adonai Eloheinu melech ha-olam...
...asher natan lasech'vee vina, l'hav'cheen bein yom uvein lai'la.
...she-asanee b'tzalmo.
...she-asanee Yisra-el
...she-asanee ben/bat choreen.
...poke-ach iv'reem.
...malbeesh arumeem.
...mateer asureem.
...zokef k'fufeem.
...roka ha-aretz al hamayim.
...she-asah lee kol tzor'kee.
...hamecheen mitz'adei gaver.
...ozer Yisra-el bigvurah.
...oter Yisra-el b'tif'arah.
...hanoten laya-ef ko-ach.
...hama-aveer shenah me-einai ut'numah me-af'apai.

שחרית לחול

מוֹדֶה אֲנִי

DID YOU KNOW THAT... It is very important that we never take things for granted. That's why every day we start out by thanking God for allowing us to wake up in the morning. Have you ever wondered how your body knows how to wake up?

מוֹדֶה/מוֹדָה אֲנִי לְפָנֶיךָ, מֶלֶךְ חַי וְקַיָּם,
שֶׁהֶחֱזַרְתָּ בִּי נִשְׁמָתִי
בְּחֶמְלָה רַבָּה אֱמוּנָתֶךָ.

מַה טֹּבוּ

מַה טֹּבוּ אֹהָלֶיךָ יַעֲקֹב, מִשְׁכְּנֹתֶיךָ יִשְׂרָאֵל.
וַאֲנִי בְּרֹב חַסְדְּךָ אָבוֹא בֵיתֶךָ,
אֶשְׁתַּחֲוֶה אֶל הֵיכַל קָדְשְׁךָ בְּיִרְאָתֶךָ.

בִּרְכוֹת הַשַּׁחַר

בָּרוּךְ אַתָּה יְיָ אֱלֹהֵינוּ מֶלֶךְ הָעוֹלָם, אֲשֶׁר נָתַן לַשֶּׂכְוִי בִינָה, לְהַבְחִין בֵּין יוֹם וּבֵין לָיְלָה:
בָּרוּךְ אַתָּה יְיָ אֱלֹהֵינוּ מֶלֶךְ הָעוֹלָם, שֶׁעָשַׂנִי בְּצַלְמוֹ:
בָּרוּךְ אַתָּה יְיָ אֱלֹהֵינוּ מֶלֶךְ הָעוֹלָם, שֶׁעָשַׂנִי יִשְׂרָאֵל:
בָּרוּךְ אַתָּה יְיָ אֱלֹהֵינוּ מֶלֶךְ הָעוֹלָם, שֶׁעָשַׂנִי בֶּן־/בַּת־חוֹרִין:
בָּרוּךְ אַתָּה יְיָ אֱלֹהֵינוּ מֶלֶךְ הָעוֹלָם, פּוֹקֵחַ עִוְרִים:
בָּרוּךְ אַתָּה יְיָ אֱלֹהֵינוּ מֶלֶךְ הָעוֹלָם, מַלְבִּישׁ עֲרֻמִּים:
בָּרוּךְ אַתָּה יְיָ אֱלֹהֵינוּ מֶלֶךְ הָעוֹלָם, מַתִּיר אֲסוּרִים:
בָּרוּךְ אַתָּה יְיָ אֱלֹהֵינוּ מֶלֶךְ הָעוֹלָם, זוֹקֵף כְּפוּפִים:
בָּרוּךְ אַתָּה יְיָ אֱלֹהֵינוּ מֶלֶךְ הָעוֹלָם, רוֹקַע הָאָרֶץ עַל הַמָּיִם:
בָּרוּךְ אַתָּה יְיָ אֱלֹהֵינוּ מֶלֶךְ הָעוֹלָם, שֶׁעָשָׂה לִי כָּל צָרְכִּי:
בָּרוּךְ אַתָּה יְיָ אֱלֹהֵינוּ מֶלֶךְ הָעוֹלָם, הַמֵּכִין מִצְעֲדֵי גָבֶר:
בָּרוּךְ אַתָּה יְיָ אֱלֹהֵינוּ מֶלֶךְ הָעוֹלָם, אוֹזֵר יִשְׂרָאֵל בִּגְבוּרָה:
בָּרוּךְ אַתָּה יְיָ אֱלֹהֵינוּ מֶלֶךְ הָעוֹלָם, עוֹטֵר יִשְׂרָאֵל בְּתִפְאָרָה:
בָּרוּךְ אַתָּה יְיָ אֱלֹהֵינוּ מֶלֶךְ הָעוֹלָם, הַנּוֹתֵן לַיָּעֵף כֹּחַ:
בָּרוּךְ אַתָּה יְיָ אֱלֹהֵינוּ מֶלֶךְ הָעוֹלָם, הַמַּעֲבִיר שֵׁנָה מֵעֵינָי וּתְנוּמָה מֵעַפְעַפָּי:

Weekday Morning Prayers

Weekday Morning Prayers

> "Praise God. It puts everything into its
> proper place and perspective."
> —Rav Nachman, LM 1:27

Blessing for putting on the tallit

Praised are You, Adonai our God, Ruler of the universe, who made us holy with mitzvot, and who gave us the mitzvah to wrap ourselves in tzitzit.

Baruch atah Adonai Eloheinu melech ha-olam asher kidshanu b'mitzvotav, v'tzivanu l'hit'atef batzitzit.

Blessing for putting on the t'fillah of the arm

Praised are You, Adonai our God, Ruler of the universe, who made us holy with mitzvot, and who gave us the mitzvah to put on t'fillin.

Baruch atah Adonai Eloheinu melech ha-olam asher kidshanu b'mitzvotav, v'tzivanu l'haneeyach t'filin.

Blessing for putting on the t'fillah of the head

Praised are You, Adonai our God, Ruler of the universe, who made us holy with mitzvot, and who gave us the mitzvah of t'fillin.
Praised be God's glorious name forever.

Baruch atah Adonai Eloheinu melech ha-olam asher kidshanu b'mitzvotav, v'tzivanu al mitzvat t'filin.

Baruch shem k'vod malchuto l'olam va-ed.

While winding the strap three times around the middle finger, say:

I will betroth you to Me forever.
I will betroth you to Me with righteousness, with justice, with love, and with compassion.
I will betroth you to Me with faithfulness, and you shall love Adonai.

V'eras'tich lee l'olam.
V'eras'tich lee b'tzedek uv'mish'pat, uv'chesed, uv'rachameem.
V'eras'tich lee ba-emunah, v'yada-at et Adonai.

שחרית לחול

שַׁחֲרִית לְחוֹל

> We always begin our day at camp with *Shacharit*. The prayers that make up *Shacharit* are divided into sections. After putting on our *tallit* and *t'fillin*, we start on page 6 with *Birchot Hashachar* where we think about waking up and coming to *Shacharit*. Next, we do *P'sukei D'zimra* where we prepare for the core of our *Shacharit* prayers on pages 8-14. Then, the core of the service starts with *Barchu* and runs through the *Sh'ma* and the *Amidah* on pages 16–38. After this, we wrap up our service with *Aleinu* and *Adon Olam* on pages 40–44.

תלית *Blessing for putting on the*

בָּרוּךְ אַתָּה יְיָ אֱלֹהֵינוּ מֶלֶךְ הָעוֹלָם אֲשֶׁר קִדְּשָׁנוּ בְּמִצְוֹתָיו, וְצִוָּנוּ לְהִתְעַטֵּף בַּצִיצִת.

תפילה של יד *Blessing for putting on the*

בָּרוּךְ אַתָּה יְיָ אֱלֹהֵינוּ מֶלֶךְ הָעוֹלָם, אֲשֶׁר קִדְּשָׁנוּ בְּמִצְוֹתָיו, וְצִוָּנוּ לְהָנִיחַ תְּפִלִּין.

תפילה של ראש *Blessing for putting on the*

בָּרוּךְ אַתָּה יְיָ אֱלֹהֵינוּ מֶלֶךְ הָעוֹלָם, אֲשֶׁר קִדְּשָׁנוּ בְּמִצְוֹתָיו, וְצִוָּנוּ עַל מִצְוַת תְּפִלִּין.
בָּרוּךְ שֵׁם כְּבוֹד מַלְכוּתוֹ לְעוֹלָם וָעֶד.

While winding the strap three times around the middle finger, say:

וְאֵרַשְׂתִּיךְ לִי לְעוֹלָם.
וְאֵרַשְׂתִּיךְ לִי בְּצֶדֶק וּבְמִשְׁפָּט וּבְחֶסֶד וּבְרַחֲמִים.
וְאֵרַשְׂתִּיךְ לִי בֶּאֱמוּנָה, וְיָדַעַתְּ אֶת יְיָ.

Weekday Morning Prayers

Introduction

We hope that your summer at Camp Solomon Schechter is filled with a lifetime of wonderful memories. This siddur has been compiled to help you appreciate the beauty of your friends, the staff, the trees, the lake, and all your experiences at Camp Solomon Schechter through the art of prayer.

Those of us who have spent many years here at Camp Solomon Schechter have grown into a community unlike any other Jewish community. Having spent countless summers in the Pacific Northwest surrounded by our natural environment, our friends, and the warmth of God, we have grown as Jews and individuals. This siddur is a product of our Jewish education at Camp Solomon Schechter.

Along with an abridged version of the traditional Hebrew text from authors within the Conservative Movement, we have included a new English translation, transliteration, and some brief commentary explaining the meaning of many of the prayers in our siddur. It is our hope to pass on to you the love of Judaism and love of camp that we have developed over our many summers at Camp Solomon Schechter.

The title of our siddur is *Sh'ma Koleinu*, Hear Our Voice. We trust that through the prayers in this siddur, all of us at Camp Solomon Schechter will be able to come together as a collective voice and that our voice will be heard.

We would like to thank everyone who gave us suggestions over the past few years on how to make a siddur that fits our camp. A special thanks to Rabbi Ron Isaacs for his guidance, inspiration, and materials to make this siddur possible. We would also like to thank Paul Schlesinger, Vice President of the Camp Solomon Schechter Board of Directors for his commitment to this project. Thanks also to you, the camper, for using this siddur respectfully to find meaning and reflection in our *T'fillot* at camp and throughout the year.

We hope that you appreciate every moment of your time at camp.

B'Shalom,

Ian Felgar, Rebecca Kltz, and Jonny Bryantseva
2001/5761

Introduction To Second Printing

Praying to God at Camp Solomon Schechter is a very special experience. In camp we are surrounded by the beauties of God's world, the magnificent lake, the majestic trees, the rushing river, and the broad pastures. The stillness of nature allows us to hear the still, small voice of our souls. And when we raise our voices in prayer, we do so as camp buddies, united in true bonds of friendship.

Rabbi Joshua Stampfer
Founder, Camp Solomon Schechter
2009/5769

As it has been since Rabbi Stampfer founded Camp Solomon Schechter in 1954, prayer is a very special and integral part of our Jewish camping experience. It has always been inspiring for me to witness so many campers, staff and visitors connecting to their friends, to their community and to the Jewish people through the Hebrew, the translations and the commentary in this special siddur.

I would like to thank all of the camp alumni, past staff and board members who have helped to create and maintain such a special community over the past 55 years. Thank you to the former campers that created this beautiful siddur and the donor that made the siddur possible back in 2001. Thank you to Dr. Zane and Celie Brown for their generosity in reprinting and rebinding this 2009 edition. I would also like to thank Donna Peha, board president, and Zane Brown Jr., past president, as well as the entire Camp Solomon Schechter Board of Directors for their continued support and guidance.

Enjoy your time here at Camp Solomon Schechter; I hope you use this siddur and the power of prayer to enhance the meaning of your experience.

Sam Perlin 2009/5769
Executive Director
Camp Solomon Schechter
"Where Judaism and Joy are One"

תוֹכֶן הָעִנְיָנִים
Table of Contents

תְּפִלּוֹת לְחוֹל		**Weekday Prayers**
שַׁחֲרִית לְחוֹל	4	Morning Prayers
סֵדֶר הוֹצָאַת הַתּוֹרָה לְחוֹל	46	Torah Service
מִנְחָה לְחוֹל	54	Afternoon Prayers
מַעֲרִיב לְחוֹל	58	Evening Prayers
תְּפִלּוֹת לְשַׁבָּת		**Shabbat Prayers**
קַבָּלַת שַׁבָּת	66	Welcoming Shabbat
מַעֲרִיב לְשַׁבָּת	78	Evening Prayers
שַׁחֲרִית לְשַׁבָּת	100	Morning Prayers
סֵדֶר הוֹצָאַת הַתּוֹרָה לְשַׁבָּת	132	Torah Service
מוּסָף לְשַׁבָּת	144	Musaf Prayers
מִנְחָה לְשַׁבָּת	166	Afternoon Prayers
הַלֵּל	192	**Psalms of Praise**
בְּרָכוֹת		**Prayers for Other Occasions**
תְּפִלָּה לִשְׁלוֹם הַמְּדִינָה	196	Prayer for Peace in Israel
תְּפִלַּת הַדֶּרֶךְ	196	Traveller's Prayer
אָבִינוּ מַלְכֵּנוּ	198	Avinu Malkenu
בִּרְכַּת הַחֹדֶשׁ	198	Blessing of a New Month
הַבְדָּלָה	200	Havdallah
בִּרְכוֹת הוֹדָאָה	202	Everyday Blessings

Copyright © 2009
All rights reserved.

ISBN: 1-4392-4597-5
ISBN-13: 978-1-4392-4597-2
To order additional copies,
please visit www.BookSurge.com

שְׁמַע קוֹלֵנוּ
Hear our Voice

סִדּוּר לְמַחֲנֶה
Camp Siddur

> In memory of
> **Noam Rogers Stampfer,** ז״ל
> May his memory be a blessing.
> March 22, 1951–June 26, 2001

Second Printing (2002/5762)

Made in the USA
Middletown, DE
24 May 2025

75868168R00117